7/8/19.

Dear Danny,

Thanks for all the inspiration.

All my best,

Adam.

Reciprocity and the Art of Behavioural Public Policy

What motivates human behaviour? Drawing on literatures from anthropology to zoology, Oliver examines how we are motivated to give and take, rather than give or take. This book reviews the evolution of reciprocity as a motivator of behaviour, in terms of its observation in non-human species, in very young humans, and in societies that we can reasonably expect are similar to those in which our distant ancestors lived. The behavioural economic and social psychology literature that aims to discern when and in what circumstances reciprocity is likely to be observed and sustained is also reviewed, followed by a discussion on whether reciprocity is relevant to both the economic and the social domains. The dark sides of reciprocity are considered, before turning again to the light, and how the potentially beneficial effects of reciprocity might best be realised. This culminates in the presentation of a new political economy of behavioural public policy, with reciprocity playing a prominent role.

ADAM OLIVER is a behavioural economist and behavioural public policy analyst at the London School of Economics and Political Science. He is a founding Editor-in-Chief of the journals, Health Economics, Policy and Law and Behavioural Public Policy. He edited the book, also titled Behavioural Public Policy (Cambridge University Press, 2013), and authored The Origins of Behavioural Public Policy (Cambridge University Press, 2017).

Reciprocity and the Art of Behavioural Public Policy

ADAM OLIVER
London School of Economics and Political Science

CAMBRIDGE
UNIVERSITY PRESS

University Printing House, Cambridge CB2 8BS, United Kingdom

One Liberty Plaza, 20th Floor, New York, NY 10006, USA

477 Williamstown Road, Port Melbourne, VIC 3207, Australia

314–321, 3rd Floor, Plot 3, Splendor Forum, Jasola District Centre,
New Delhi – 110025, India

79 Anson Road, #06–04/06, Singapore 079906

Cambridge University Press is part of the University of Cambridge.

It furthers the University's mission by disseminating knowledge in the pursuit of education, learning, and research at the highest international levels of excellence.

www.cambridge.org
Information on this title: www.cambridge.org/9781108480208
DOI: 10.1017/9781108647755

© Adam Oliver 2019

This publication is in copyright. Subject to statutory exception and to the provisions of relevant collective licensing agreements, no reproduction of any part may take place without the written permission of Cambridge University Press.

First published 2019

Printed in the United Kingdom by TJ International Ltd. Padstow Cornwall

A catalogue record for this publication is available from the British Library.

Library of Congress Cataloging-in-Publication Data
Names: Oliver, Adam J., author.
Title: Reciprocity and the art of behavioural public policy / Adam Oliver, London School of Economics and Political Science.
Description: Cambridge, United Kingdom ; New York, NY : Cambridge University Press, 2018. | Includes bibliographical references and index.
Identifiers: LCCN 2019008396 | ISBN 9781108480208 (hardback : alk. paper)
Subjects: LCSH: Policy sciences – Psychological aspects. | Economics – Psychological aspects. | Reciprocity (Psychology)
Classification: LCC H97 .O453 2018 | DDC 320.6–dc23
LC record available at https://lccn.loc.gov/2019008396

ISBN 978-1-108-48020-8 Hardback
ISBN 978-1-108-72714-3 Paperback

Cambridge University Press has no responsibility for the persistence or accuracy of URLs for external or third-party internet websites referred to in this publication and does not guarantee that any content on such websites is, or will remain, accurate or appropriate.

About the author

Adam Oliver is a behavioural economist and behavioural public policy analyst at the London School of Economics and Political Science. He has published and taught widely in the areas of health economics and policy, behavioural economics and behavioural public policy over the past twenty years. He is a founding Editor-in-Chief of the journals, *Health Economics, Policy and Law* and *Behavioural Public Policy*. He edited the book, also titled *Behavioural Public Policy* (Cambridge University Press, 2013), and authored *The Origins of Behavioural Public Policy* (Cambridge University Press, 2017).

For two Charlies: Darwin and Oliver.
The latter, named after the former, was worth the wait.

Contents

List of Figures and Tables	*page* xi
Preface	xiii
Acknowledgements	xvii

1	Setting the Scene	1
	Types of Reciprocity	3
	A Simple Experiment	7
	To What End?	12

2	Animals and Infants	19
	Non-Primates	20
	Non-Human Primates	26
	Infants	33

3	A Pinch of Anthropology	38
	Kin or the Group	40
	Reciprocity in Tribal Communities	45
	The Undernourishment of Reciprocity	52

4	A Dash of Behavioural Economics	57
	A Little Theory	59
	Prisoners, Ultimatums and Dictators	62
	The Other Games People Play	66
	Beyond Abstraction	72

5	The Domain of Reciprocity	76
	A Fair Exchange?	77
	Fostering a Fair Exchange	82
	A False Dichotomy	87

6	The Dark Side of Reciprocity	93
	Resentment	95
	Retaliation and Retribution	99
	Cronyism, Fundamentalism, Nationalism and Other Isms	105
	Ten Lessons	109
7	Nurturing Reciprocity in Public Policy	111
	The Importance of Emphasis	112
	The Case for Decentralising	115
	The Case for Reducing Inequality	123
8	Reciprocity-Informed Policy Design	128
	Fair Effort for Fair Pay, and Trust Between Buyers and Sellers	130
	Non-Competitive Trade	134
	Reputation Once More	137
	Messaging Reciprocity	143
9	Towards a Political Economy of Behavioural Public Policy	147
	Addressing Internalities	148
	The View from Nowhere	151
	Reciprocity and Flourishing	158
	Budging Phishing	161
10	Summing Up	166
	Principal Arguments	167
	Encore	174
	References	178
	Index	191

Figures and Tables

FIGURES

1.1	Practical priming with the all-seeing eye	*page* 16
6.1	A consequence of cronyism	106
8.1	The Careggi performance target	141
9.1	The requirements of libertarian paternalism	150
9.2	The requirements of behavioural regulation	163

TABLES

2.1	Matching pennies	30
4.1	Behavioural economic theories of reciprocity	61
4.2	The prisoner's dilemma	62
4.3	The centipede game	67
4.4	The trust game	68

Preface

Towards the front of *East of Eden*, in a note – almost a love letter – to his publisher, Pascal Covici, John Steinbeck (1963) wrote:

Dear Pat,
You came upon me carving some kind of little figure out of wood and you said, 'Why don't you do something for me?'
I asked you what you wanted and you said, 'A box'.
'What for?'
'To put things in'.
'What things?'
'Whatever you have', you said.
Well here's your box. Nearly everything I have is in it, and it is not full. Pain and excitement are in it, and feeling good or bad and evil thoughts and good thoughts – the pleasure of design and some despair and the indescribable joy of creation.
And on top of these are all the gratitude and love I have for you.
And still the box is not full.

I have been working on the ideas presented in this book for seven or eight years, and have had the opportunity to study many areas that I am genuinely interested in (and wish I had more expertise), from anthropology to zoology, lexicographically speaking. I published some of my initial thoughts on the topic of reciprocity in an article that appeared eventually in the *American Review of Public Administration* (Oliver, 2018), but I felt that the themes that I raised merited a book-length treatment. No author can genuinely call their own book a must-read, but for me this book became almost a must-write. I cannot say that the book that I hope you are about to read is an *East of Eden*, but I can relate to Steinbeck's note: it may not be perfect, but I have put a lot of what I have into it.

MOTIVATION AND CONTENTS

The literature on reciprocity is immense, rich and multidisciplinary. Indeed, in that reciprocity is perhaps humanity's most fundamental and widespread social norm, it sometimes seems, to me at least, that almost all readings relate to it in some way. Given that I cannot read everything, the readings that I have referred to in this book are necessarily selective. I can only apologise to those who believe that I have excluded arguments, evidence, information or policy implications that they deem relevant to this book, and I urge them to take up the mantle of reciprocity in their own writings.

Despite the rich literature on reciprocity, efforts to collate the principal arguments from across the different relevant disciplines into a single space are relatively scarce. Moreover, and somewhat bizarrely, efforts to inform the design of public policy with this fundamental motivator of human behaviour have, until recently, been lacking. Rather, over the past several decades, the literature on motivation in public policy has tended to focus on whether people are pure altruists or selfish egoists (with the latter assumption generally triumphing), and yet that we take from *and* give to others is a more realistic generalisation of human behaviour than arguments that we unremittingly take from *or* give to others. In recent years, however, with the rise of behavioural public policy, there has been increasing recognition in the policy discourse that the standard model of rational behaviour, underpinned by the assumption of egoism, is not fully reflective of actual human behaviour, and a closer consideration of reciprocal motivations is coming to the fore.[1] In short, a paradigm shift is perhaps occurring in this field of analysis, and the book before you is intended as a contribution to that effort.

---

[1] At a teachers meeting at the London School of Economics and Political Science in 2007, Julian Le Grand proposed that he would teach a new postgraduate course that combined behavioural insights with public policy, and requested suggestions for a title for the course (a course that I now direct). Mara Airoldi suggested the title, Behavioural Public Policy, which Julian embraced. I cannot dismiss the possibility that someone else had previously used this term, but it was in that meeting that I first heard it.

The main motivations for writing this book are thus twofold: to outline the role of reciprocity from a multidisciplinary perspective, and to add to the efforts of making this concept more central in considerations of public policy design. The structure of the book is as follows. First, the various definitions of reciprocity will be summarised, and then the evolution of the phenomenon will be considered, in terms of its observation in non-human species, in very young humans, and in societies that we can reasonably expect are similar to those in which our distant ancestors lived. Some of the behavioural economic and social psychology literature that aims to discern when and in what circumstances reciprocity is likely to be observed and sustained will then be reviewed, before a discussion of the relevant domain(s) of reciprocity – i.e. economic and/or social – is offered. Reciprocity has a dark side – indeed many darks sides – and these will be considered, before focusing again on its potential benefits, and how these may best be realised. Some ways in which reciprocity might more specifically inform the design of public policy interventions will be presented, before a new political economy of behavioural public policy – of which reciprocity is a fundamental part – falling within, or at least alongside, the liberal economic tradition, is proffered. The book ends with some concluding thoughts.

NOTES ON STYLE

I have tried to write this book in a style that will be accessible and interesting to a multidisciplinary audience, and to experts, policy makers, students and interested laypersons. I have pitched it somewhere between popular science and a technical academic text, in the spirit of Daniel Kahneman's (2011) *Thinking Fast and Slow*.

When the occasion calls for it, I have used the terms 'she' and 'her' rather than 'he' and 'him'. Following a coin toss, I used the masculine terms in my previous book, and it was thus the turn of the feminine. British English is used throughout.

Footnotes are used in all of the chapters. The reader will be able to understand my arguments from the main text, but I like to think that the footnotes provide digressions and a little more nuance, and, indeed, that they enrich the narrative, and thus some readers may find them useful.

At the end of each chapter, in the form of a few questions, I have provided some *Food for Thought*. This again mirrors Kahneman's *Thinking Fast and Slow*; clearly, I think that he sets a good example. If I have provided at least a few people with some food for thought in the pages that follow, then I feel I will I have done my job.

Acknowledgements

The following people have in various ways served as sources of personal inspiration and kindness to me in the period over which I worked on this book, and I hope they feel that I have, in some form or other, reciprocated: George Akerlof, Tim Besley, Gwyn Bevan, Steve Birch, Larry Brown, Richard Cookson, Joan Costa-Font, Michael Gusmano, Mike Jones-Lee, Rudolf Klein, Julian Le Grand, Graham Loomes, Ted Marmor, Bob Sugden, Cass Sunstein, Albert Weale and Joe White. I owe thanks also to Phil Good at Cambridge University Press, and of course to Keti who, to me at least, is an unconditional altruist.

1 Setting the Scene

There is a huge multidisciplinary literature on the significance of reciprocity to the functioning of societies, some of it dating back many hundreds of years. Indeed, to the extent that reciprocity can be thought of an exhortation to treat others as you wish to be treated yourself, the importance of this so-called golden rule as an ethical imperative is as old as the history of recorded thought, and is central to many of the world's major religions. In Luke 6.31 of the New Testament, for instance, Jesus asks us to do unto others as we would have them do unto us, and the Jewish religious leader, Hillel the Elder, alive at around the same time as Christ, reportedly went as far as to say that the golden rule is the *whole* of the Torah. In his classic book, *The Gift*, the social anthropologist Marcel Mauss (1954) noted that the Latin *do ut des* and the Sanskrit *dadami se, dehi me*, which both can be translated to 'I give in order that you may give', are found in Western and Eastern religious texts, and in the quasi-religious *Analects of Confucius* we are told that what we do not wish for ourselves we should not wish for others. Much of the above alludes, if sometimes loosely, to what is now known as reciprocal altruism or conditional co-operation; i.e., to repay kindness with kindness, and be willing to incur a cost in the expectation that it will be repaid in kind. Negative reciprocity, in the form of punishing harmful acts, akin to taking an eye for an eye, is embedded in the Old and New Testaments (e.g. Exodus and Matthew), the Torah, the Qur'an and, as we will see, in many more recent sources besides. Some may contend that the golden rule is too idealistic to be taken seriously in practice, but according to the evolutionary biologist Robert Trivers (1971), the notion that underlies the rule – namely, reciprocity – is observed in all known cultures.

Simple acts of reciprocity are of course older than recorded thought and, since they are common in the animal kingdom, we can state with some confidence, predate humans. The reader will know, for instance, that cats lick each other and primates, literally and metaphorically, scratch each other's backs. This type of instinctive, attitudinal reciprocity is common among humans and between species also; for example, a person who has a door held open for her might unthinkingly hold the next door ajar in return, and a dog who licks its owner's hand may receive a pat on the head. There is not much, if any, pre-calculated deliberation involved in these acts. They are a type of direct reciprocity (Nowak, 2011), which refers to some kind of to and fro between two partners in a dyadic – i.e., a one to one – exchange. Tit for tat is also a form of direct reciprocity – i.e., if you help me, I will help you, and if you stop helping me, I will stop helping you.[1] The political scientist Robert Axelrod (1984) once famously – at least in social science circles – reported that tit for tat is the optimum strategy for human co-operation, although others have since concluded that it is a poor strategy when the information about the payoffs or behaviour of one's partner is less than perfect, or when the group is large and the number of people willing to co-operate is small (Henrich and Henrich, 2007).[2] Leaving this aside, attitudinal reciprocity appears

[1] Nowak (2011) also refers to what might often be a more calculated form of tit for tat that he defines as generous tit for tat, in which a person never forgets a good turn and occasionally forgives a bad turn. Also, since standard tit for tat is vulnerable to people misunderstanding others' intentions, which could lead to endless rounds of retribution, Boyd (1989) and Novak and Sigmund (1992) propose contrite tit for tat, where one side retaliates only if the other side has defected in two consecutive rounds, and forgiving tit for tat, where one side automatically forgives one third of the defections committed by the other side. On the flipside, in order to discourage defections from live-and-let-live truces between British and German soldiers during, for instance, mealtimes in the trenches of World War I, it was known on both sides that any rogue shell would be met by two in response (Sapolsky, 2017). These truces demonstrate that reciprocity can hold between enemies in the most extreme circumstances.

[2] Talcott Parsons (1951) noted, perhaps somewhat optimistically, that once a stable relationship of mutual benefit – akin to tit for tat, or rather tat for tat – has been established, it is self-perpetuating, and no additional mechanisms are needed to reinforce it.

to have arisen earlier in the evolutionary chain than a more deliberative form of reciprocity, conferring some form of advantage to those animals that behaved as such. In humans, attitudinal reciprocity may have served as the kernel for the later tendency towards more complex, co-operative endeavours.

So far, then, I have referred to reciprocal altruism, negative reciprocity, attitudinal reciprocity and direct reciprocity, and when one delves into the rich multidisciplinary literature on this topic, these and other definitions of reciprocity, sometimes with more than one term referring to the same concept, frequently arise. Given this confusion of terminology, it seems apt to spend a little time outlining the main concepts of reciprocity, before honing in on those that will inform the rest of this book.

TYPES OF RECIPROCITY

In a book published in 2008, the French economist Serge-Christophe Kolm wrote:

> Reciprocity is to treat other people as other people treat you, voluntarily and not as a result of a binding exchange agreement ... Good social relations in general, which are essential for the amenity and value of a society, are sustained by reciprocity ... It is no surprise, therefore, that most social reformers have advocated a greater role for reciprocity as the alternative to coercive hierarchy, selfish exchange, and the utopia of unconditional altruism. (Kolm, 2008, pp. 1–2)

One could contend quite reasonably that coercive hierarchy, in the form of command and control policies, selfish exchange, informed by standard economic theory, and unconditional altruism, in informing the creation and development of many welfare states in the post–World-War-II era, have had a powerful influence on public policy design, and that the 'greater role for reciprocity' has generally gone somewhat unheeded. Kolm, to emphasise the richness of reciprocity, goes on to classify this notion into the following three types, all of which go beyond mere instinctive attitudinal reciprocity and rely more on deliberation and stored memory:

1. **Balance or Matching Reciprocity.** The motivation here, according to Kolm, is to return a gift with the aim of restoring some property of balance or fairness between the exchange partners.
2. **Liking Reciprocity.** Here, the return gift is motivated by a positive affective sentiment towards the initial giver, a feeling that may arise when the initial giver's gift or favour is perceived to have been offered benevolently. Kolm maintains that the sentiments underlying liking reciprocity are those of altruism and affection, and it is plausible that the relationship embedded in this type of exchange matters over and above the actual goods exchanged, or, in other words, the exchange has an intrinsic and not merely instrumental value.
3. **Continuation Reciprocity.** This is akin to exchange driven by self-interest, whereby all partners benefit by continuous positive reciprocal acts, and with retaliation to deter unfavourable actions – which Trivers (1971) termed moralistic aggression – as its negative counterpart.[3] If the number of people who are willing to punish transgressors in a particular population is too small, egoistic actions become more profitable and may drive out reciprocal altruism.[4] Many might see continuation reciprocity as the

---

[3] Some people are willing to pay a personal cost to punish transgressors and are hence called altruistic punishers, but given that neural imaging studies have shown that people often appear to gain pleasure in punishing and taking revenge (Gospic et al., 2011; Strobel et al., 2011), perhaps these punishers are not always as altruistic as they might on the face of it appear. Moreover, although incurring an immediate cost, the possibility that altruistic punishers expect their actions to reap longer term gains for themselves cannot be discounted (Trivers, 1971). Nowak (2011), who tends to believe that punishment is counterproductive, prefers to call this costly rather than altruistic punishment, partly because he believes that the punisher can, in fact, bear some cost to themselves and partly because he takes the view that punishment in real life is hardly ever altruistic – that punishment can mark an escalation in conflict and is often motivated by anger or greed, or to suppress or exploit others. Sapolsky (2017) concurs, believing that punishment should never be considered a virtue.

[4] The sociologist Alvin Gouldner (1960, p. 173) defined egoism as 'a salient (but not exclusive) concern with the satisfaction of one's own needs'. He therefore sees reciprocity, when driven by long-term mutual self-interest, as being egoistical, writing that 'the norm of reciprocity enlist[s] egoistic motivations in the service of social system stability'. However, in this book, egoism will be taken to mean *the exclusive* and somewhat shortsighted concern with the satisfaction of one's own wants and/or needs. It can be thought of as a highly selfish form of self-interest, with an egoistic actor willing to transgress group dynamics to benefit herself entirely whenever the

principle motivation for the reciprocal altruism and negative reciprocity mentioned earlier – i.e., it is in the self-interest of all exchange partners that these actions occur. This was the view taken by the Scottish Enlightenment philosopher David Hume, who in his *A Treatise of Human Nature* (1740) saw reciprocity as being motivated not by kindness, but because one expects the other person to return in kind in the future. Kolm himself, however, unlike the fairness and altruism embedded in balance and liking reciprocities, does not believe that actions driven by self-interest are pure forms of reciprocity.

Putting to one side Kolm's assertion that continuation reciprocity is not in fact a pure form of reciprocity, he does recognise that the three motivations defined above coexist across people, and often within a single individual. Moreover, he alludes to two further types of reciprocity, which are less about fundamental initial motivations of fairness, altruism and self-interest in a direct dyadic exchange, and are instead focused upon how people's reactions to these initial exchanges might have knock-on effects across a wider community:

4. **Generalised Reciprocity**. This is the notion that having benefited from somebody's help, a person is more likely to help other people, and is defined as indirect reciprocity by Sapolsky (2017). We can transport ourselves to a ready example of indirect reciprocity, whereby a car driver, on being let into the flow of traffic by another driver, will, one would hope, be more likely to give way to other users of the road. Thus, indirect reciprocity can involve a large number of actors, where, rather than the dyadic relationship in direct reciprocity, the individual's relationship is that between themselves and society in general, and thus this type of reciprocity affords wider co-operation within a group. We will see later in this book that fostering indirect reciprocity ought to be an important consideration in public policy.

---

opportunity arises, and therefore differs from the enlightened self-interest that often drives reciprocal relationships. It is typically (if, admittedly, not necessarily correctly) taken that the implicit assumption in standard economic theory is that human self-interest is egoistic rather than enlightened, and much of the time, enlightened self-interest will require somewhat more sophisticated – if often still almost instinctive – strategic decision-making and lower rates of time preference (i.e a tendency to be patient) than selfish egoism. Also, as an aside but as will be discussed in more depth in Chapter 9, it is assumed here that the objective of an individual's enlightened self-interest is decided by the individual herself, and may differ across individuals.

5. **Reverse Reciprocity**. Here, Kolm argues, people who are known to help others are themselves helped by others still, because they are thought of as deserving, a phenomena that is also often known as indirect reciprocity (and thus for the purposes of this book, acts of generalised reciprocity and reverse reciprocity will be both labelled as indirect reciprocity). A person's reputation is therefore fundamental to the operation of reverse reciprocity, which is an important reason why reputation has evolved to be such an important part of most people's psyche. To paraphrase Napoleon, men will die for a bit of ribbon to be placed on their chests, or to quote directly the biologist Martin Nowak (2011, p. 54):

> Thanks to the power of reputation, we help others without expecting an immediate return. If, thanks to endless chat and intrigue, the world knows that you are a good, charitable guy, then you boost your chance of being helped by someone else at some future date. The converse is also the case. I am less likely to get my back scratched, in the form of a favour, if it becomes known that I never scratch anybody else's. Indirect reciprocity now means something like 'If I scratch your back, my good example will encourage others to do the same and, with luck, someone will scratch mine'.

Reputation serves as a proxy for experience[5]; Nowak (p. 67), quoting the evolutionary biologist David Haig, goes on to state, 'For direct reciprocity you need a face. For indirect reciprocity you need a name'. Ebay and Amazon sellers – to name just two domains – rely on publicised feedback to generate a positive reputation, in the hope that buyers will 'co-operate' with them, and if good reputations spread quickly enough, co-operation in a society has a better chance of

---

[5] This notion applies to goods and services as well as people. For instance, there is a small noodle shop in central London called Kanada-Ya, that always has a large number of people outside it queuing for a table. I have no idea if the food is any good, but the queue signifies that it must be, and on passing it I always want to taste the noodles that it has to offer (although not so much as to join the very long queue). Similarly, the scarcity value that people attach to goods that appear to be running out – e.g., 'only two left in stock' – may be underpinned by the thought that, although we do not know it directly, the apparent high demand for the product indicates that it must be good.

emerging and continuing. I shall return to the importance of reputation to reciprocity and co-operation at several points in this book. As noted in the quote from Nowak, indirect reciprocity (and for that matter all of the other types of reciprocity mentioned above), can also have a negative counterpart. That is, a person who feels maligned by one person may also be more likely to malign other people – think of the car drivers – and a person who is unhelpful to others may garner a poor reputation and, as a consequence, may be shunned – or worse – by one and all.

As stated above, Kolm acknowledged that the fundamental motivations for acting reciprocally – i.e., for the sake of fairness, altruism and self-interest – can coexist, and indeed may intertwine (e.g. the notion of a fair exchange to promote the self-interest of all trading partners). It is very difficult, if not impossible, to tease out the relative impacts of these types of motivation on reciprocal behaviours, but one of the most repeated and robust experiments in the field of behavioural economics – the so-called ultimatum game – has uncovered reciprocal patterns in respondent groups in many countries that can plausibly be attributed to at least some of the types of reciprocity outlined above. As a precursor to various discussions offered later in the book, and as an illustration of how some of the motivations outlined above might drive people's choices in simple controlled contexts, it may not be without merit for the reader to be given an ultimatum.

A SIMPLE EXPERIMENT

In the ultimatum game, first reported by the economist Werner Güth and his colleagues (1982), each participant is assigned as either a 'proposer' or a 'responder'. Proposers and responders are paired and typically remain unaware of one another's identity. The proposer is given an amount of money, which can be any amount but is often in the range of £10–20 (or $), and is asked for the share of her endowment that she is willing to give to her responder. The proposer is told that if the responder accepts the share offered, then the proposer is left with the remainder, but if the responder declines then both parties receive nothing.

The argument is often proposed that, according to standard economic theory, with its underlying assumption that people are invariably entirely selfishly, or egoistically, self-interested, the proposer should offer a tiny percentage of her endowment, because she will want to keep as much of the money as possible, and responders will accept tiny offers, because they will consider anything at all to be better than nothing. However, the general finding across multiple studies is for the mean offer from proposers to exceed 40 per cent of their endowment, for modal offers to be 50 per cent, for offers of less than 30 per cent to be frequently rejected by responders and for offers of less than 20 per cent, although rare, to be rejected half of the time (for reviews see Camerer and Thaler, 1995; Henrich et al., 2005; Kahneman, Knetsch and Thaler, 1986; Roth, 1995).

Some economists, including Kenneth Binmore, maintain that these results do not, in fact, necessarily undermine the descriptive validity of standard economic theory, by arguing that it is not axiomatic in economics that utility increases with money holdings, and that whether utility maximisation equates to income maximisation is an empirical question (Binmore, 2005). They rightly claim that the experimental approach to understanding social norms is common among game theorists, that standard theory is more nuanced than critics often give it credit for and that standard theory requires only that people are consistent in their choices. Behavioural economists and others have amply demonstrated that this latter assumption is, at the very least, heroic, but it is true that standard theory merely requires that people maximise *something* (i.e. not necessarily money). Economists could of course raise many other objections to the findings of the ultimatum game, not least in relation to its external validity. For example, it is uncommon in real life that people are given what may be viewed as essentially 'free' money (i.e. windfall money), and proposers and responders might both react differently to the figures summarised in the previous paragraph in the more realistic context of proposers being required to do something to earn their initial money holdings.[6]

Nonetheless, it can reasonably be contended that the ultimatum game is a simple device that demonstrates that people are influenced by different reciprocal motivations in particular contexts; that man is less *homo economicus* in the common understanding of the term, and more *homo reciprocus*, in the words of the sociologist Howard Becker (1956). For instance, many proposers in the typical ultimatum game are motivated to offer a substantial share of their endowment by the desire to maximise their final holdings, given their knowledge that if they offer an amount that is deemed unfair by the responder, they will end up with nothing.[7] That is to say, that they are aware that responders, implicitly driven by balance reciprocity, are motivated to respond negatively to very low offers, and thus the proposers, driven by something resembling continuation reciprocity, offer an amount that they feel will be just sufficient to avoid punishment, thereby – in their mind – maximising their expected final holdings.[8] If this occurs, the proposer is therefore fundamentally self-interested, but is sensitive to the possible reactions of other human beings to her decisions.

---

[6] In recent unpublished experiments that I have conducted that replicate the ultimatum game with the exception that proposers have to undertake tasks to earn their initial endowments (and with responders being aware of this fact), proposers tend to offer shares of their endowments that are somewhat smaller – although still substantial – than that generally observed, and responders are typically willing to accept nothing (or very close to nothing). The responders' reactions were motivated by something akin to balance reciprocity; i.e., they took the view that since the proposers had earned and thus deserved the money and that they themselves had done nothing, it would be unfair to punish the proposers for low offers.

[7] Gintis et al. (2005) report a variant of the ultimatum game where rejection by responders left only them, and not the proposers, with nothing, which led to responders never rejecting offers, suggesting that rejection is driven entirely by the desire to punish. In this variant, proposers made much smaller but still positive offers, implying a residual of fairness amid the self-interest.

[8] The ultimatum game is often a one-shot game, and thus in these circumstances contrary to what the 'continuation' in continuation reciprocity implies, the proposers and responders are not forging a longstanding relationship based on mutual self-interest. However, they are attempting to forge an arrangement that leads, or continues, to a final outcome where they receive allocations of the endowment that both find acceptable.

As earlier noted, a condition of anonymity between the proposer and responder is usually assumed in the ultimatum game, but in many social and economic exchanges the parties are aware of each other's identity. If the participants knew each other in the ultimatum game, we might expect liking (or disliking) reciprocity to play a role, perhaps motivating the proposer to offer more of the endowment, and/or for their offer to be motivated by affection rather than self-interest, and for the responder to be slower to punish. To a certain extent, liking reciprocity can also perhaps be biologically manipulated, and in non-anonymised circumstances, strengthened in the ultimatum game. For example, the neuroeconomist Paul Zak exposed proposers in a version of the ultimatum game to a nasal spray containing oxytocin (Zak, 2012). Oxytocin is the hormone that prepares female mammals for childbirth and lactation, helps mothers to bond with their offspring and is often labelled as a facilitator of trust. Zak reported that this increased offers by 80 per cent compared to placebo. He further reported that women, who as one might expect naturally produce more oxytocin than men, tend to be more generous in these somewhat abstract games, although Henrich et al. (2005) did not observe any strong or consistent effect of sex on ultimatum game responses. Zak also noted that infusions of testosterone – which blocks the binding of oxytocin to its receptors – was associated with ultimatum game offers that were 27 per cent less generous compared to placebo. Before concluding that oxytocin should be released into the water supply, however, the neuroendocrinologist Robert Sapolsky (2017) warns that this hormone has a dark side. For instance, when the players in co-operation games remain anonymous to each other and are placed in different rooms, oxytocin *diminishes* generosity. It therefore appears that oxytocin strengthens the bond with those you know, but turns you against those who, in an evolutionary sense and particularly at times of childbirth and rearing, you might perceive as a threat. Furthermore, in the right circumstances, testosterone has a pro-social bright side. For instance, the neurobiologist Christoph Eisenegger, with colleagues including the economist Ernst Fehr, reported that when the ultimatum game is repeated and thus one's reputation further on in the experiment might depend on being fair and is thus a source of pride, proposers are *more* generous if given testosterone in advance (Eisenegger et al., 2010).[9,10]

Therefore, the case is made that the relative driving forces of the different types of reciprocity on human decision-making are likely to be mixed and highly contextual, even within the same overarching framework of something as simple as the ultimatum game, and one can only imagine how contextual the observation of these different motivations will be in something as complex as the real world.[11] In this book, I will pay relatively little further attention to whether

---

[9] Sapolsky (2017, p. 115) goes on to note that 'oxytocin enhances charitability – but only in people who are already so. This mirrors testosterone's only raising aggression in aggression-prone people. Hormones rarely act outside the context of the individual and his or her environment'. Sapolsky explains that the effect of genes on behaviour is also heavily dependent on a person's environment. For example, some people have a particular sequence of gene that makes them relatively unresponsive to dopamine, a hormone associated with impulsive behaviours. It has been shown that children with this sequence are less generous than the average child if they have an insecure attachment to their parents, but if they have a secure attachment to their parents, they are more generous than the average. A lesson here is to be cautious about the generalisations that can be readily found in popular science books. Zak also writes in his book that he insists that all visitors must hug him, to feel the benefits of the associated oxytocin release. For multiple reasons, a lesson there is not to follow suit.

[10] Dr Eisenegger was killed by a venomous snake bite in Namibia in 2017. As well as an obvious human tragedy, this was a tragedy for his scholarly field.

[11] It is possible to think of further types of reciprocity to those mentioned above. For instance, there is a form of self-reciprocation where one can reward or sanction oneself if one undertakes or fails to undertake an action that may be deemed in some sense good. For example, I may promise myself that if I go to the gym I will reward myself with a doughnut. Behavioural economists sometimes classify observations similar to this as irrational spillover effects, in that the reward may undo the good behaviour (i.e. in terms of net calorie intake in relation to the gym and the doughnut) (e.g. Dolan and Galizzi, 2015). Sapolsky (2017) attributes similar spillovers to humans being able to carry a finite cognitive load. That is, since willpower is a finite resource, any attempt to regulate our social behaviour (say, engage dutifully in recycling behaviours) might make the frontal cortex of our brains work hard, and immediately after our performance on a different frontal cortex-dependent task may suffer (e.g. we might turn the heating or air conditioning up higher than is necessary). However, spillovers appear to relate to automatic actions rather than the pre-planned self-reciprocation to which I refer. For example, I may want a doughnut and, ideally, I want to go to the gym, but the gym requires an effort in the moment. I am not concerned with my net calorie intake, but denying myself the doughnut until I have been to the gym will ensure that I exercise today. There is nothing irrational about that.

reciprocity is driven specifically by fairness, altruism or self-interest, although in Chapter 5 I will touch upon work that examines whether reciprocal actions are motivated by the distribution of outcomes or by people's intentions (or both). The point that I want to convey here is that with these different types of reciprocity the terminology used in relation to this concept in the literature is many and mixed. Moreover, occasionally the same terminology is used to define different concepts and different terminologies have been used to define the same concept. This is a recipe for confusion; thus, for purposes of clarity in relation to the remainder of this book, I will proffer my ingredients now, simply and clearly (hopefully). I will use the term reciprocal altruism to refer to those circumstances where a kind action is rewarded with kindness (subject to some concern with outcomes), and the term negative reciprocity where unkindness is met with punishment. Despite the possible objections noted earlier, I will call a person who is engaged in negative reciprocity an altruistic punisher, and thus, even if the reader disagrees with the use of this terminology, my meaning is clear. I will use attitudinal reciprocity for the automatic reactional exchanges that are common in the animal kingdom and direct reciprocity for the dyadic exchanges that occur between partners. Finally, in relation to non-dyadic exchanges, and as earlier noted, I will group generalised reciprocity and reverse reciprocity under the umbrella term of indirect reciprocity; that is, where a person's actions towards others are influenced by how still others have acted towards her, and where a person's reputation, rather than the direct observation of her actions, influences how others treat her. But aside from our individual altruistic, fairness-related and self-interested concerns, are there bigger reasons – reasons that go beyond the *self* – for our reciprocal motivations?

TO WHAT END?

Embedded in the earlier quote from Serge-Christophe Kolm (2008, p. 1) was the line, 'Good social relations in general, which are essential for the amenity and value of a society, are sustained by reciprocity'. That, in a nutshell, may be the fundamental benefit of reciprocal actions: to the extent that reciprocity sustains the societies that we are all part of, to have people behave in these ways is presumably often good for their *selves*, and it is good for everyone else too. The evolutionary biologist Joseph Henrich extends this notion beyond mere social sustenance when he argues that an 'approach to explaining our species' ecological dominance focuses on our prosociality, our abilities to co-operate intensively across many different domains and extensively in large groups. Here the idea is that natural selection made us highly social and co-operative, and then by working together we conquered the globe' (Henrich, 2016, p. 11). Henrich's main focus is on culturally transmitted information – i.e., the human ability to pass on learning from generation to generation that no other animal seems to match – but the evolved social norm of reciprocity, which is a nutrient for co-operation, is one of these cultural transmissions.[12,13,14]

This is not to argue that all people will behave reciprocally, nor that any single person will do so all of the time, but it is to recognise that a tendency for most people to reciprocate much of the time strengthens the groups in which we live. That this social norm has evolved over tens of thousands of years has resulted in people complying with it without really acknowledging explicitly why they do so;

---

[12] Henrich (2016) suggests that humans developed their particular co-operative tendencies because we are ground apes and were forced to band together due to the threat from predators. The survival chances of these groups improved when their members behaved co-operatively, and co-operation was facilitated by reciprocation.

[13] The definition of culture has a complex history, but for our purposes, following Sapolsky (2017), we can take it to mean the non-genetic transmission of knowledge on how we do and think about things.

[14] Fehr and Gächter, S. (2000a, p. 166) define a social norm as "1) a behavioural regularity; that is 2) based on a socially shared belief of how one ought to behave; which triggers 3) the enforcement of the prescribed behavior by informal social sanctions." They contend that the altruistic punishment of free riders helps to enforce social norms and is one of the most important consequences of reciprocity (see also Boehm, 2012). Fehr and Fischbacher (2004) and Kurzban et al. (2007) appear to concur, claiming that third party punishment of transgressors is required in order for social norms to survive – direct dyadic punishment is not sufficient, particularly as societies become larger and more atomistic, potentially creating more opportunities for egoism.

that is, it now seems almost part of human nature.[15] In terms of the general implausibility of widespread pure altruism, the social psychologist Jonathan Haidt (2012) has gone so far as to suggest that the general human reaction to prefer to give something for something rather than something for nothing can partially explain the relative success of right-of-centre compared to leftist political parties, at least in the United States and the United Kingdom, in modern times. However, given the temptations for people to act egoistically, the authors of the great religious and ethical codes (for instance) probably knew that reciprocity should not be taken for granted, and that this social norm needs to be reinforced normatively. Hence, the pronouncements alluded to in the introduction of this chapter. In this sense, and as acknowledged by none other than Charles Darwin (1879), the normative may have been driven by practices that had evolved gradually and descriptively.[16] If it is possible to place such monumental arguments in a nutshell, religions may therefore have been designed, in part, to reinforce the importance of a behavioural motivation that most humans, much of the time, accept intrinsically, and which strengthens the group collective. As a signpost to some of the discussion in later chapters, it may be telling that these codes developed markedly in an era of heightening interfaith competition, and that with the growth in their number of followers rendering the direct observation and punishment of transgressors into egoism ever more infeasible, and with the increasing atomisation of many societies, the importance to the functioning of these groups of the all seeing eye – the ultimate altruistic punisher – was, and remains, profound (an

---

[15] Henrich (2016) also notes that people comply with a host of social norms even when their understanding of why the norm originally developed is lacking, such as the taboo on eating pork, or seafood when pregnant, in some cultures, or buying rounds of drinks in others.

[16] The philosopher Cristina Bicchieri (2006) distinguishes norms of justice from other social norms by arguing that insofar that their normative legitimacy is acknowledged, we have a preference for abiding by them. For example, if the norm of reciprocity is recognised as being good for the functioning of society, we will have a relatively strong preference for abiding by it. Perhaps those in authority can therefore manufacture particularly strong norms by lending them normative force, which may be used for good or evil.

example of using the concept of the all-seeing eye(s) in a practical application in the London Borough of Southwark is pictured in Figure 1.1).[17] In short, as societies became bigger and more atomised, religious codes may have developed as an attempt to maintain the bonds of humanity.

It is therefore more than plausible that reciprocity aids co-operation and is thus beneficial to groups. In that public policy is in large part centred on group performance, maintaining and fostering reciprocity ought to be a central public policy concern because an erosion of reciprocity, even if not absolute, could be severely detrimental to the cohesion of the group. Engaging in reciprocal action is often effortful and, as earlier noted, there is evidence that suggests that people are less likely to be pro-social after performing a task that places strain on the frontal cortex (Sapolsky, 2017). Therefore, given that public policy contexts are often challenging for those working within them, it would seem to make sense to make it as easy as possible for people to act reciprocally in these environments, and certainly to avoid crowding out their reciprocal tendencies. Gintis et al. (2005) concur with the view that reciprocity is essential for group cohesion in that they argue that a high level of co-operation can only be attained when there is a sufficient proportion of strong reciprocators – i.e., people who are both reciprocal altruists *and* altruistic punishers – in the

---

[17] The concept of an all-seeing eye is being used, in a sense, in experiments on what is known as priming. To illustrate, consider a study reported by Bateson, Nettle and Roberts (2006), who focused on office workers who were allowed to help themselves to tea or coffee in a shared kitchen on the understanding that they would make voluntary contributions to pay for further supplies. For a period of ten weeks, a poster was displayed next to the suggested price list, with the picture alternating each week between an image of flowers, and an image of a pair of eyes. The contributions were three times higher in the 'eye weeks' than in the 'flower weeks', indicating that the reminder of being watched, albeit directly unseeingly, was sufficient to motivate people to contribute more money. Incidentally, the defunct Presidio Modelo prison complex in Cuba, inspired by the ideas of Jeremy Bentham, was based on a similar principle; see www.atlasobscura.com/places/presidio-modelo. People can also be primed in other ways. For example, Cohn, Fehr and Maréchal (2014) prompted bank workers using words on a questionnaire to get them to think about their banking identity and found that this increased the likelihood of them cheating by 20 per cent in a coin toss game that had financial rewards than if they were not primed as such.

FIGURE 1.1 Practical priming with the all-seeing eye

population. On the basis of evidence from controlled experiments, Fehr and Fischbacher (2005) contend that 40–50 per cent of people are strong reciprocators, implying that 50–60 per cent of people are not, although the percentage of strong reciprocators may well be much higher if the question is focused on who is a strong reciprocator some, but not all, of the time. Moreover, the sociologist Toshio Yamagishi (1986) suggests that, depending on their personality type, people adopt different roles to maintain co-operative endeavours, with less trusting individuals less likely to be reciprocal altruists than their more trusting counterparts, but more likely to be altruistic punishers, and thus although strong reciprocity in a single individual may be relatively rare, strong reciprocity within a population is likely to be commonplace. The reader is unlikely to find it difficult to think of circumstances where acquaintances appear to have been motivated by selfish egoism; on the flipside, the anthropologists Eric Smith and Rebecca Bliege Bird (2005) note that people occasionally undertake generous acts, such as those associated with charity and self-sacrifice, that are not contingent on reciprocity. According to this reasoning, pure altruism is sometimes evident, although these acts may be done to enhance reputation so as to indicate that the person is worthy of co-operation. Moreover, extreme self-sacrifice often tends to be associated with the belief of being rewarded in the afterlife. This said, to varying degrees, it is likely that most people are egoistically selfish, unconditionally altruistic and – not or – reciprocally motivated depending on the circumstances, but for the success of a group, our co-operative and reciprocal tendencies – our sense of fairness in exchange relationships – appear to be of considerable importance.

To conclude, what I have hoped to convey in this chapter is that reciprocity, both in the descriptive sense that it can be observed and in the normative sense that it ought to be demonstrated, can be found almost everywhere. The different types of reciprocity – for example, direct and indirect forms of reciprocal altruism and negative reciprocity – are essential to intragroup cohesion and co-operation, and in that public sector services are essentially group environments, with relationships within and between purchasers, providers, governments and users, they are heavily reliant on reciprocal relationships if they are to perform well. Yet even with the aid of a hypothetical abstraction as simple as the ultimatum game (let alone the complexities of the real world), the extent to which the different types of reciprocity are observed in people's behaviours, or indeed whether any type of reciprocity is observed at all, will be driven heavily by the contexts or environments – or what the nudge theorists Richard Thaler and Cass Sunstein (2008) might call the choice architecture – that they face. This is because the context cradles the meaning of the interaction, and the meaning that people attach to the way the context is designed, described or framed drives their behavioural responses. Therefore, public policies, organisations and institutions should be designed carefully to reinforce and crowd in – and certainly not crowd out – reciprocal motivations and actions.

To reiterate then, given the right circumstances, many, perhaps most, people will engage in reciprocal relationships with those around them, but how deep is this motivation within us? Looking a little at the behaviours of infants and other animals might offer up some clues as to whether reciprocal tendencies are, to a degree, innate.

FOOD FOR THOUGHT

1. Do people act reciprocally purely for the purpose of self-interest?
2. Do altruistic punishers hold groups together?
3. Does the ultimatum game relate at all to the real world?

2 Animals and Infants

In Chapter 1, I referred to attitudinal reciprocity and it being common in the animal kingdom, including among humans and between species. As with most common behaviours, there are likely to be good evolutionary explanations for why this occurs. Cats may lick each other, for instance, particularly around the back of the neck where it is hard for them to reach themselves, in order to remain clean and relatively free of parasites. It may even be the case that these simple acts of instinctive reciprocity served as the kernel – the evolutionary link – to more complex, deliberative, memory-based forms of reciprocity that are thought by some to be the preserve of human beings; this chapter addresses whether this latter belief is justified.

Inferring the nature of our distant ancestors by studying behaviours in non-human primates has a long history, and was an approach adopted by the zoologist Konrad Lorenz (1966) and the playwright Robert Ardrey (1966), among others. Some believe that a way in which to discern whether the roots of human morality predate our cultural institutions is to extend our study beyond the boundaries of our species (see Boehm, 2012; Sapolsky, 2017). In the spirit of this tradition, in this chapter, I will consider some of the evidence on whether non-human primates, and occasionally other animals, appear to demonstrate forms of reciprocity that go beyond the mere attitudinal. If evidences of such behaviours are convincing, we might conclude that the tendency towards deliberative reciprocity, by being core to non-human activities, is not something that has been learned merely within human societies, but is deeper, and is foundational to the way in which various categories of animals have organised themselves. It may lend support to the notion that deliberative reciprocity, if not exactly innate, was learned so long ago that its learning may have predated the emergence of modern humans, and may thus be considered practically innate to our species. If that is not convincing, it might still lend support to the notion that reciprocal actions are necessary to the proper functioning of groups.

On the subject of whether reciprocity is learned or innate, some attention in this chapter will also be paid to whether very young children show signs of behaving reciprocally almost instinctively, or at the very least, whether they develop concerns, such as an attention to reputation, that appear not to be taught and that might be essential for indirect reciprocal behaviours to occur. But let us first consider other animals.

NON-PRIMATES

Sir Alex Ferguson, the famed former manager of Manchester United and one of the most successful sports coaches of all time, used to occasionally call a halt to training sessions and ask his players to look to the sky. He would point to the V formation of migrating geese on their 4,000 mile journey, and explain that each bird would take a turn at the front, before joining the following flock, so that they all, by behaving reciprocally, maximised their chances of reaching their destination safely. It was a perfect machine, he would allegedly say, designed to achieve a final goal, and then he would tell his players that if they could do the same they could win the league. Eleven players running around, doing their own thing, acting egoistically, would not win anything.

Although Sir Alex has lectured at Harvard Business School, he is not, of course, a scholar, at least not in a formal sense, and thus some might readily dismiss his musings. Yet since long ago, learned individuals have speculated similarly, maintaining that animals mutually act to help each other. More than one hundred years ago, for instance, the Russian activist and philosopher Peter (actually, Pyotr) Kropotkin (1902/2014, p. 8), wrote

> It is not love, and not even sympathy ... which induces a herd of ruminants or of horses to form a ring in order to resist an attack of

wolves; not love which induces wolves to form a pack for hunting; not love which induces kittens or lambs to play, or a dozen of species of young birds to spend their days together in the autumn; and it is neither love nor personal sympathy which induces many thousand fallow-deer scattered over a territory as large as France to form into a score of separate herds, all marching towards a given spot, in order to cross there a river. It is a feeling infinitely wider than love or personal sympathy – an instinct that has been slowly developed among animals and men in the course of an extremely long evolution, and which has taught animals and men alike the force they can borrow from the practice of mutual aid and support, and the joys they can find in social life.

Kropotkin further argued that when animals have to struggle against a scarcity of food, competition results in calamity for the whole species in terms of health and vigour, and thus that no progressive evolution of the species can be based on intense competition.[1] He contended that mutual aid therefore emerged as a law of nature – an argument in favour of the pre-human origin of moral instincts – and referred to Charles Darwin to support his views:

In the *Descent of Man* [Darwin] points out how, in numberless animal societies, the struggle between separate individuals for the means of existence disappears, how struggle is replaced by co-

[1] Perhaps more than anything else, Kropotkin (1902/2014) is disdainful of competition, because 'competition is not the rule either in the animal world or in mankind. It is limited among animals to exceptional periods, and natural selection finds better fields for its activity. Better conditions are created by the elimination of competition by means of mutual aid and mutual support. In the great struggle for life – for the greatest possible fullness and intensity of life with the least waste of energy – natural selection continually seeks out the ways precisely for avoiding competition ... Don't compete! – competition is always injurious to the species, and you have plenty of resources to avoid it!' (pp. 50–1). Competition, which might be necessary in times of scarcity in order to try to ensure short-term survival, also points to a very strong focus on the immediate moment (i.e. a very high discount rate), akin to what behavioural economists have termed present bias. Such a strong focus on the immediate moment might generally be viewed as myopic in circumstances where extreme scarcity is not apparent, and where a more considered co-operative effort might bring greater longer term rewards to the group.

operation, and how that substitution results in the development of intellectual and moral faculties which secure to the species the best conditions for survival. He intimated that in such cases the fittest are not the physically strongest, nor the cunningest, but those who learn to combine so as mutually to support each other, strong and weak alike, for the welfare of the community. (Kropotkin, 2014, p. 12)[2]

Kropotkin used the example of the eusocial insects to also contend that negative reciprocity plays a forceful role in maintaining group cohesion in the animal kingdom. 'If an ant which has its crop full has been selfish enough to refuse feeding a comrade', wrote Kropotkin (1902/2014, p. 18), 'it will be treated as an enemy, or even worse. If the refusal has been made while its kinsfolk were fighting with some other species, they will fall back upon the greedy individual with greater vehemence than even upon the enemies themselves.' Kropotkin believed that societies would not exist for any gregarious animal without interference in favour of the wronged, and that a collective sense of justice becomes a habit.

Ants are often referred to as a species that engage in reciprocal and co-operative behaviours more generally, with the great American biologist Edward O. Wilson (1971) believing that these behaviours in the eusocial insects are now caused by genetic evolution rather than learning or cultural forces. Martin Nowak draws on an interesting comparison that Wilson made between humans and leaf cutter ants, in that both owe their civilisation to agriculture. Nowak (2011, p. 168) states that:

What is remarkable is that while our relationship with plants catapulted our species out of its hunter-gatherer lifestyle 10,000

---

[2] Much later, Martin Nowak seemed to agree. 'Co-operation', he wrote, 'is the master architect of evolution' (Nowak, 2011, p. xviii). Darwin sometimes offered seemingly contradictory statements in his writings, but Kropotkin is interpreting at least some of Darwin's ideas correctly. Moreover, as Kropotkin implies, it is worth emphasising that when Darwin wrote 'fitness' he did not (necessarily) mean physical fitness, but rather fitness (i.e. suitability) to an environment.

years ago, some social insects achieved this transition 60 million years earlier. There may be parallels between the scenarios of animal and human eusocial evolution, and they are, we believe, well worth examining to shed light on how we made the step from wandering tribes of hunter-gatherers to hamlets, towns, and cities.

Wilson had written that superorganisms, such as ant colonies, arose from the initial formation of groups. However, the ant colony, rather than the ant, can now be thought of as the individual organism (and therefore not a group), with the ants acting more like cells supporting the larger organism than separate organisms doing their own thing. A collection of selfish ants, like a collection of cancerous cells, might thus eventually kill the body. Moreover, ants in a colony, by virtue of there being one queen, are technically all siblings, and therefore co-operation, it could be argued, is driven by their kinship.[3] Wilson believed that genetic mutations prevented ants from leaving their nests, which guaranteed the persistence of those initial 'groups', and emergent traits arose due to the interaction of colony members which, shaped by natural selection and environmental forces (including intense inter-colony competition), eventually led to sophisticated co-operation that benefits the nest, such as the construction of fungi gardens and the herding of aphids. In light of all that human beings have achieved, many of us undoubtedly think that we are the pinnacle of evolution and that we do not have much room to manoeuvre to further evolve, but in terms of co-operative instincts we may be tens of millions of years behind the eusocial insects. An intriguing possible implication is that at some point in our evolutionary future humans may become as genetically co-operative as ants, with the societies in which we live becoming superorganisms and each of us behaving as an individual cell. But we are not there yet.

Some may contend that these speculations are entering the realm of science fiction, and even if the conjectures are plausible,

---

[3] There are exceptions. For example, nests within wood ant supercolonies contain ants that are not all kin (Helanterä, 2009). See www.youtube.com/watch?v=RdPsVpD6b08.

our global collective lack of co-operation will probably destroy the world before we have ever evolved sufficient co-operative tendencies to save it. Moreover, examining a species that is so far genetically advanced than us in terms of its co-operative behaviours offers few lessons regarding contemporary non-related human beings' receptiveness towards acting reciprocally and co-operatively, and therefore perhaps cannot inform us on how to structure our societies or policy making contexts to bring out the best in people. Moreover, and more importantly, Kropotkin's view that ruminants and horses, for example, will bunch together due to the instinct of mutual aid when under attack is dismissed by most modern evolutionary theorists and animal behaviouralists (Sapolksy, 2017); instead, individual, as opposed to group, selection, where each animal is acting in its own rather than the group's interest, in line with the evolutionary biologist Richard Dawkins' (1976) arguments in his best seller, *The Selfish Gene*, is the generally more respected thesis.[4]

Nonetheless, Kropotkin's views, which, to reiterate, he expressed more than a century ago, are interesting in that they mirror the notion of group selection advocated by the English zoologist V. C. Wynne-Edwards, who received some attention in the 1960s (see Wynne-Edwards, 1986). As intimated above, Wynne-Edwards' ideas were ultimately dismissed in favour of individual selection by most evolutionary theorists (in large part due to the observation in numerous species of competitive infanticide following a change in group leadership), although in recent years, group selection theory, at least in relation to human populations, has been re-visited and increasingly

---

[4] Individual selection posits that the ruminants bunch together not to ensure some kind of mutual benefit but because by doing so each animal is minimising its own chances of being eaten. Sapolsky (2017, pp. 333–4) writes that 'Individual selection fares better than group selection in explaining basic behaviours. A hyena bears down on some zebras. What would the nearest one do if she's a group selectionist? Stand there, sacrificing herself for the group. In contrast, an individual selectionist zebra would run like hell. Zebras run like hell. Or consider hyenas that have just killed a zebra. Group selection mind-set – everyone calmly takes turns eating. Individual selection – frenzied free-for-all. Which is what occurs.'

accepted as a possibility by many people working in this field. We will return to group selection theory throughout this book.[5]

Others have contended that observations of mutualistic symbiosis – i.e. that of different species acting to offer each other long-term benefits – are examples of deliberative direct reciprocity in the animal kingdom. For example, Robert Trivers (1971) comments on the symbiosis between reef cleaner fish and their hosts, with the host getting cleaned of parasites and the cleaners having access to a stable, ample food source, free from the fear of becoming food themselves. There are numerous similar examples, some involving symbiosis between animals and plants. For instance, fig wasps are parasites of fig flowers, and they are also the only means of pollination and seed setting for these plants, so insect and plant both gain from their relationship (Axelrod and Hamilton, 1981). Beyond the eusocial insects, there are also some other examples in the animal kingdom of different members of the same species assuming different tasks so as to benefit the whole group. One member of a pod of killer whales, for example, has been observed

---

[5] Although those who address group selection often take it to mean circumstances in which an animal behaves unselfishly for the good of the group, Nowak offers a somewhat more nuanced definition. Nowak (2011, p. 93) states: 'Group selection makes no assumptions about whether individuals are co-operative or selfish, let alone whether genes themselves are truly selfish. Instead, it simply says that intense between-group competition will favour mechanisms that blur the distinction between group and individual welfare if they improve performance or fitness at the group level'. Nowak's definition implies that in group selection theory it is the outcome rather than the motivation that is assumed to have been the driver of apparently co-operative behaviours. For instance, group selection theory, according to Nowak, does not postulate that ruminants herd when under attack because each individual is trying to minimise its own chances of death, nor because the group of individuals choose to give each other mutual aid to protect the group, but because herding evolved as it is beneficial to the group in these circumstances, and that ruminants that did not develop this tendency were, over time, killed off. Some animals appear to act for the benefit of the whole group, while at the same time prioritising their own progeny. For example, dominant female ostriches incubate all (up to about 40) of the eggs from their herd, but by identifying the pattern of pores on the shells, take particular care of their own eggs. Kropotkin himself did not believe that, except in times of scarcity, there was much intra-species competition, but he does not deny that interspecies competition is common (e.g. the ruminants versus the wolves), which, akin to group-selection theory, he may have taken as the driver of within-species co-operation.

blowing bubbles to scare fish to the surface of the ocean where other members of the pod stun the fish with their tails (Henrich, 2016).

However, possibly the best example of reciprocal altruism among non-primates was reported by the biologist Gerald Wilkinson (1984), who conducted a study on food sharing among wild vampire bats in Costa Rica.[6] Wilkinson observed that when a bat has been successful in obtaining food during a hunt, which, for each individual bat, does not happen every night, it will regurgitate blood into the mouth of an unsuccessful non-related peer; interestingly, there is reciprocation between the same unrelated bats on a future night when their success levels are reversed. Thus, kinship ties are not driving this reciprocal behaviour, and it is not, of course, a simple instantaneous attitudinal response. It is apparently a co-operative behaviour that has evolved for the benefit of the group.

All in all, though, there does not appear to be much uncontested (or even lightly contested) evidence or support for the notion of a deliberative form of reciprocity among non-primates, although it is also probably fair to say that our knowledge of behaviours in this realm of the animal kingdom is, to understate it, incomplete. However, most research efforts devoted to studying strong reciprocity among non-human animals has to date focussed on primates, and here the evidence is mixed, depending partly on the species studied and partly on the researcher's interpretation of the behaviour that he or she observes.

NON-HUMAN PRIMATES

Mutual grooming is common among primates, but that will not be news to most readers. It brings to mind the English idiom, 'you scratch my back and I'll scratch yours', which essentially signifies an act of reciprocal altruism, although the origin of the phrase may well have nothing to do with monkeys or non-human apes.[7] As argued by the

---

[6] For further arguments and evidence, both for and against those originally proposed by Wilkinson, see Carter and Wilkinson (2013).

[7] The term probably originated from implicit agreements between sailors in seventeenth century England that if one of them were to receive a whipping for being, for example, disobedient or absent, then the other, if assigned the role of punisher, would whip the

anthropologist Joan Silk (2005), however, the extent to which mutual grooming is more than an act of attitudinal reciprocity is not known definitively. Nonetheless, Silk maintains that it is at least possible that this behaviour is practiced to afford protection, to build coalitions, to receive food and to gain access to newborns over which many female primates take a strong interest.

The Dutch primatologist Frans de Waal is less guarded in insisting that great apes and monkeys display behaviour that suggests something stronger than attitudinal reciprocity.[8] de Waal is fond of studying the behaviour of New World capuchin monkeys, which are a little further removed from humans than are apes (i.e. chimpanzees, bonobos, gorillas and orangutans).[9] One of his experiments has two capuchins placed in a cage, separated by wire mesh (de Waal, 2010). If both monkeys were required to pull on a counterweighted tray in order for only one of the two monkeys to reach a cup of apple slices, the monkey in receipt of the apple will push more of it through the wire mesh to the 'helper' than when he secured the apple entirely via his own efforts.[10] If the helper is not rewarded as such, he is less likely to help out if the task is repeated, and thus one might argue that the threat of negative reciprocity looms large, which again hints at an attitude that is beyond the mere reflexive.

A further example of capuchin monkeys (arguably) behaving reciprocally can be viewed in a film clip narrated by the naturalist and national treasure, Sir David Attenborough.[11] In the film there are two monkeys – Virgil and Vulcan – that are separated by a see-through barrier. Virgil has a pot of hazelnuts, and Vulcan has a rock that is needed to open the top of the pot. Vulcan sees Virgil circling the box

---

former only lightly (i.e. would merely scratch him), on the understanding that similar would happen if their roles were reversed.

[8] An entertaining TED talk in which de Waal describes some of his research can be viewed at www.youtube.com/watch?v=GcJxRqTs5nk.

[9] It is perhaps important to note that humans did not descend from the other apes, but rather share a common ancestor with them.

[10] I will refer to monkeys and apes as males. It seems appropriate.

[11] A man of impeccable taste, Sir David chose to grow up in Leicester. The film clip can be found by searching 'Attenborough monkey co-operation'.

and through a window in the barrier, passes (or, rather, throws) the rock to him. After struggling, Virgil eventually manages to open the box with the rock. Since he is physically separated from Vulcan he could, without immediate consequences, keep all of the hazelnuts for himself. However, through the window he hands three of the six nuts that were in the box to Vulcan, which, implicitly within the film clip, is attributed to Virgil reciprocating; i.e. by offering a fair share of the nuts as 'payment' to Vulcan for providing the rock.[12]

The experiments of the like undertaken by de Waal have been subject to much criticism, most notably in relation to the fact that the monkeys are known to each other (Henrich, 2016). From that line of argument, to test properly reciprocal exchanges, and to control for the confounding influences of kinship and other personal relationships, the monkeys would have to be strangers to each other. For instance, would Virgil have shared any of the hazelnuts if he had not known Vulcan at all, and, if not, then his tendency towards rewarding help would apply to only limited circumstances and would not relate very closely to many of the reciprocal exchanges that are observed in often large, atomised human societies. Others may contend, however, that many important reciprocal exchanges are not between partners who are anonymous to each other, and some may invariably be underpinned by a pre-existing deep personal relationship between the participants. Moreover, it is plausible that reciprocal relationships between kith and kin were an evolutionary stepping stone to reciprocal exchanges between strangers. On the presumption that humans are more evolutionarily advanced than capuchins, that these monkeys perhaps demonstrate a kind of reciprocity that is based upon memory of help and hindrance and is therefore more than instinctively attitudinal – even if observed only between individuals that are familiar to each other – seems noteworthy.

Placing this methodological point of contention aside, de Waal (2010) further contends that, based on his observations of a class of

---

[12] It ought to be noted, however, that Vulcan is considerably bigger than Virgil, and thus some hierarchical effects may have been at work.

primates that are a little closer to us, the chances of a captive chimpanzee receiving a share of food that has been handed to another chimpanzee will depend on whether he has administered a favour, such as grooming, to the food-laden chimpanzee within the previous half an hour to two hours. Interestingly, this tendency is lessened within close kin, where prior favours may be expected, weakening a kin-based explanation for the observed reciprocity. Moreover, de Waal argues that among wild chimpanzees, a male's chance of receiving a share of captured prey appears to depend on his role in the hunt rather than his dominance within the group, perhaps to serve to incentivise full co-operation in hunting expeditions, an argument that is in tune with group selection theory.[13]

The developmental psychologist Michael Tomasello, who has worked extensively on studying the cognitive and cultural differences between humans and the other great apes, rejects de Waal's explanations for chimpanzee behaviour.[14] Tomasello (2009) takes the view that chimpanzees are invariably highly selfish (see also Boehm (2012), who is of the view that dominance plays a very important role in determining the share of meat that each chimpanzee receives following a successful hunt). Tomasello is sceptical of memory-based reciprocity in other primates and argues that what seem to be organised hunts by chimpanzees are really just animals acting individually according to what seems to be the best action for them to take for their own benefit in the moment (Tomasello et al., 2005). This line of reasoning indicates that Tomasello is more supportive of individual selection than group selection, at least in relation to non-human primate behaviour, and also suggests that chimpanzees may be closer to the standard homo economicus portrayal of individual behaviour being driven by

---

[13] The anthropologist Bernard Chapais (1995) has observed something resembling a kind of kin-based group selection among Japanese macaques, where females seem to try to maximise selfishly their own rank among their kin on the one hand, and yet work towards co-operating with their kin to improve their group's rank relative to non-kin groups on the other.

[14] Tomasello has less to say about New World monkeys.

Table 2.1 *Matching pennies*

		Matcher	
		Left	Right
Mismatcher	Left	(4, 0)	(0, 2)
	Right	(0, 2)	(1, 0)

egoistic self-interest than, perhaps, are humans (see, for example, Oliver, 2017). As we saw in Chapter 1, in the ultimatum game, reciprocal behaviours can lead to choices that contrast with the predictions of standard economic theory, if we accept that the theory is underpinned by notions of selfish egoism. Interestingly, there is some evidence that chimpanzees are more economically rational than humans in similarly abstract co-operation games.[15]

For instance, consider Table 2.1, which is a representation of the outcomes on offer in a game called 'matching pennies' (Henrich, 2016). In matching pennies, a 'matcher' and a 'mismatcher' are paired with each other over several rounds, and in each round the participants select either 'left' or 'right'. The matcher receives a reward only when her choice of left or right matches that of the mismatcher. For example, if both matcher and mismatcher choose left, Table 2.1 indicates that the matcher receives four units and the mismatcher receives nothing (in the four payment schedules in the table, the first number represents the matcher's reward and the second number is the mismatcher's payment). In contrast, the mismatcher receives a reward only when her choice of left or right is different to that of the matcher. For instance, if she chooses right and the matcher chooses left, Table 2.1 shows that she receives two units and the matcher receives nothing. Indeed, it can be read from the table that the mismatcher receives two units for successful mismatching irrespective of the choice. According to the rules of economic rationality, the

---

[15] Incidentally, chimpanzees never reject in the ultimatum game (Henrich, 2016).

matcher should randomly each of left and right 50 per cent of the time, because if she becomes predictable, she leaves herself open to exploitation by the mismatcher. For example, if she normally goes for left, then the mismatcher will invariably choose right, and if the matcher usually picks right, the converse will occur. The mismatcher should choose left only 20 per cent of the time because if she makes that choice more often it becomes profitable for the matcher to also choose left most of the time. This would then cause an unstable equilibrium because the matcher could get exploited, and thus, rationally, she should go back to choosing left only 50 per cent of the time. The only economically rational stable equilibrium – i.e. the Nash equilibrium, named after the Nobel and Abel Laureate, John Nash, of *A Beautiful Mind* fame – for the outcomes summarised in Table 2.1 is thus for the matcher and the mismatcher respectively to play left 50 per cent and 20 per cent of the time. Martin et al. (2014) found that when faced with this matching pennies game and with currencies in money and apple cubes, there was a seven-fold greater deviation from economic rationality in humans than in chimpanzees.

On the basis of this evidence, might it then be that chimpanzees are better than humans at learning and strategy in this simple abstract game, and that, compared to humans, their egoistic self-interest pushes them into more closely conforming to the rules of economic rationality? Perhaps, but this does not necessarily mean that their choices were unequivocally *better* than those made by humans.[16] As almost pure speculation, perhaps the human matchers and mismatchers were trying to search for a fair, reciprocal strategy – an approach possibly driven by what might be termed enlightened self-interest, rather than egoistic selfishness. For example, if the matchers and mismatchers could have somehow alighted on a strategy where

---

[16] Chimpanzees may be less guided emotionally by, for example, feelings of empathy and sympathy than humans. Sapolsky (2017) notes that people with damage to their ventromedial prefrontal cortex, which drives the impact of emotion on decision-making, show poor judgment in their choice of friends and partners, and tend not to change their behaviours following negative feedback. That is, they often make bad decisions.

the matchers chose left all of the time and the mismatchers chose left 33 per cent of the time, then, after repeated rounds, both parties could have received an equal share; or if the matchers chose left all of the time and the mismatchers chose left half of the time, then in half of the rounds both parties would be sure to achieve the maximum outcome that they could each attain in this experimental design. In short, an evolved reciprocal relationship might have produced a stable non-Nash equilibrium that both parties would consider fair. It is unlikely that chimpanzees would ever reach such an implicit agreement, and even in humans, without allowing the parties to communicate directly with one another to strategise and build up a bond of trust, such an outcome may be optimistic. But it really should be no surprise that a game designed to demonstrate our fundamental motivations of egoistic self-interest does not produce the expected outcomes if we are not actually motivated as such. Chimpanzees may perform 'better' (against economic theory) in some of these games, not because they are better strategisers, but because they are indeed less interested in the actions and outcomes of others.[17]

All in all, then, there are quite profound disagreements among primatologists, biologists, psychologists and evolutionary theorists as to whether non-human primates behave reciprocally and co-operatively, or whether they are fundamentally egoistically self-interested. Frans de Waal is perhaps the key proselytiser of the prosocial-oriented thesis in this domain, and his experiments, particularly using New World monkeys, despite their possible methodological flaws, do plausibly uncover some memory-based reciprocal actions that may have laid some groundwork for more sophisticated reciprocal behaviours further down the evolutionary chain. But, as noted above,

---

[17] The economists and Nobel Laureates George Akerlof and Robert Shiller, in their 2015 book, *Phishing for Phools*, invoke the visual image of each human having a little monkey sitting on his or her shoulder, with the monkey being the representation of the emotions driving our decisions, overcoming our inner reason. Assuming that reason equates to egoistic utility maximisation (admittedly, much of the time, a strong assumption, as intimated above), perhaps a more accurate image is that of a chimpanzee with a little human on his shoulder.

many remain unconvinced about whether these co-operative tendencies are generalisable beyond a few exceptional examples. Sapolsky (2017, pp. 270–1) states, for instance, that 'with few exceptions, nonhuman culture is solely about material culture (versus, say, social organization)', although he also contends that the use of negative reciprocity to sustain co-operation is evident in several species; this is shown, for example, 'when a male baboon who is being an aggressive brute to a female is chased out of the troop for a while by the victim and her relatives' (p. 635). However, many of those who take the view that reciprocal altruism is rare in the animal kingdom do nevertheless believe that this motivation lies very deep within human beings, perhaps even being driven at the biological level. One way of trying to ascertain just how ingrained reciprocal tendencies are in people is to study the behaviour of those over whom life hasn't yet had the chance to take much of a hold.

INFANTS

Although a sceptic of co-operation in non-human primates, Michael Tomasello (2009) contends that humans possess the mental apparatus that enables reciprocity. Differing slightly from, although still quite similar to, Henrich's (2016) view that human co-operation was forged by the need for collective protection on descending trees, Tomasello speculates that humans developed shared intentions first among two or three people when foraging, then eventually scaled up these actions in hunter-gatherer societies, where the promise of capturing large game on any single day was far from secure (cf. the vampire bats), and in response to threats from others. Victory went to the most cohesive groups, and shared intentionality, according to Tomasello, predated language.

Tomasello notes that, from a very young age, children start to care about their reputations. As mooted in Chapter 1, a concern for reputation and reciprocity go hand in hand in that reputational information is a key factor in initiating and sustaining co-operation between non-kin. The political economist and, at the time of writing, only female Nobel Laureate in the Economic Sciences, Elinor Ostrom (1998), wrote that people have an incentive to acquire a good reputation for keeping promises and for performing acts that appear immediately selfless because this makes them appear trustworthy, and trustworthy people will engage with other trustworthy people in mutually beneficial social exchanges. Similarly, Leimar and Hammerstein (2001), borrowing from the economist Robert Sugden (1986), refer to the importance of good standing, and note that this is particularly relevant for initiating and sustaining indirect reciprocity, which is, of course, important in large, atomised organisations and societies.[18] A partial explanation for the tendency for people to comply with social norms, including the norm of reciprocity, is that this strengthens a person's reputation.

Henrich (2016) reports an experiment where very young children – pre-schoolers – appear to show some sensitivity towards reputation or standing.[19] Specifically, infants were required to watch a film clip in which two adults play with a toy in different ways. A number of bystanders also appear in the film, and they are shown to pay more attention to one of the adults than the other, which Henrich defines as a prestige-cue. The two adults also select a different unfamiliar food and a different coloured drink. After watching the film, the pre-schoolers were allowed to play with the toy, and choose between the food and drinks that they had viewed on the clip. The children were thirteen times more likely to use the toy in the way the person with the prestige-cue had used it, and four times more likely to choose the food and drink that she had chosen, compared to the adult who had been relatively overlooked by the bystanders. Although the children did not consciously express it, they tended to follow the actions of the person who they implicitly associated with greater standing. As language is

---

[18] i.e. Tom has never had any direct dealings with Harry but is willing to undertake an act that benefits him so long as Harry is in good standing. As an attempt to foster a good (or otherwise) reputation, people also engage in self-signalling, to indicate how they want to be perceived (e.g. fair, generous, Scrooge-like).

[19] Non-human primates have also been known to be influenced in their behaviours by those to whom they attach prestige (see Sapolsky, 2017, p. 457).

learned, this intrinsic concern with reputation can fuel efficient indirect reciprocity.[20]

That humans very early on in their lives are influenced by the attention that people receive from others is an indication that reputation matters, although it could matter for several, perhaps interconnected, reasons. For instance, we may implicitly want to learn from those who appear competent, and while our attempts to be cooperative with those persons might implicitly strengthen the group (which is plausibly one reason why such behaviours evolved), our motivation, at least in part, for wanting to learn their skills is to advantage ourselves. This may be another instance where it is difficult to tease apart the influences of group and individual selection. Henrich (2016, p. 119) contends:

> [H]umans reliably develop emotions and motivations to seek out particularly skilled, successful, and knowledgeable models and then are willing to pay deference to those models in order to gain their co-operation, or at least acquiescence, in cultural transmission. This deference can come in many forms, including giving assistance (e.g. helping with chores), gifts and favors (e.g. watching their children), as well as speaking well of them in public (thus broadcasting their prestige).

Henrich also notes that although kindergarteners will usually follow the fruit choices of relatively older children, they will follow the choices of relatively younger children if the latter demonstrate themselves to be superior at problem solving. All in all, a concern for competence, which is perhaps often entwined with a concern for

---

[20] Martin Nowak (2011) argues that for *indirect* reciprocity to work efficiently, it needs gossip, linked, as it is, to creating reputations, and Samuel Bowles (2016) contends that persuasion, gossip and ridicule all play a part in sustaining social norms (Sapolsky [2017] notes that anthropologists have estimated that two-thirds of everyday conversation in societies in general is gossip); indirect reciprocity, according to Nowak (p. 171), is the midwife of language. Others have suggested that it is indirect reciprocity that distinguishes humans from other animals because animals rely on direct observation (Ainslie, 2005), but the reader will now be aware that many are sceptical that other animals engage in direct deliberative reciprocity also.

reputation, matters to people at a very early age, as an implicit means to ensure individual advantage, and with an end that may benefit the group.[21]

If we move on from a concern with reputation to a more direct consideration of reciprocity, there is some evidence that suggests that children as young as four react similarly to adults in the ultimatum game (Lucas, Wagner and Chow, 2008) and that by the time they are eight months old, negative reciprocity, in the form of preferring puppets that retaliate against antisocial puppets over those that seemingly punish helpers, is observed (Henrich, 2016). That said, there is other evidence that indicates that young children react egoistically in economic games, and only react in accordance with a concern for reciprocity as they get older (Harbaugh and Krause, 2000; Murnighan and Saxon, 1998), suggesting, perhaps, that when placed in a position of a proposer, it takes a good deal of time for them to learn the strategy of enlightened self-interest, or, in other words, to recognise that pure egoism is likely to be punished. A possible reason for the differences observed between at least some of these results is that Lucas et al. used stickers as the currency for their respondents, whereas Harbaugh and Krause used money; for very small children, it is plausible that stickers may be more relatable as a means of transaction. More work needs to be done in this area, but if the Lucas et al. results were to prove generalisable, it would suggest that the tendency towards being motivated to act reciprocally is something that lies very deep within human beings.

---

[21] Many behavioural phenomena that are likely to have evolved for good reasons can, with a bit of imagination, be applied to particular situations to reveal apparently strange behavioural patterns. In the 1950s, the social psychologist Solomon Asch directed a number of studies that showed that people would often – about one-third of the time – conform to a majority point of view even when they knew that view to be incorrect. An amusing example of an Asch-like experiment that demonstrates behavioural conformity in the confines of a lift can be viewed by searching 'Candid Camera Asch'. Some people have forged careers out of revealing apparent biases in people's behaviours in circumstances that are very different to those in which the phenomena driving those biases evolved.

To conclude, seemingly group-orientated behaviour occurs throughout the animal kingdom; fish swarm, cows herd and birds flock, but all of this may be driven by individual rather than group selection. There are some examples of non-human primates demonstrating a form of reciprocity that goes beyond the mere attitudinal, but this has generally been observed only among subjects who already know each other, which nonetheless is of interest in that it may have served as a step towards more complex forms of reciprocity. Although our knowledge of the behavioural intentions of non-primates remains quite limited, a deliberative form of reciprocity in the wider animal kingdom is, according to most experts, rare. Very young humans, however, appear to show some tendencies towards reciprocal altruism and altruistic punishment. Moreover, there are suggestions that they are influenced by a person's reputation or standing, a crucial factor that underscores the proper functioning of indirect reciprocity. Thus, although there is some scattered evidence in support of reciprocal altruism, altruistic punishment and reputational concerns in other animals, it is humans who are the masters in this regard. But has it always been thus?

FOOD FOR THOUGHT

1. How plausible is group selection among humans and non-human animals?
2. Are Frans de Waal's methods fatally flawed?
3. Why might human infants be influenced by reputation and standing?

3   A Pinch of Anthropology

Some of the great philosophers of the Enlightenment wrote on, and disagreed about, the character of Man in the state of nature. In *Leviathan*, for instance, Thomas Hobbes believed that the natural state of humans was that of every man for himself (and, presumably, every woman for herself), each egoistically engaged in a war against all. In an attempt at civilising and protecting themselves, Hobbes took the view that people create mutually beneficial contracts, with the reputation gained for fulfilling the terms of the contract that one engages in when there is some assurances that the other party will do the same being a valuable thing, particularly when self-preservation depends on alliances (see also Sugden, 2018). That is, people will wish for a reputation of being a good reciprocator/co-operator, as this is likely to serve their enlightened self-interest. Hobbes thus believed that a gift, good or service is given only on the expectation that there will be some return, and a person will fulfil the terms of the contract only if she expects her exchange partner to do likewise. According to Hobbes, enlightened self-interest will serve as the beginning of benevolence, trust and mutual aid.[1] In short, as Robert Sugden (2018) contends, Hobbes is essentially postulating the contractarian argument that each individual will better serve her own interests by engaging into and maintaining mutually advantageous relationships with others.

---

[1]   The selfish egoism that Hobbes attributes to state-of-nature Man is attune to what many assume underpins modern rational choice theory and neoclassical economics. That is, in an exchange relationship, each party would, if given the chance, exploit the other for their own gain. Enlightened self-interest, on the other hand, assumes a reciprocal relationship – a fair exchange, which is important if one wants to maintain a relationship over time. This type of self-interest is likely to be better aligned with the views of the classical economists, particularly, in the English-speaking world, Adam Smith, on whom more later.

Hobbes has had many critics, but perhaps the most notable was the Genevan philosopher, Jean-Jacques Rousseau. Rousseau (1755/2009) referred to Man in the state of nature as a savage. He did not believe that humans were necessarily noble or moral, but he did express the view that they were often admirable, in common with other apes, in being self-sufficient and focussed on surviving. Rousseau maintained that although Man could be violent in defence, there were no natural warlike tendencies; these tendencies, he believed, had been created by modern societies and political systems.

Thus, Hobbes believed that a contract was rationally agreed upon and imposed for the betterment of all; Rousseau believed that modern political systems did not necessarily serve for the betterment of anybody. David Hume, introduced in Chapter 1, held views that were perhaps more closely aligned with those of Hobbes, although with an important distinction. Although Hume (1739–40/1978), like Hobbes, believed that we have moved towards enlightened self-interest, he contended, with echoes of Darwin,[2] that social institutions and moral practices have evolved over a long history, rather than being consequent on an original rationally imposed political agreement, and refers to native societies in North America to argue that these laws of nature are recognised and self-enforcing even in stateless societies. With further resonance with Darwin, in relation to the latter's suggestion that religious codes normatively reinforce practices that evolved for the common good, Hume intimates that a public system of enforcement is merely a back-up device for rules that have evolved organically, and that, much of the time, the enforcement is not needed since the rules are nonetheless honoured.

Sugden (2018) also sees Hume's argument to be in the same spirit as that of Hobbes, arguing that the content of conventions in both theories is focussed on reciprocity; i.e. each individual constrains her actions as part of a general practice in which others constrain theirs, and this rests on a general sense of common interest. If there

---

[2] Although, since Darwin came later, perhaps Darwin echoed Hume.

was a breakdown in reciprocity, society would not be able to function, and everybody would suffer as a consequence. Thus, according to Sugden (2018), both Hobbes and Hume saw mutual advantage as a central explanatory and normative concept, albeit with Hobbes seeing the descriptive as following the normative and with Hume charging vice-versa. If Hume's view is the more accurate, however, it suggests that the tendency towards reciprocal actions lies deep within us – an evolved social norm – and that it is somewhat less fragile and tenuous than relying on mutually enforced contracts *à la* Hobbes.

Hume and Rousseau both referred, to some extent, to societies that they considered somewhat primitive at the time that they were writing to support their arguments – i.e., respectively, native North Americans and Caribbeans. As noted in Chapter 2, attempting to infer the nature of our distant ancestors by studying the behaviours of other animals – in particular, the non-human primates – has quite a long history. In this chapter, following these philosophers, I will try to infer the nature of our slightly less distant ancestors by looking briefly at the behaviours in extant tribal communities in the hope of gaining some insights into whether reciprocal tendencies are merely principally a product of relatively recent cultural practices or whether they are more foundational to human actions.[3] Before doing so, however, I would like once again to reflect upon group selection, not this time in contrast to individual selection, but rather in opposition to prioritising one's kin.

KIN OR THE GROUP

In perhaps the most famous allusion to kin selection, the British geneticist J. B. S. Haldane, referring implicitly to the importance he attached to shared genes, reportedly said that he would gladly lay down his life for two brothers or eight cousins. But let me begin this section with a quote from Sapolsky (2017, p. 499), a view that he claims is also supported by Henrich et al. (2005), that posits where

---

[3] But without using the terms 'primitive' and 'savages'.

humans' reciprocal nature, particularly in relation to strangers co-operating with each other in large societies, evolved from:

> Our moral anchoring in fairness in large-scale societies is a residue and extension of our hunter-gatherer and nonhuman primate past. This was life in small bands, where fairness was mostly driven by kin selection and easy scenarios of reciprocal altruism. As our community size has expanded and we now mostly have one-shot interactions with unrelated strangers, our prosociality just represents an expansion of our small-band mind-set, as we use various green-beard marker shibboleths as proxies for relatedness.[4]

In short, this view says that our tendencies to reciprocate with those we don't know grew out of our need to reciprocate with those to whom we are related.

Henrich later modified, or rather supplemented, this view slightly. Henrich (2016) noted that for decades the leading evolutionary researchers, following Haldane, have argued that humans co-operate efficiently because of the evolutionary forces of kin selection. However, in augmenting rather denying this view, Henrich contends that in small, nomadic hunter-gatherer societies, which have dominated human history, group members across whom co-operation is the norm consist of many non-related individuals, and therefore culturally constructed norms augmented our innate kin-driven tendencies.[5] What drove the culturally constructed norm of reciprocity? – according to Henrich and an increasing number of like-minded scholars: group selection.

---

[4] In this sense, green-beard markers are not gender-specific, and can merely be thought of as a characteristic or characteristics that a person has and with which another person identifies, thus motivating the second person to attempt to reciprocate/co-operate with her.

[5] Henrich (2016) remarks that in order to explain co-operation in tribal societies, affinal relationships between in-laws are more important than those between genetically related kin. It has been estimated that in extant hunter-gatherer societies, which are highly co-operative, only about 40 per cent of people within bands are blood relatives (Kim et al., 2011).

To recap, group selection theory – which allows an individual A to dominate individual B but contends that a group of Bs may well dominate a group of As – postulates that competition between groups necessitates a sufficient level of reciprocation, prosociality and consequent co-operation within groups if the group is to survive. The competition is necessary to sustain the co-operation.[6] Henrich (2016, p. 170) remarks:

> [H]istory suggests that all prosocial institutions age and eventually collapse at the hands of self-interest, unless they are renewed by the dynamics of intergroup competition. That is, although it may take a long time, individuals and coalitions eventually figure out how to beat or manipulate the system to their own ends, and these techniques spread and slowly corrode any prosocial effects.[7]

Henrich (p. 174) later notes that 'much ethnography and ethnohistory ... indicates that the copying of institutions and rituals from more successful groups is commonplace'. That intergroup competition may motivate intragroup co-operative endeavour and innovation, and that the more successful groups might then offer examples of good practice to the less successful, is a potentially important insight for the appropriate design of public policy institutions, and is a point to which I will later return.

Henrich (2016) – like Sapolsky (2017), as noted in Chapter 2 – is, in the main, sceptical of the proposition of deliberative acts of co-operation among unrelated non-human animals, and believes that humans are special in their behaviours, being influenced heavily by culturally evolved social norms.[8] Henrich and Henrich (2007) go as far

---

[6] The geographer Jared Diamond has argued that the intense intergroup competition between European countries from the fifteenth century onwards was a principle reason why they went on to conquer the world. It is also often said that due to the intense intergroup competition during World War II, British society across and within the various social groups was unusually cohesive, although given the spike in crime during the War (see, for example, Legg, 2017), the spirit of camaraderie, if it did exist at all, clearly didn't infect everyone.

[7] In Chapter 7, I shall highlight the importance of emphasising reciprocity in the policy rhetoric if one wants to sustain reciprocity in action.

[8] Apropos Chapter 2, although Sapolsky (2017) generally limits group selection to humans who have traditionally had to compete for hunting grounds, pastures and

as to say that cultural adaptations can even influence biological predispositions, and over relatively short periods of time; for example the mutation towards milk sugar tolerance through lactase persistence among human adults spread throughout and benefited those societies that domesticated dairy animals 6,000–10,000 years ago. Henrich (2016) contends that the products of human cultural evolution, such as fire, cooking, tools, clothing and language, become the source of selection pressure and thus genetically shape our minds and bodies. Similarly, according to Henrich and Henrich (2007), the development of co-operation perhaps modified human biology in ways that are beneficial to the survival of our species (which might explain the sensitivity to reputation and reciprocal altruism in infants).[9] In short, Henrich (2016) argues that, over the course of eons, cultural practices, including the tendency to reciprocate, have shaped human psychology and biology through a culture–gene co-evolutionary process (known as co-evolutionary theory), and that people who were relatively more selfishly aggressive were largely selected against and that those who were relatively more social were rewarded. This (Humean rather than Hobbesian) view – that over time our norms and practices amplify or suppress our innate motivations – differs from that held by luminaries in the field of evolutionary theory, such as Richard Dawkins and Steven Pinker, who believe, *à la* Haldane, that co-operation in small-scale hunter-gatherer societies is

water sources, he does offer a striking non-human example, by noting that if one were to take the most prolific egg layers from several groups of chickens and put them together in the hope of forming a super group, egg production will be minimal. This is because each hen that was dominant in its own group was so because it was aggressive; if one were to place several aggressive hens together, they would spend their lives pecking each other, reducing overall fertility in the group. Sapolsky (2017, p. 363) writes that 'this is the circumstance of a genetically influenced trait that, while adaptive on an individual level, emerges as maladaptive when shared by a group and where there is competition between groups'. This is group selection theory in action. Another example can perhaps be found in those species, such as meerkats, that have sentinels that release an audible signal to warn their group of an approaching danger, even if this brings that particular individual to the attention of the threat.

[9] Incidentally, primate brain size (and cortex-to-brain ratio) and the social complexity of their groups are correlated, although we can of course say nothing about causation.

caused entirely by direct genetic selection rather than a culturally evolved psychology.[10]

As also noted in Chapter 2, those, like Henrich and Sapolsky, who see merit in group selection theory as an explanation for intragroup co-operation between non-kin, at the very least in relation to some human behaviours, although still perhaps in a minority, have witnessed a broader acceptance of their view among evolutionary theorists over recent years. Notable proselytisers of group selection include David Sloan Wilson and Edward O. Wilson (2007), Jonathan Haidt (2012),[11] and Martin Nowak (2011),[12] and Samuel Bowles and Herbert Gintis (2011) have been busy trying to convince economists of this perspective. Gintis et al. (2005, p. 30), for instance, wrote that 'prosocial norms evolve not because they have superior fitness within groups, but because groups with prosocial norms outcompete groups that are deficient in this respect'; moreover, Joan Silk (2005) has commented that while a person individually may benefit from giving less than she receives, too much self-interest is bad for the evolutionary success of the group. It is perhaps important to reiterate, though, that group selection theory does not prescribe that everyone will be reciprocal and co-operative all of the time. It makes room for what might be viewed as egocentric selfish acts, and requires merely that there is sufficient strong reciprocity within the group in order for the group to survive. It thus allows a mix of motives, not only at the interpersonal level but also at the intrapersonal level. Be that as it may, there is a long and large anthropological literature that purports to show people behaving seemingly reciprocally, often

---

[10] It is worth noting that Steven Pinker, in *The Better Angels of Our Nature* (2011) and more recently in *Enlightenment Now* (2018), offers an essentially Hobbesian view that the Enlightenment brought order and progress in place of the violence that was the condition of mankind for eons, and that this has led to longer, healthier and more prosperous lives worldwide.

[11] Haidt, a prominent social psychologist, in his book, *The Righteous Mind*, concurs that intense intergroup competition, with intragroup gratitude and vengeance, will continually strengthen loyalty, sanctity and reciprocity in successive generations.

[12] Nowak (2011) expresses the view that for group selection to work efficiently, there cannot be too much migration between groups; i.e. there has to be group loyalty.

among non-kin, in tribal communities, and it behoves me now to present at least a snapshot of that.[13]

RECIPROCITY IN TRIBAL COMMUNITIES

To re-emphasise the point that hunter-gatherer societies have dominated human history, anatomically modern humans emerged 200,000 years ago, whereas agriculture has origins that stretch back about 12,000 years. Hunter-gathering thus captures about 95 per cent of modern human history, give or take the odd per cent. Therefore, in terms of the behaviours of all humans living today, those that developed in our hunter-gatherer existence are likely to remain relevant. Without the aid of time travel, we cannot of course directly observe our ancestors, but we can at least study existing tribal communities in the hope of gaining some insight into how our ancestors may have behaved and organised themselves. However, whether hunter-gatherers, pastoralists, agriculturists or horticulturists, caution is required when using extant tribal communities as models for our prehistoric past, because, for example, tribal groups today often live in degraded habitats that force more resource competition, and the modern world places increasing pressures on these peoples, pressures that our forebears would not have faced.[14]

Notwithstanding that caveat, and even ignoring the generalisations of, for example, Rousseau and Hume, the study of behaviour in tribal communities to gain insight into our own actions and circumstances has a long history. Peter Kropotkin (1902/2014, p. 72), for instance, with perhaps another implicit nod to group selection theory, concluded:

---

[13] Although some scholars might object to the use of the word 'tribe' as a general term, it is used throughout this book just as a simple way to define what may be thought of as pre-modern societies. No offence is intended.

[14] The 2018 BBC documentary, *My Year with the Tribe*, shows that the Korowai tribe in Papua, Indonesia, play to foreign expectations of what tribal life is imagined to be when people visit them rather than revealing the reality of their lives. See www.bbc.co.uk/programmes/b0b09812.

The savage is not an ideal of virtue, nor is he an ideal of 'savagery'. But the primitive man has one quality, elaborated and maintained by the very necessities of his hard struggle for life – he identifies his own existence with that of his tribe; and without that quality mankind never would have attained the level it has attained now.

However, arguably *the* classic (and indisputably *a* classic) early text in this field – a text that has served as foundational for the study of reciprocity – was authored by the French sociologist Marcel Mauss (1954), and titled *The Gift*. Many tribal communities make sacrifices to the gods in the hope that they will reciprocate (by bestowing prosperity, and delivering from evil), but Mauss was interested principally in a different type of reciprocity. Drawing on tribal communities from all around the world but with a particular focus on the indigenous peoples of the Pacific North-West, he wrote that although gift giving in and between tribal communities often appears voluntary, gifts are not normally acts of pure altruism. Rather, they are given and repaid under obligation, and thus they lend the act of reciprocating a moral dimension, because if a group (or an individual) is obligated to return a gift and does not do so – or returns one that is, in some sense, of substantially inequivalent value – then the view from those to whom they are obligated is likely to be that they have acted unfairly. An inadequate return gift risks also creating feelings of superiority, dominance, subordination and subservience between the parties involved. This type of reciprocity is akin to Kolm's notion of balance reciprocity, referred to in Chapter 1.

Mauss contended that gifts that were meant to instil a sense of obligation arose out of what is known as total prestation, where clans, and individuals and groups within clans, share everything.[15]

---

[15] Kropotkin (1902/2014) noted that within tribal communities everything is shared in common. For example, among the Hottentots, he noted, a man does not begin eating, if he is alone, until he has shouted loudly three times an invitation to anyone close to come and share his meal.

Mauss argued that, in total prestation, gifts often have a sort of spiritual meaning. For instance, he noted that in Melanesian and Polynesian cultures, gifts are never completely separated from the man who gives them; a gift is seen as part of oneself, and the recipient must give something of themselves in return. If they fail to do so, they will think that (the spiritual) part of themselves may be lost. The sociologist Anthony Heath (1976) wrote that Mauss saw the typical gift exchange in the tribal communities he focussed on as intermediate between total prestation and the modern economic transaction, with them still being instilled with the sense of duty and obligation mentioned in the previous paragraph. Gifts in the gift exchange are also often rich in meaning, paying attention to the preferences and tastes of the receiver, similar (at least ideally) to Christmas and birthday presents exchanged in developed societies.

Mauss maintained that almost indissoluble alliances are forged through the gift exchange. A person cannot easily refuse a gift, because, to reiterate, to do so means losing dignity due to showing a fear of having to repay. At times, such refusal can even be tantamount to a declaration of war. Although Mauss recognised that the gift exchange has survived at particular moments in developed countries (remember Christmas?), he believed that exchange driven by the law and economic interest via money transactions is inferior, as it is without the rich meaning and felt obligations of the gift exchange.

Having said all of this, there are strong suggestions that people within tribal communities will sometimes refuse gifts, precisely because they do not wish to become beholden to others, a sentiment summarised in an Inuit proverb, relayed (several times) by Serge-Christophe Kolm (2008, e.g. p. 36): 'The gift makes the slave as the whip makes the dog'. Sometimes, it seems, gifts offered can be the most expensive things that one can imagine. Henrich et al. report some empirical support for this conjecture after running the ultimatum game in several tribal communities; they wrote:

> [A]mong the Au and Gnau of Papua New Guinea many proposers offered more than half the pie, and many of these offers were rejected. The making and rejection of seemingly generous offers, of more than half, may have a parallel in the culture of status-seeking through gift giving found in Au and Gnau villages and throughout Melanesia. In these societies, accepting gifts, even unsolicited ones, implies a strong obligation to reciprocate at some future time. Unrepaid debts accumulate, and place the receiver in a subordinate status. Further, the giver may demand repayment at times or in forms (e.g. political alliances) not to the receiver's liking, but the receiver is still strongly obliged to respond. As a consequence, excessively large gifts, especially unsolicited ones, will frequently be refused. (Henrich et al., 2005, p. 811; Gintis et al., 2005 make a similar point.)

This implies that in some tribal communities, it would be wise to refrain from making offers that might be perceived as too generous in the ultimatum game or more generally. Indeed, lower-than-typical offers have been observed in other tribal groups. Henrich (2000), for instance, reported that Machiguenga horticulturists offered an average of only 26 per cent of their endowments, with a modal offer of 15 per cent, a group who also rarely reject the offers made to them (Henrich et al., 2005).[16] Henrich (2016) contends that in the smallest-scale human societies, people tend to offer little and rarely reject in the ultimatum game because they lack social norms for money exchange with strangers.

Given the intense levels of reciprocity and co-operation in tribal communities commented upon by Kropotkin, Mauss and others since

---

[16] Henrich (2016) reveals that in tribal communities, there tends to be more monitoring of co-ethnics, and thus in the ultimatum game people often pay more to punish co-ethnic than non-co-ethnic offers. This resonates with the observation, reported in Chapter 2, that non-human apes may expect unconditional favours from close kin but not from non-kin. It ought to be noted that Henrich et al. (2005) also report that ultimatum game responses across many cultures are similar to those typically observed in developed countries.

them,[17,18] Sapolsky (2017) expresses some surprise that people appear to sometimes reject and even punish generous offers in these communities, an act that he terms 'antisocial punishment'. He speculates that this behaviour may be caused by responders attempting to up the ante, sending a signal that causes everyone to be more generous than they would like to be, and, while plausible in some situations, a more likely explanation, particularly since it is often already highly generous offers that are rejected, is that people will often, as aforementioned, resist a perceived exercise of power by others. This resonates with self-determination theory, developed originally by the psychologists Edward Deci and Richard Ryan (1985; 2000), that distinguishes between autonomous actions and behaviours that are perceived to be controlled or influenced by factors external to the self. Self-determination theory postulates that actions that are perceived as supporting autonomy – i.e. supporting that which people would wish to do themselves – are likely to be more effective than those that attempt to steer people from a path that they would ideally like to take, and there are lessons here for those who wish to incorporate more strongly reciprocal altruism in the design of public policy.[19]

---

[17] For example, in hunter-gatherer tribes, meat is shared out across successful and unsuccessful hunters, a fact that resonates with Wilkinson's (1984) study of vampire bats, referred to in Chapter 2. Among hunter-gatherers, there is evidence from as far back as 200,000 years ago that meat was shared out fairly (Sapolsky, 2017), and the sharing of meat was an important catalyst to co-operation (it has been argued that plant foods are less commonly shared, because their gathering is consequent more on effort than on luck and thus their sharing would encourage free-riding rather than insurance (Pinker, 2018)). As might be the case with chimpanzees, the dominant individual in a hunt does not necessarily receive the largest share; the meat is typically shared out by a third party (see also Henrich, 2016). As will be discussed later in this book, third party arbitrators will often play a crucial role in securing and maintaining reciprocal relationships in public policy sectors. For instance, see Ostrom (2000, p. 149), who, in relation to co-operative endeavours, notes that 'The presence of a leader or entrepreneur, who articulates different ways of organizing to improve joint outcomes, is frequently an important initial stimulus'.

[18] Richard Thurnwald (1932) was another early notable commentator and believed that the principle of reciprocity was a primordial driver that pervades almost every aspect of life in tribal communities.

[19] Examples of antisocial punishment, or the *ex post* wish that one would have chosen antisocial punishment after the fact, are not difficult to find in popular culture. For

Sapolsky (2017) does nonetheless contend that overt intimidation and power mongering are issues among nomadic hunter-gatherers – indeed, more so than attempts at covert cheating – and, along with murder, sorcery, stealing, greed, treachery and the breaking of sexual taboos, are actions that are subject to a most extreme form of negative reciprocity; namely, perpetrators can be killed. The threat of negative reciprocity in these communities serves to enforce group norms.[20] This point is further highlighted by Henrich (2016, p. 188), who also touches on the importance of reputation to the operation of reciprocity in relation to the inhabitants of the Yasawa Islands:

> When someone, for example, repeatedly fails to contribute to village feasts or community labor, or violates food or incest taboos, the person's reputation suffers. A Yasawan's reputation is like a shield that protects them from exploitation or harm by others, often from those who harbor old jealousies or past grievances. Violating norms, especially repeatedly, causes this reputational shield to drop and creates an opening for others to exploit the norm violator with relative impunity. Norm violators have their property (e.g., plates, matches, tools) stolen and destroyed while they are away fishing or visiting relatives in other villages; or they have their crops stolen and gardens burned at night. Despite the small size of these communities, the perpetrators of these actions often remain anonymous and get direct benefits in the form of stolen food and tools as well as the advantages of bringing down a competitor or dispensing revenge for past grievances. Despite their selfish motivations, these actions sustain social norms, including

[20] example, in the television series *The Sopranos*, restaurant owner, Artie Bucco, soon regrets accepting the help he received from his friend and mob boss, Tony Soprano, after his restaurant is burned down, not least because Tony then implicitly expects his future meals to incur no charge. Or, in the Costa Books Award-winning novel, *Eleanor Oliphant Is Completely Fine*, the title character, on being offered a drink by a man at a party, retorts, 'No thank you ... I don't want to accept a drink from you, because then I would be obliged to purchase one for you in return, and I'm afraid I'm simply not interested in spending two drinks' worth of time with you' (Honeyman, 2017, p. 200). Although some hunter-gatherer groups have very high homicide rates.

cooperative ones, because – crucially – perpetrators can only get away with such actions when they target a norm violator, a person with his reputational shield down. Were they to do this to someone with a good reputation, the perpetrator would himself become a norm violator and damage his or her reputation, thereby opening themselves up to gossip, thefts and property damage.

Henrich et al. (2005) earlier also reported that across small-scale cultures – hunter-gatherers, pastoralists, horticulturists etc. – the higher the degree of market integration between tribes, the greater the pro-sociality, at least as measured by generosity in economic games such as the ultimatum game. Indeed, Gintis et al. (2005) suggest that the degree of market integration in these societies can explain 50 per cent of the difference in co-operation and sharing in experimental games. Might it therefore be that the act of trading strengthens the tendency towards reciprocal altruism and thus the concerns of, for example, Mauss – that modern market economies crowd out people's sense of obligation to each other – are unfounded? This is a question to which we will later return, but Sapolsky (2017) questions whether small-scale societies with little market integration are relatively less prosocial in the broad sense of the term. Sapolsky argues that we know that people within these societies are reciprocal with respect to obligations, duties and favours, and share such diverse goods and services as meat, childcare and wisdom, but because they are not familiar with money they may simply not know how to respond to the ultimatum game.[21] Henrich et al. (2005) further observed that the bigger the group, and the larger the proportion of people within the group who belong to a world religion such as Christianity or Islam, the greater was the tendency towards third party punishment of transgressors. This is in tune with some of the postulates relayed in Chapter 1; namely, as societies become bigger and opportunities for acting egoistically increase, religious codes may be developed or embraced to reinforce reciprocity (via, in this case, indirect negative reciprocity).

---

[21] As noted earlier, Henrich (2016) recognises this possibility.

This thus provides some evidence that normative proclamations affect observed behaviour, and that although, following Hume, the tendency towards acting reciprocally may have evolved over a great many generations, (in a partial nod to Hobbes) the opportunity to act upon our baser motivations might weaken our prosocial actions over time unless the latter are nourished.[22]

THE UNDERNOURISHMENT OF RECIPROCITY

Unfortunately, the prosocial norms of reciprocity are indeed sometimes insufficiently nourished, an example of which was reported not in a small-scale tribal community but in a poor region of southern Italy, by the political scientist Edward Banfield, in the 1950s. Banfield spent an extended period living in and studying the people of this rural Italian community, but found little community spirit. For example, in offering a typical view by, in this instance, quoting a teacher, Banfield (1958, p. 20) wrote:

> No one in town is animated by a desire to do good for all of the population. Even if sometimes there is someone apparently animated by this desire, in reality he is interested in his own welfare and he does his own business. Even the saints, for all their humility, looked after themselves. And men, after all, are only made of flesh and spirit.

Moreover, the desire to avoid being obligated to another person by accepting a favour was widespread, with Banfield (p. 115) noting that:

> The peasant who works for another keeps a careful record of his hours. Even trivial favors create an obligation and must be repaid. When a visiting social scientist said he planned to leave the key to

---

[22] In an early work, the anthropologist Bronislaw Malinowski (1932) held the view that conformity to a moral code is upheld by social machinery, and not by psychological force. That the norm of reciprocity has evolved over tens of thousands of years (at least), that our brains might thus now be wired to be receptive towards acting reciprocally, but that this may be undermined if our social structures and institutions do not continue to nurture this tendency, suggests that in our current state, reciprocity could be psychologically *and* sociologically upheld.

his house with a neighbor for a few days while he was away, his landlord pointed out that such a thing would be foolish. 'You would needlessly create an obligation which you would have to repay'.

Banfield does acknowledge some circumstances when a self-interested form of reciprocity appears to be at work, but these are usually underpinned by differential levels of power between those concerned, and thus the relatively poor, even if they would wish to, found it difficult to refuse the requests made of them. For instance, he notes that (pp. 75–6):

> When a gentleman of Montegrano buys a melon or a basket of tomatoes in the public square, he hands it wordlessly to the nearest peasant boy, woman, or man, who carries it to his home as a matter of course. He hands his burden to any peasant with whom he is acquainted, and there is no thought on either side of payment for a specific service. The peasant wants to be polite and amiable (*civile*) and he knows that a time will come when the gentleman can give or withhold a favor or an injury.

Overall, Banfield called the citizens among whom he lived 'amoral familists', who were interested only in their families and thus were generally not concerned with broader reciprocal relationships – or charity, or even justice – with non-kin. People seemed to fear and distrust anyone outside the family; kin selection appeared to be at work. Why was this? One possible explanation is that the society was very poor, and thus the people within it had adopted the selfish disposition that, excepting those who were closely related to them, they would look out for number one. This is perhaps not the only, or even the primary, explanation, however, as others have observed reciprocal behaviours among non-kin to solve collective action problems in poor communities (e.g. Ostrom, 1998).[23] A second explanation is that it was

---

[23] Some hunter-gatherer tribes reportedly have an abundance of food sources, at least. For instance, Pinker (2018, p. 23) writes that: 'the Hadza of Tanzania, who live in the ecosystem where modern humans first evolved and preserve much of their lifestyle, extract 3,000 calories daily per person from more than 880 species.'

an isolated, rural community, and therefore the intergroup competition that is so central to group selection theory was absent. Third, the fear of negative reciprocity for selfish transgressions was weak. The law was generally ignored, and without the threat of punishment Banfield observed, for example, that merchants did all they could to exploit their customers. Banfield (1958, p. 137) felt that in this society, positive and reputational signals, while being marginally effective, were simply not enough to encourage co-operation, and that therefore the threat of harder forms of punishment was required:

> [T]he desire to be liked or admired, is also a curb on aggression ... but its importance is by no means as great as the others. One would be ashamed (i.e., embarrassed) to be caught stealing, for example, but the risk of being ashamed is a light thing in comparison to that of going to jail or being beaten. One likes to be considered a fine fellow ... But the satisfaction of being thought well of would not, for most people, outweigh any advantage that could be had without danger by trickery or other unfair means. In short, the desire for the good opinion of others is a supporting but not a leading motive.

As Banfield himself acknowledged, the lack of enlightened self-interest, manifested by a lack of widespread reciprocal altruism (itself perhaps caused by a lack of altruistic punishment), was a principal reason why this Italian community was economically backward, and in relation to the previous paragraph, he also somewhat contradicted himself by arguing quite forcefully that a focus on cultivating good personal reputations had an important role to play in reversing these circumstances. He concluded that:

> The individual must define self or family interest less narrowly than material, short-run advantage. He need not cease to be family-minded or even selfish, but – some of the time, at least – must pursue a 'larger' self-interest. For example, he might prefer to take some of his income in prestige or in the intrinsic satisfaction of organizational behavior as a 'game' rather than in material reward.

Or he might forego present for future advantage, for example by establishing a reputation for fair dealing. (p. 158)

Assuming that it had existed in the distant past, Banfield paints a convincing picture that reciprocity had atrophied in this backward society.[24]

To conclude this chapter, then, behaviours underpinned by much of what we would define as reciprocity – i.e. direct and indirect reciprocal altruism, and negative reciprocity – are clearly evident in tribal communities, and, notwithstanding that these communities have been influenced by the modern world, we can conclude with reasonable confidence that the societies in which our ancestors lived demonstrated these traits. Gift giving was used to bind and obligate; people shared for the betterment of the group and, ultimately, of themselves; and the threat of negative reciprocity to discourage transgressions from accepted practices, selfish egoism and an intention to exert power over others, are all widely observed. Hume's arguments that these behaviours, which are still fundamental to human motivation, developed over eons because they serve people well are therefore convincing; they support observations of enlightened self-interest, and much else (e.g. balance and liking reciprocity), but Banfield's study of a poor Italian community demonstrated that reciprocal altruism is far from inevitable, to the detriment of almost everyone, if the institutions and environment are not shaped to reinforce and sustain it. And thus perhaps Hobbes was also partially right, in that we need to be vigilant against the movements of the darker angels of our nature.

---

[24] Even if the coexistence of little reciprocity and backwardness is convincing in this case, it is important to keep in mind that we can conclude, at most, correlation rather than causation. That is, we do not know if the lack of reciprocity caused the lack of development, or if the lack of development caused the lack of reciprocity. But Banfield clearly thought that more enlightened self-interest would give the society the best chance to develop.

FOOD FOR THOUGHT

1. Does Hobbes or Hume provide the more plausible account for human co-operation?
2. Would you give your life for eight cousins?
3. Will reciprocity wither if it is not watered?

4 A Dash of Behavioural Economics

As highlighted in the preceding chapters, Joseph Henrich and others have used behavioural economic tools such as the ultimatum game to uncover reciprocal motivations in tribal communities (and elsewhere). Most behavioural economists, however, have tended to focus upon people, and particularly students, living in modern societies when experimenting with these sorts of economic games, and there are many such games.[1] The main ones will be described in this chapter, with the intention of offering some insight into the extent to which core reciprocal motivations have been inherited by, as it were, modern man (and woman).

A disclaimer is perhaps warranted at the outset, however, in that some economists, and not without foundation, claim that the evidence gleaned from these economic games does not, in fact, challenge standard economic theory. As noted in Chapter 1, for instance, Kenneth Binmore (2005) contends that it is not axiomatic in economics that utility equates to money, whether utility maximisation equals income maximisation is an empirical question, and that all that is required in standard theory is consistency in preferences and for individuals to maximise *something* (that maximises utility). He also claims though that, with experience, people are likely to tend towards income maximisation in economic games. Even if this latter point is not observed, the psychologist George Ainslie (2005), among others, notes that the idea that there will be times when emotion can compete with money and other goods in an individual's utility function should not be

---

[1] Occasionally, researchers are criticised for using students as their respondents, but, believe it or not, students are people. Moreover, economics students are often used, a subgroup that one might expect to show strong conformity to the assumptions of standard economic theory in their decision-making behaviours; but they invariably do not.

controversial, which suggests that a richer understanding of utility than that which is often taken to be the standard economic position can incorporate the findings of the behavioural economic experiments.

Binmore and Ainslie thus make the reasonable point that utility may often depend upon more than mere money – i.e. that people can have exotic preferences. Binmore (1999) implies, for instance, that responders may gain utility from punishing proposers who offer little in the ultimatum game, whose behaviour contravenes the social norm of signalling cooperative intentions regarding resources that they have no real personal claim over. Indeed, if people gain utility from a desire to be prosocial, fair and/or reciprocal, then the assumption of utility maximisation in standard economic theory can also incorporate the findings that will be explored in the following sections. Parking to one side for the moment the contention that it is always reasonable to expect that people do, and indeed should, maximise utility,[2] there is a risk that placing too many arguments in the utility function will lead to it 'explaining' every conceivable behaviour; any behaviour could then simply be classified, somewhat emptily, as an attempt to maximise utility. For the purposes of this chapter, and indeed the rest of this book, the widely accepted assumption that orthodox economic theory is underpinned by the notion of selfish, egoistic utility maximisation, an assumption that has, as we shall see, been influential in policy formation, will be retained. In contrast, the reader will be able to discern that the findings that have been uncovered by behavioural economists do at least imply that people are often driven by some form of enlightened self-interest, where we give in order to gain, rather than selfish egoism, where we are assumed to take and take again.

Most behavioural economists have probably concluded that reciprocity is at work in practice. But do they believe that it works in theory?[3] Let us briefly consider some theory first.

---

[2] Sugden (2018) contends that it is not reasonable to assume that a third party knows what people want from life, and we should refrain from normative judgments pertaining to the outcomes that people ought to aim for; he terms utility, welfare or happiness maximisation 'the view from nowhere', an argument to which we will later return.

[3] The old joke of, 'ok, so it works in practice, but does it work in theory?' is often used to try to ridicule economists, but it is a perfectly sensible question to ask if one accepts

A LITTLE THEORY

As noted earlier in the book, behavioural economists had in the 1980s reported reasonably substantive empirical evidence on the ultimatum and other economic games that appeared to conflict with the assumption of selfish egoism in people's decision-making behaviours, and from the early 1990s they began to offer theoretical modifications of standard economic theory to incorporate these (then) quite recently uncovered preference patterns. Perhaps the first substantive contribution in this line of inquiry was offered by a young Matthew Rabin in 1993. In a nutshell, Rabin's model assumes that people are willing to sacrifice their own material wellbeing in order to help those who they believe to be kind, and to punish those who they view as unkind, but that the propensity to act in these ways diminishes as the material cost of the required sacrifice increases. A decade later, the economists Martin Dufwenberg and Georg Kirchsteiger (2004) likewise incorporated the observation that people care about the intentions of co-players in economic games in their model of economic behaviour. A person's kindness, they postulated, depends on her intentions, and thus when a person wishes to reciprocate kindness with kindness, she must form beliefs about the other person's intentions.

The models developed by Rabin (1993) and Dufwenberg and Kirchsteiger (2004) are therefore exclusively intention-driven and say little about reciprocal motivations in relation to differential outcomes. That is to say, they assume that people do not consider whether they end up with more or less than an exchange partner/opponent; rather, they assume that people's perception of intentions is determined by whether the partner could have given them more or less. Indeed, there is experimental evidence that a concern for intentions, as opposed to

---

that theory is not fixed. Theorising potentially gives the explanation as to why something has (or has not) worked, which in turn offers the potential to generalise the findings to other contexts and settings. If your mind is set to do so, there are more valid points on which to ridicule economists (for example, many of them take the view that 'my preferred theory is right, and if it doesn't work in practice then people are just making the wrong decisions').

outcomes, predominates in that responders' choices often depend on what proposers could have done, but chose not to do. For example, in an ultimatum game, a typical responder is more likely to accept an offer of (8, 2) – i.e. eight to two in favour of the proposer – if the only alternative for the proposer was to make an offer of (9, 1) than if the only alternative was (5, 5) (Falk, Fehr and Fischbacher, 2003), although in the real world intentions might not always be so easy to discern.[4] Similarly, the economist Armin Falk and his colleagues (2008) also reported that responders are less likely to punish when proposers' actions are determined randomly than when they have greater agency over their choices, again suggesting that responders are concerned with intention.[5]

Falk and Fischbacher (2006) also propose a formal theory of reciprocity, which, like those mentioned above, allows identical outcomes to trigger different reciprocal responses. They contend that their model explains why outcomes tend to be perceived as fair in dyadic, bilateral exchanges but often as highly unfair in competitive markets, because the intentions in the latter, according to these authors, are often perceived to be egoistically selfish, further undermining reciprocity. However, unlike Rabin (1993) and Dufwenberg and Kirchsteiger (2004), Falk and Fischbacher (2006) argue that in

[4] In relation to Chapter 2, Nowak (2011) states that group selection theory makes no assumptions about individual intentions with respect to selfishness or prosociality, and that it is outcomes that drive reciprocal behaviours. However, humans clearly do care about intentions in deciding whether to reciprocate, so either Nowak is wrong (at least vis-à-vis group selection in human populations), reciprocity in humans is not explained by group selection, or humans have evolved beyond the mere concentration on outcomes when undertaking reciprocal acts. Perhaps humans developed so as to seek a reason for conforming to a social norm that arose organically in relation to it serving outcomes entirely, or perhaps intentions serve as signals for what the likely, if not inevitable, final outcomes will be.

[5] Further, Kahneman, Knetsch and Thaler (1986) reported that when their respondents were asked if they would prefer to share $12 equally with a person who had made an unequal proposal in a prior ultimatum game, or $10 with someone who had previously made an equal proposal, nearly three-quarters chose the latter, which can be interpreted as a focus on intentions over outcomes. However, if people are hardwired to make short-term sacrifices for possible longer-term gains, this may lead them to reward people who they think are more in tune with generating those longer-term gains, even in games that end before long-term gains can be realised.

Table 4.1 *Behavioural economic theories of reciprocity*

	Rabin (1993)	Dufwenberg & Kirchsteiger (2004)	Falk & Fischbacher (2006)
Intentions matter	✓	✓	✓
Outcomes matter	✗	✗	✓

addition to intentions, outcomes also play a sometimes decisive role in driving reciprocal exchanges, in that people tend to compare their payoffs with those of others when deciding how to respond in exchange relationships. Perhaps a responder will be more likely to respond favourably to a proposer whom they perceive as having poor intentions, or whose intentions they cannot observe, if the final distribution of outcomes is relatively equal than if it is wide. If reciprocity is driving mutual self-interest, as assumed by scholars from, for example, Hume (1739–40/1978) to Sugden (2018) – to reiterate, if enlightened self-interest is the driver – then presumably there must be some attention paid to the distribution of outcomes. The road to hell, after all, may well be paved with good intentions.[6]

Table 4.1 summarises the factors that are assumed to matter in the theories of reciprocity summarised in this section, but let us now turn to the economic games that behavioural economists (and others) have designed to try to challenge the notion that selfish egoism predominates.

---

[6] As outlined in Chapter 1 (and since), context matters. In some situations, we might be motivated by another's intentions (e.g. by not giving way to an inconsiderate driver – liking and balance reciprocity), in others by outcomes (e.g. in negotiating a fair price for eight giant Madagascan prawns at the local fishmonger, hypothetically – balance and continuation reciprocity), and sometimes by outcomes and intentions (e.g. in deciding what to buy a sibling for Christmas, based partly on gifts received in the past – balance, liking and continuation reciprocity). It may be that outcomes and intention play different roles in social versus economic exchanges. As also noted in Chapter 1, although highly contextual, all of the above may be rooted in motivating prosociality, to ultimately benefit all. The social versus the economic as theatres of reciprocity, both of which are of interest to behavioural economists incidentally, will be considered in Chapter 5.

Table 4.2 *The prisoner's dilemma*

		Prisoner A	
		Do not inform	Inform
Prisoner B	Do not inform	(1, 1)	(0, 3)
	Inform	(3, 0)	(2, 2)

PRISONERS, ULTIMATUMS AND DICTATORS

Perhaps the most famous economic game of all, developed in the 1950s not by behavioural economists but by mathematicians working at the Rand Corporation in California, is the prisoner's dilemma. The prisoner's dilemma was actually drawn up to show why two (economically) rational people might not co-operate with each other when it is in both their interests to do so and has been applied across the social and biological sciences; indeed, it has been written about so much that it will only be considered briefly here. The payoffs in a basic construct of the prisoner's dilemma are summarised in Table 4.2, which, in defining the two players as prisoners locked in separate rooms and each having to decide whether to inform on the other in relation to the committing of a crime, remains true to the original spirit of the game.

Table 4.2 shows that if neither Prisoner A nor Prisoner B informs on each other, then both will be sentenced to one year in prison (thus, in relation to these outcomes, the lower the better). If A does not inform but B informs, then A will receive a three-year sentence and B will be released immediately. The other strategy combinations and consequent outcomes in the table can be read similarly. Careful scrutiny of the table reveals that, no matter what B does, it is always in A's best interests to inform, at least purely in terms of the outcomes summarised. That is, if B does not inform, then A will be released immediately if she informs and will serve one year if she does not inform, and if B informs, then A will serve two rather than three years if she informs. Similarly, it is always in B's best interests to inform irrespective of what A does. Therefore, the only stable equilibrium – i.e. the Nash equilibrium – is for both prisoners to inform, even though both would be better off if they implicitly co-operated in not informing.

At least, inform-inform is the economically rational stable equilibrium if the prisoner's dilemma is played just once, or for a known number of rounds. If, however, people are exposed to an unknown number of prisoner-dilemma-type scenarios where in each round each partner in the game has to decide whether or not to co-operate – for example, when apes (including humans) are deciding whether or not to share their meat following a hunt, knowing that they will have to make regular, similar decisions indefinitely into the future – then the prisoner's dilemma, assuming that the partners can forge or stumble upon an initial position of mutual co-operation, may proceed to a game of tit for tat in which joint co-operation becomes a stable equilibrium.[7] Maintaining co-operation in the prisoner's dilemma is therefore perhaps secured by the threat of punishment, and that non-co-operation will sacrifice better long-term outcomes for only a short-term gain. Although the initial act of co-operating may, in some circumstances, have been forged by an act of reciprocal altruism, we will learn in Chapter 5 that Adam Smith, to name but one great figure in the history of intellectual thought, believed the threat of negative

---

[7] As noted in Chapter 1, however, tit for tat is an optimum strategy only under a limited set of circumstances. Moreover, when dealing with actual prisoners or criminals, a code of honour that forbids informing may secure co-operative behaviours that are damaging to a society in general, an example of the dark side of reciprocity that will be discussed in Chapter 6. Relatedly, people are, as perhaps expected, more likely to co-operate in the prisoner's dilemma with people who they consider to be part of their in-group, and less likely to co-operate with those who they perceive to be a threat to their 'own'. This effect can be biologically enhanced. For example, with a nod to Chapter 1, the psychologist Carsten de Dreu and his colleagues (2010) found that when people were given a sniff of oxytocin before facing a prisoner's dilemma with a person they viewed as an outsider, they were more likely to be uncooperative, due principally to a concern that co-operation could threaten their in-group.

reciprocity to be a more important force in sustaining co-operative behaviours.

Perhaps the most robust findings reported by behavioural economists in relation to reciprocity are those uncovered with the ultimatum game, but these have already been discussed at some length in previous chapters. Suffice to remind readers here that in the standard ultimatum game, proposers tend to offer, on average, 40–50 per cent of the money endowments that they are bestowed with, and that offers of 20–30 per cent are frequently rejected by responders, when widely accepted wisdom contends that standard economic theory requires that proposers and responders should offer/accept very small amounts of the endowment (see, for example, Gintis et al., 2005; Henrich et al., 2005; Kahneman, Knetsch and Thaler, 1986).[8] As mentioned in Chapter 1, a possible explanation for why people tend to make such high offers in the ultimatum game is less to do with reciprocal altruism than it is to avoid being punished. That is, the proposers are aware that the responders will react negatively to any offer that they perceive as unfair, thus leaving the proposers with nothing. In short, proposers, familiar with negative reciprocity, offer an amount that they believe will not fall victim to that aspect of human nature, and thus maximise – or perhaps satisfice – in relation to their final expected reward.

The relative extent to which the proposers' responses in the ultimatum game are motivated by a positive sense of reciprocal altruism, or the threat of negative reciprocity, can be to some extent elucidated by looking at results from the so-called dictator game. In the dictator game, proposers are asked simply for the amount of their endowment that they are willing to give to the other party, and both parties then leave with their respective shares. The threat of negative reciprocity is therefore absent. Here, compared to the ultimatum game, the distribution of offers

---

[8] It is sometimes contended that recipients will be less likely to reject small proportions when the stakes are substantial, but research in developing country contexts has demonstrated that similar rejection rates are observed when the initial money allocation is as high as three months income (Cameron, 1999). More work is required on this issue, though.

tends towards zero; the modal offer is typically at 0–20 per cent (with often around 20 per cent of proposers offering zero), and with average offers at 20–30 per cent of the endowment (Falk and Fischbacher, 2006; Forsythe et al., 1994; Henrich et al., 2005).[9] Therefore, although the share offered in the dictator game is normally quite a bit lower than that observed in the ultimatum game, an average offer of 20–30 per cent remains quite substantial, suggesting either that at least some proposers are indeed motivated by a positive sense of fairness, or that some have a concern about the threat of negative reciprocity that is so hard-wired that it influences answers even when the threat is not, in fact, present (or both of the above).[10] Gintis et al. (2005, p. 25) contend that 'strong reciprocity is an historically evolved form of enlightened self- and kin-interest that falsely appears altruistic when deployed in social situations for which it was not an adaptation'. Overall, though, the threat of negative reciprocity in the ultimatum game clearly does cause of lot of behaviour that could be confused as generosity.

Notwithstanding the above, some have questioned whether the results of the dictator game (and indeed the other economic games summarised in this chapter) translate to real world settings; i.e.

---

[9] Henrich et al. (2005) report that offers as low as zero are rarely offered by people in tribal communities, perhaps due to a perceived concern regarding the connotations that an extreme lack of generosity may bring forth in small communities.

[10] Of course, some proposers may be motivated by pure altruism, although the cynical may conclude that proposers are still getting something out of offering a non-negative amount of their endowments, whether it be with respect to their reputation for example (i.e. wanting to give a good impression to the experimenter), or to the warm glow of giving. Although it still remains plausible that some proposers are more concerned with distributional fairness in final outcomes than reciprocal altruism, Fong, Bowles and Gintis (2005) report an experiment that paired several dictator proposers with real-life welfare recipients and found that significantly more money was allocated to recipients who expressed strong work preferences than those who expressed weak work preferences, indicating that the proposers preferred giving to those who were more willing to offer something back. Also, since proposers in the dictator game, like the ultimatum game, are offered windfall money, some of them may think it only fair that they offer a proportion to the other party; their answers may well be different if their endowments were earned (as indeed was observed by Cherry, Frykblom and Shogren (2002), who reported that earned money is associated with less generosity in the dictator game).

whether these games have external validity. For example, the economist Nick Bardsley (2008) has suggested that the propensity for many people to offer a proportion of their endowment is simply an artefact of the design of the dictator game, where allowing the respondents to only give (and not take) may introduce an expected norm of behaviour by which proposers are guided. Bardsley reported that if the proposers who otherwise appeared generous are allowed to take from others, they will indeed do so, implying that we cannot draw inferences about people's general motivations from the dictator game and suggesting once again that in terms of people's behaviours, context matters. Unless care is taken in designing the policy environment, it is thus likely that reciprocal altruism can be crowded out, which could be detrimental for the policy's intended target group.

THE OTHER GAMES PEOPLE PLAY

To support the claim that economic games have legs, behavioural economists have also studied the centipede game. For illustrative purposes, consider a game that has four stages, I to IV. There are two players in the game, A and B. In stage I, A chooses to 'take' or 'pass'. If she takes, she receives 80 per cent of an initial endowment of five units of some material outcome, such as money. If she passes, the endowment doubles in size, and B gets to choose whether to take or pass. Likewise, if B takes, she gets 80 per cent of the growing endowment, but can pass back to A if she chooses, the endowment is again doubled and the process is repeated until either one of the two players takes, or the four stages are completed. To aid exposition, consider Table 4.3.

Thus, the table indicates that if A takes in stage I, she will receive four units leaving one unit to B, but if she passes then B, in stage II, will have the opportunity to either take eight units and leave two units to A or pass, moving us on to A's choice in stage III, etc. If the players were to proceed to the end, A would receive sixty-four units to B's sixteen units, leaving both players considerably better off than if the game had ended at the beginning. However, through backward induction, we can see that B would be better off taking in phase IV than

Table 4.3 *The centipede game*

	Takes	Passes
I (A decides)	(4, 1)	II
II (B decides)	(2, 8)	III
III (A decides)	(16, 4)	IV
IV (B decides)	(8, 32)	Finish
Finish	(64, 16)	

passing, and a rational A would therefore expect B to take if they reached that point. Since A would be better off taking in stage III than if the game was to end with B taking in stage IV, it is assumed that A would take if she got as far as stage III; but a rational B would know this and she would thus be better off taking in stage II. Through backward induction and full rationality, a selfish person would always decide to take; rational choice theory therefore predicts that the game will end with A taking in stage I. However, Richard McKelvey and Thomas Palfrey (1992) reported an experiment where 93 per cent of players passed in stage I, 62 per cent passed in stage II, 35 per cent passed in stage III and 25 per cent passed in stage IV. This not only challenges the notion that players will necessarily tend towards selfish egoism – it also suggests that many players were not particularly inequality averse, since the absolute difference in units received by A and B widens as they proceed through the stages. Perhaps these results indicate that most people cannot work out the intricacies of backward induction – that their rationality has bounds. Or perhaps the players will tend to co-operate, at least up to a point, to try to ensure that each will receive a larger number of units than if the game had ended early. That is, A will trust that an initial good turn will be met – and, if these results are anything to go by, often will indeed be met – in turn by B.

Speaking of trust, there is an eponymous economic game that also involves two players, A and B.[11] Again, the payoffs can be taken as some

---

[11] To illustrate, I use here an example taken from Sugden (2018).

Table 4.4 *The trust game*

Player A						
Holds	→	(0, 0)				
Sends	→	→	→	Player B		
				Keeps	→	(−1, 5)
				Returns	→	(2, 2)

unit of material outcome. As summarised in Table 4.4, player A can 'hold', in which case both players receive nothing, or 'send' to player B. B can then 'keep' or 'return'. If she keeps, she receives five units while A then loses a unit, whereas if she returns then both players receive two units. Egoistic self-interest dictates that B will keep, and an economically rational A would expect that; thus, according to standard economic theory, A will always hold, and the game ends at (0, 0).

However, although egoistic behaviour in experimental trust games is far from rare, Sugden (2018) notes that significant proportions of respondents respond in ways that generate mutual benefit in situations where pure selfishness would fail to do so. In short, reciprocal altruism is often observed, but unlike Rabin (1993) and Dufwenberg and Kirchsteiger (2004) discussed earlier, Sugden (2018) does not attribute this to the considering of two acts of kindness. Rather, he attributes A's sending to her wishing to signal a co-operative intention, and B returning to reciprocate that willingness to co-operate so as to play a part in mutually beneficial schemes.[12]

Finally, for here, there is the public goods game, which involves three or more players. Each player is given an equal number of tokens (that have a money value), and each is asked to choose a proportion of their tokens to place in a public account. The tokens that the players have in their private accounts retain their exact value, but the value of the

---

[12] As noted in Chapter 3, in tribal communities high offers are sometimes rejected. This may not be motivated by a desire to punish or by a lack of kindness, but as a means to signal an unwillingness to co-operate. Somewhat similarly, rejecting inadequate offers may be a signal from the responder that she considers the proposer to be a person who is not worth her time (see Chapter 3, footnote 19).

public account tokens are multiplied by a factor of m, where 1 < m < n, with n being the number of players in the game. The final payoff, in terms of tokens, to each player is whatever they have in their private account plus an equal share of the number of tokens in the public account.

Now, consider the following example from Samuel Bowles (2016, p. 135): 'there are five members of the group and the multiplication factor is two (the amount in the pot is doubled by the experimenter before being redistributed to the subjects)'. Assume that each player has five tokens. The best *collective* strategy is for all players to put all of their tokens into the public account: this would double the monetary value of the tokens that they together own and, collectively, they cannot do better than that. However, because m/n < 1, the best strategy for an egoistically selfish player is to refrain from giving any of their tokens to the public pot. For instance, if player A was to give up one token, it would be doubled in size but then divided between the five players, and thus A would receive back only 2/5 of a token from that action. Or if A was to give all five of her tokens, she would similarly receive back only two tokens directly in return. In short, no matter how many of her tokens she gives to the public pot, she would receive fewer directly in return, and therefore egoism would preclude her from giving anything. Individual selfishness thus conflicts with opportunities for mutual benefit.

Sugden (2018) contends that three conclusions can be drawn with respect to the experimental evidence on the public goods game. First, so long as m/n is not too close to zero, a substantial proportion of players make significant positive contributions to the public pot, contrasting with egoistic self-interest.[13] Second, if the game is played either sequentially, where players contribute in turn, or is played repeatedly, each player's contribution tends to be positively correlated to the previous contributions of other respondents, an apparent form of tit for tat. Third, over repeated games, the contributions to the public pot tend to decline towards zero, a result that may be explained by the interaction of free

---

[13]   Student respondents in public goods games contribute a mean of 40–60 per cent to the public pot, but there is wide variance with most players contributing either everything or nothing (Henrich et al., 2005).

riders, who never contribute, with conditional co-operators, who, because of the free riders, gradually withdraw their co-operation (Bardsley and Moffatt, 2007; Fischbacher and Gächter, 2010; Henrich et al., 2005).[14] Thus, a relatively small amount of egoism within a group can, over time, destroy group co-operation, which is somewhat worrying and may underline the importance of the role that altruistic punishers play.

Conveniently, the economist Benedikt Herrman and his colleagues (2008) ran a repeated public goods game that was modified to include the opportunity to punish transgressors. In their experiment, players were anonymised but were assigned identification numbers, and the amounts given to the public pot by each player, listed only by their ID number, was publicised to all of the players in the game. In the punishment game, each player was then allowed to sacrifice some of their own personal payoff to punish other players; the authors also ran a non-punishment game as a control. With and without punishment, the authors found that players contributed substantial proportions of their endowments in the first period, in common with other public goods games, and, also in accordance with common observation, without the threat of punishment co-operation soon faded. With the threat of punishment, however, contributions stayed consistently high.

Similarly, Fehr and Gächter (2000b) conducted an experiment where strangers could punish those whose contributions to public goods were perceived by them as unfair.[15] They ran ten rounds of their game, and punishers were moved on in successive rounds so that they could not benefit from any subsequent increase in contributions from those whom they punished (both punisher and punished were aware of this experiment design). Fehr and Gächter reported that contributions to the public pool increased markedly

---

[14] Although Isaac, Walker and Williams (1994) found that the greater the number of times a public goods game is repeated, the greater the extent to which co-operation is sustained; for example, if a game is repeated sixty times, they found that co-operation decayed less than if it was repeated ten times, implying that co-operation can be learned.

[15] Incidentally, among behavioural economists, Ernst Fehr is the leading contributor to the empirical study of reciprocity.

over the successive rounds when stranger punishment was possible, and decreased when no opportunity to punish was allowed.[16] Thus, the threat of negative reciprocity appeared to sustain co-operative behaviours, an observation that holds even if the proportion of altruistic punishers in a group is small. The effect of punishment on co-operation was, however, stronger when players were certain that the punisher remained within their group in successive rounds, suggesting that the impact of negative reciprocity on co-operation is more robust in groups that are coherent and permanent (cf. Chapter 3, footnote 12), a finding that has implications for the structural design of public policy sectors, discussed in later chapters.

Gächter, Kölle and Quercia (2017), across a series of experiments, found that reciprocal altruism was stronger when creating a new than when sustaining an existing public good, perhaps because some egoists or optimistic conditional co-operators saw the benefits of getting things going, but acted on their egoism or became disillusioned once things were up and running. Negative reciprocity was much higher in the sustaining than in the creating condition, maybe because of a recognition that people will try to transgress once things are up and running, but given the goodwill required to get things going, punishment at an early stage may risk being perceived as coercive and, hence, counterproductive, highlighting once more the context-dependent nature of reciprocity (see also Rand, Yoeli and Hoffman 2014).

Overall, regarding negative reciprocity in public goods games, Sugden (2018) concludes that the experimental evidence suggests that if the cost of punishing is low relative to the cost of being punished, and if the individuals who are punished are not given the opportunity to retaliate, high rates of contribution can be sustained. Nowak (2011), however, strikes a cautionary note, arguing that in real life people usually know who is punishing them and therefore

---

[16] Carpenter and Matthews (2012) also found that contribution levels in an experimental public goods game increased substantially when it was recognised that altruistic punishment exists.

reprisals can be expected. Thus, in many circumstances it might be wise for all relevant parties to agree upon sanctions for bad behaviour in advance, and for there to be an arbitration body that has representatives or input from all concerned groups, that moderates expectations and punishes transgressors, and indeed that punishes those who inappropriately assume the role of retaliator themselves. As aforementioned, the influence of punishment in public goods games highlights the importance of context on human decision-making, and this must lead us to at least question whether the findings gleaned from the economic games discussed in this section (and the previous one) are at all valid in the more complex, messy real world.[17]

BEYOND ABSTRACTION

Although typically not quite the real world, some behavioural economists have designed experiments that are somewhat less abstract than those described above, to lend them at least a flavour of reality. For example, Ernst Fehr (again), Gächter and Kirchsteiger (1997) conducted an experiment where respondents were asked to assume that they were employers or employees. The standard economic assumption that inspired their experiment is that those placing themselves in the position of employees would be entirely self-regarding, and will therefore choose a zero-cost effort level in a hypothetical contract irrespective of the wage offered to them, an assumption that had been earlier challenged by George Akerlof (1982), who speculated that a wage higher than the minimum necessary would often be perceived by employees as, in some sense, a gift, and they would consequently work harder than self-interest

[17] The economists Matteo Galizzi and Daniel Navarro-Martinez, in an article forthcoming at the time of writing, report that answers in economic games bear little correlation to socially orientated decision-making behaviours in the real world. To contest this conclusion in part, one might say that experimentally controlled contexts may reveal deep behavioural drivers, uncontaminated by a real world that pulls people in many conflicting directions, with some real-world contexts having been designed almost to drive out reciprocal behaviours. As noted in Chapter 3, we may be hard-wired for reciprocity, but the wiring still needs regular maintenance.

dictates.[18] Standard economic theory also postulates that those assuming the employer position will anticipate that employees will choose a zero-cost effort level and thus offer no more than the minimum wage. However, Fehr et al. found that the higher the wage offered by employers, the higher the effort level to which employees committed. Although it ought to be noted that the amount of effort given, although considerable, was not as much as the amount of effort agreed upon (suggesting an element of selfish egoism at work), Fehr et al. attributed their results to employer recognition that employees will be predisposed towards strong reciprocity, and thus made quite generous wage offers.[19] The anticipation of strong reciprocity therefore probably made both the employers and the employees better off than they otherwise would have been; an important lesson for public sector labour markets is that it may be the case that you get what you pay for.

In offering some support that the behaviours observed in economic games translate to real-life decision making, Fehr and Leibbrant (2011) studied the actions of shrimp fishermen. They reported that those shrimpers who showed themselves to be more co-operative in a public goods game tended to punch significantly larger holes in their shrimp traps (compared to the lesser co-operative), which, by releasing immature shrimps, serves to protect future stocks for the community. Similarly perhaps, the economist Devesh Rustagi

[18] To recall Chapter 2, it has been shown that capuchin monkeys may also respond to fair 'wages'. For example, in one study, two capuchins, separated by wire mesh, were each required to give a pebble to a human in order to receive a grape in return. One of the capuchins then received a piece of cucumber, which is much less preferred than a grape. This would have been fine if the cucumber was given to both monkeys from the beginning of the experiment, but now the cucumber-receiver knew that the other capuchin received a grape. He thus rejected the cucumber, in the knowledge that others were receiving something better (Brosnan and de Waal, 2003). If these behaviours relate also to humans, which they surely do, then a lesson here is that if, as an employer, you have to disclose your wage structures, you ought to make sure that they are perceived by your employees as fair, otherwise they might well reduce their effort levels.

[19] In that offering what may be perceived as generous wages might be a signal of intentions, all of the theoretical models presented earlier can explain why employers are often reluctant to hire workers at less than the prevailing wage, a reluctance that has been observed in real labour markets (e.g. Bewley, 1999).

and his colleagues (2010) reported that conditional co-operation in public goods games in Ethiopia was associated with a tendency to plant more trees, which again may be an indicator of concern for the future of the community (but refer back to footnote 17).

In the chapters that follow, we will focus more intensively on reciprocal behaviours in broad policy contexts, but it seems fair to conclude that experimental economic games often reveal that a core human motivation is a desire to act reciprocally and co-operatively, but that unless the context is conducive to these tendencies, the motivation can erode.[20] Context, again, is everything. For instance, whether the game is repeated, whether it allows altruistic punishment, whether the person you play against is known, liked, disliked, a member of one's 'in-group', an outsider or anonymous, to name but a few factors, all influence a player's apparent levels of generosity.[21] Moreover, on the question of whether it is intentions (and whether those intentions are signals of kindness or co-operativeness) or outcomes that are driving reciprocal behaviours, it is surely often a bit of both, which will again be context-dependent. We do, it seems, sometimes respond favourably to kindness and unfavourably to those who are mean, and we do sometimes want to signal a wish to be co-operative, and hope that people might respond positively to that. But at least with respect to much of the driver of strong reciprocity – that is, the continuation reciprocity that secures mutual benefit – over an extended period, intentions alone will not be enough to sustain mutual co-operation. All parties will want to see what's in it – materially – for them, or for those they wish to serve.

---

[20] In a series of economic games, Charness and Rabin (2002) reported data that suggests that reciprocal altruism plays little role in helping behaviours – i.e. respondents were no more likely to show kindness towards those who had demonstrated a nice prior action than towards those who had been neither kind nor unkind. But negative reciprocity, in the form of respondents being less likely to help those who had previously been unkind, was evident.

[21] Ostrom (2000) reported, furthermore, that face-to-face communication in public goods games and other types of social dilemmas is more likely than anonymous interactions to lead to sustained levels of co-operation.

FOOD FOR THOUGHT

1. Do intentions or outcomes, or intentions *and* outcomes, drive reciprocal actions?
2. Is punishment of selfishness necessary to sustain long-term co-operation?
3. Are the results of experimental economic games relevant to real-world considerations?

5 The Domain of Reciprocity

As touched upon in Chapter 3, anthropologists have written extensively about the role that reciprocity plays in tribal communities, with Marcel Mauss (1954) and others, for instance, writing that the gift exchange serves as a mechanism to ensure that mutual obligations are met, being, in essence, the glue that binds society, and societies, together. In this formulation, the gift exchange was therefore more than a means by which to bestow mutually beneficial material transactions; it was rich in meaning in relation to obligations, duty and dignity, it forged indissoluble alliances, and it carried baggage in these respects that the modern economic exchange does not. As aforementioned, Anthony Heath (1976) interpreted Mauss' concept of the gift exchange in tribal communities as something intermediate between total prestation and the modern economic transaction.

Many thus take the view that the reciprocity embedded in the gift exchange is not applicable to the modern market economy. Mauss himself believed this, contending that without felt obligations that bind people together, exchange driven by the law of economic interest via money transactions is inferior to the gift exchange. Others, particularly adherents to standard economic theory, maintain that ridding transactions of these obligations and appealing to egoistic self-interest is beneficial for everyone, (selectively) recalling the spirit of Adam Smith (1776/1999, p. 104), who wrote that 'Society may subsist among different men, as among different merchants, from a sense of its utility, without any mutual love or affection; and though no man in it should owe any obligation, or be bound in gratitude to any other, it may still be upheld by a mercenary exchange of good offices, according to an agreed valuation'. Smith's (1776/1999) imagination of the market exchange between the butcher, the baker and the brewer in *The*

Wealth of Nations – local artisans producing relatively simple, easily understood goods with limited opportunities to exploit information asymmetries – was driven as such. Whether Smith is likely to have thought that 'mutual love or affection' should be absent from the often complex, imperfect exchanges that are a feature of modern societies and economies is a question to which we will return.

Nonetheless, one cannot deny that many, perhaps most, market exchanges in modern economies are atomised and that they tend to occur between (often anonymous) strangers. These circumstances are far removed from the gift exchanges that occur between kin – or at least between people who are well known to each other – that are typical in small tribal communities where reciprocity flourished. From this, it might be concluded that a concern with reciprocity – with a mutually fair exchange – as an underlying motivation for our conduct should be restricted to social exchanges, where people are generally charged with looking out for each other (even if they are often also strangers to each other), and not applied to the dog-eat-dog world of the modern market economy.[1] But there are those who maintain that the story is a little more complex and nuanced than that.

A FAIR EXCHANGE?

In agreement with Mauss, others draw a distinction between economic and social policy in relation to human interactions and transactions.[2] The British social policy analyst Richard Titmuss (1970/1997), for instance, in his *magnum opus*, *The Gift Relationship*, argued that social policy differs from economic policy

---

[1] The reader will remember from Chapter 1 that Serge-Christophe Kolm (2008) does not believe that exchange driven by mutual self-interest – what he calls continuation reciprocity – is a pure form of reciprocity, and thus, through his lens, assuming that atomised modern market exchanges are driven by such interests, they would not be classified as being underpinned by reciprocal concerns. Many, including me, however, are not so restrictive.

[2] This section will focus on whether economic transactions are underpinned by the notion of a fair exchange, although the reader may also interpret the subheading as an indication of whether I am offering a reasonable argument for debate.

in that it centres more on institutions that create integration and discourage alienation, and, before him, the American sociologist Peter Blau (1964) had maintained that the difference between a social exchange and an economic exchange is that in a social exchange, although a return is expected, it is usually a future obligation that is not precisely specified, and the nature of the exchange should not be bargained but should be left to the discretion of the giver.[3] These writers thus appeared to believe that trust and reciprocal altruism are fundamental to social but not to economic exchanges.

As an aside, the philosopher Michael Sandel (2013) draws a distinction between the social and the modern economic exchange by arguing that there are things that money simply cannot buy, such as friends and Nobel Prizes, and there are things that money can buy but arguably should not, such as kidneys and children.[4] However, one could contend that everything is in some sense exchanged, either for money or for something else, depending on what the partners to the exchange want or feel is appropriate. Nobel Prize committees, for instance, may want evidence of a lifetime of profound intellectual contribution in exchange for the honour that they bestow; friends mutually offer support and understanding; one normally needs to demonstrate a capacity for good parenting if one wishes to adopt a child; even kidneys require an element of good behaviour. Perhaps everything can be exchanged reciprocally, and sometimes – not always – money serves as a convenient mode for one half of the exchange relationship to accept and to be used in turn, of course, in future exchanges. Reciprocity is thus in the nature of the exchange, rather than in the items or services that are actually exchanged, and requires an attentiveness to what the other partner wants. Some objects of exchange may have little monetary value but have a lot of psychological value to the receiver, and if a sense of fairness

---

[3] Heath (1976) contended that a social exchange is much more formalised than Blau suggests. For example, the division of labour in the family is often proscribed rather than left to discretion, and thus according to this line of argument, the distinction between economic and social exchanges may be on a continuum rather than a dichotomy.

[4] Although the award of a Nobel Prize might 'buy' you some friends (and enemies).

in an exchange between two partners genuinely holds (and no third party is harmed), one might contend that it is nobody else's place to hold either partner in moral contempt. However, this requires the exchange partners to be operating from a level playing field. As Sandel convincingly contends, if one of the partners is in dire need because of their background circumstances, then they may be participating in an exchange due to some degree of coercion. Essentially, an asymmetry in power would hereby afford an opportunity for one of the partners to act not reciprocally but egoistically, a point to which we will return in Chapter 6.

Unlike Mauss and Titmuss, the economists Luigino Bruni and Robert Sugden (2008; 2013) do not draw a strong distinction between the social and economic domains as arenas for reciprocal actions. Indeed, they perceive the possibility for reciprocal orientations in market transactions to be compatible with economic efficiency, and draw on Adam Smith's contemporary, the Italian economist Antonio Genovesi (1765–67/2005), to support their argument. According to Bruni and Sugden, Genovesi maintained that markets are based on the human tendency towards mutual assistance, that reciprocity is central to economic exchange, and that each party to a market exchange needs to understand and respect what the other party wants; Genovesi did not believe that there is a difference between market relationships and those governed by civil society.

Before concluding that, within economic thinking, Genovesi was an outlier, let us briefly return as promised to the writings of Adam Smith, not so much in relation to *The Wealth of Nations*, but to his intellectually richer earlier work, *The Theory of Moral Sentiments*. Here, Smith wrote extensively on what are, in essence, reciprocal motivations, providing descriptions of what are now known as reciprocal altruism and altruistic punishment:

> Actions of a beneficent tendency, which proceed from proper motives, seem alone to require reward; because such alone are the approved objects of gratitude, or excite the sympathetic gratitude of

the spectator. Actions of a hurtful tendency, which proceed from improper motives, seem alone to deserve punishment; because such alone are the approved objects of resentment, or excite the sympathetic resentment of the spectator. (Smith, 1759/2009, p. 95)[5]

Smith was particularly convinced that the tendency towards negative reciprocity was a crucial feature of the human motivation to co-operate. He wrote (1759/2009, pp. 104–5), for instance, that 'Nature has implanted in the human breast that consciousness of ill desert, those terrors of merited punishment which attend upon its violation, as the great safeguards of the association of mankind.' But he also appeared to take the view that feelings of love and gratitude are optimal in binding the members of society together, by maintaining (1759/2009, pp. 103–4) that 'All the members of human society stand in need of each others assistance, and are likewise exposed to mutual injuries. Where the necessary assistance is reciprocally afforded from love, from gratitude, from friendship, and esteem, the society flourishes and is happy.'[6]

How does this square with Smith's (1776/1999) views in *The Wealth of Nations*, noted earlier, where he writes that society may subsist from a sense of utility, without any mutual love or affection, and without any bonds of gratitude? It is of course possible that Smith believed that social and economic exchanges are driven by fundamentally different considerations, with the former driven by kindness and unkindness, gratitude and resentment (cf. footnote 5) and the latter driven more out of a concern with outcomes and utility, with reciprocal actions, *à la* Sugden (2018; see Chapter 4), a form of signalling that

[5] These particular moral sentiments – that reciprocal altruism is manifested in gratitude for beneficence and negative reciprocity in punishment for hurt (i.e. reward for kindness and punishment for unkindness) – are incorporated in all of the behavioural economic theories of reciprocity summarised towards the beginning of Chapter 4, but were the exclusive concern for Rabin (1993) and Dufwenberg and Kirchsteiger (2004) only.

[6] Talcott Parsons (1951) similarly wrote that if people fail to consider the other person in an exchange relationship when they make their decisions, the stability of the relationship will be undermined; he contended that a stable social system requires some mutuality of gratification.

one wishes to co-operate. This would again highlight the highly contextual circumstances in which different forms of reciprocal considerations drive actions. However, in *The Wealth of Nations*, which is of course focused on economic exchange, Smith may have to some degree underplayed the extent to which market imperfections, particularly asymmetries of information and power, would pervade post eighteenth century modern market economies, not to mention modern public sector services. Smith's argument in favour of self-love, mutual indifference and moral neutrality between trading partners might indeed work well in perfect markets where trading partners are equally free to act on their own interests, and may be particularly suited to artisans producing relatively simple goods and who rely on repeat custom for their business success, but these circumstances are perhaps better characterised by beer and bread than health and education. Thus, it is at least plausible that had Smith predicted the reach of market imperfections, then he may have included explicitly in his writings on economic exchange the emphasis on the importance of reciprocity that is so central to his discussion of social relationships in *The Theory of Moral Sentiments*.

However, even if Smith did see the necessary drivers of behaviour in social and economic relationships as fundamentally different from each other, it is clear that he saw a fair exchange – in the sense of the parties to an exchange being treated acceptably in what they receive as judged by themselves and reasonably as judged objectively – as foundational (see also Pinker, 2018, p. 13). In economic exchange, as with his friend, David Hume, he thus appeared to be in favour of prudent, or enlightened, self-interest, and not egoistical avarice, a point, to reiterate, supported by his contemporary disciple, Robert Sugden (2018), who contends that if someone wishes to gain wealth through market transactions, she has to find ways of transacting that benefit both herself and the person with whom she is trading. Over complex goods and services, with the asymmetries of information and power to which I have already alluded, encouraging selfish egoism will risk breaking a relationship that might have otherwise served all parties well, or sustaining an unequal relationship where one party is exploiting the other.[7] In short, in such circumstances, a fair exchange requires all parties to have an appreciation and concern for the circumstances and position of those with whom they are engaged.

FOSTERING A FAIR EXCHANGE

Given the above, what might then be the best conditions for fostering a fair exchange? Sugden (2018), drawing heavily on another great British classical economist and philosopher, John Stuart Mill (1859/1972; 1861/1972; 1869/1988; 1871/1909), sees little distinction here between social and economic transactions, suggesting that co-operation for mutual benefit should go all the way down from international trade and the institutions of civil society to the relationships between spouses. In developing Mill's concept that the market is a community of advantage, Sugden identifies what he sees as three key components of the liberal tradition of economic thought (of which he, Smith and Mill are parts):

1. In a well-ordered society, co-operation for mutual benefit should be a principle that governs all aspects of social (and economic) life.

---

[7] In the relationship between a buyer and a seller, where there is not perfect symmetry of information, it is perhaps typical for the seller to hold the advantage, but this will not always be the case. A buyer of insurance, for example, is likely to hold better information regarding her risk factors than the seller. To sustain co-operation, it is therefore important to nurture reciprocity by all parties. A specific example where this, to a degree, failed, was when Uber drivers were criticised quite severely for raising their rates following the terrorist attack on London Bridge in 2017, a behaviour that Michael Sandel (2013), and many others, would probably find morally objectionable. But one ought to perhaps keep in mind that if these drivers were paid a fair rate all of the time there might be less inclination, or even need, for them to hike their fees during periods of high demand (a situation compounded until recently by Uber drivers, at least in London, being forbidden from accepting tips). Reciprocity has to work both ways. (Admittedly, the morality of the practices of the Uber company, as opposed to the individual drivers, may be more legitimately scrutinised in relation to all of the above.) Incidentally, on the subject of tipping, I once found myself in a restaurant in Paris where I wanted to pay more for a meal than the owner was willing to accept, but admittedly that particular disagreement with respect to the preferred direction of the exchange is probably quite rare.

2. The competitive market is a network of mutually beneficial transactions, and competitive markets belong to the class of institutions in which individuals co-operate for mutual benefit.[8]
3. Each individual can judge what counts as her benefit, and thus there ought to be no paternalism in these institutional arrangements.

All three components are instructive, the first as it implies that mutuality pervades social *and* economic exchanges, the second because is posits that the underlying motivation in market exchanges is not necessarily selfish egoism, and the third because it contends that the best judge of how good an action is for a person is not a policy maker, but is the person herself.[9] Sugden calls the assumption of utility maximisation, generally held both descriptively and normatively in neoclassical economics and rational choice theory, 'the view from nowhere'.[10] It might reasonably be contested that the behavioural patterns identified by behavioural economists and psychologists over the past several decades place a question mark against whether people generally have the mental aptitude to judge what

---

[8] Sugden is, of course, not alone among more contemporary economists to align with this view. Nobel Laureate Kenneth Arrow (1972, p. 357), for instance, noted that 'Virtually every commercial transaction has within itself an element of trust, certainly any transaction conducted over a period of time. It can be plausibly argued that much of the economic backwardness in the world can be explained by the lack of mutual confidence'.

[9] Respect for individual choice is shared by classical and neoclassical economists, but for the latter, unlike the former, it is generally assumed that people will, and should, egoistically strive to maximise their own utility.

[10] Here, I will use the terms utility, welfare and happiness interchangeably. Although Sugden uses the term 'the view from nowhere' pejoratively, he borrowed it from the philosopher Thomas Nagel (1986), who believed utility maximisation to be an appropriate position to take in moral reasoning. An argument is often given that if one desires anything, then one desires it for one's happiness, but if one asks why one desires happiness, then the answer is that it is to be happy. Thus, happiness, or welfare or utility, is the end. But this, of course, assumes that happiness, or the maximisation of happiness, is indeed what one is aiming for: I find it fulfilling to write this book, and my wildest ambition is for the reader to find it fulfilling to read it. But both of us could probably gain more happiness by doing something else. The neoclassical economics roots in welfare maximisation stem from the founding father of British utilitarianism, Jeremy Bentham (1781/1988), and thus, from a neoclassical economist's perspective, it is not exactly a view from nowhere, although one may contend that Bentham himself adopted this view from nowhere.

counts as their own benefit – whatever that might be – much of the time.[11] Sugden (2018), however, himself one of the world's leading behavioural economists, insists that these behavioural findings are not fatal to the liberal tradition, principally because we cannot hope to really understand the reasons why people behave and choose in the ways that they do and that, therefore, what might appear unreasonable, flawed, biased or irrational from a neoclassical perspective, may be a perfectly reasonable decision for the person actually deciding. For instance, the general findings from the economic games reviewed in Chapter 4 may often conflict with the standard rational choice theory assumption of egoistically driven individual utility maximisation, but if they are a consequence of people wanting to signal their co-operative tendencies, then from the perspective of the liberal economic tradition (or at least some variants of it) they are perfectly reasonable. Sugden's preferred approach is therefore a contractarian one: i.e. in evaluating a social institution, a contractarian asks not whether aggregate welfare is maximised, but whether each person is willing to accept the rules of the institution, provided that everyone else accepts those rules. In a nutshell, Sugden's preferred approach is not to seek to maximise utility, but is rather to maximise opportunities, or choices.

The debate on what may be classified as the behavioural economic phenomena is not, however, limited to whether they cause people to make decisions that are sub-optimal to themselves; it also focuses on whether individuals or organisations implicitly use these phenomena in ways that impose harms on others. If we take present bias, for instance – i.e. the observation that people attach a very high weight to the immediate moment, and quickly and heavily discount the future (to a much more pronounced degree than that generally assumed in applications of standard economic theory) – then a case can be made that payday loan companies (i.e. companies that offer short-term loans at high rates of interest) implicitly make use of this

[11] For relatively recent accounts that detail many of these behavioural patterns, see Kahneman (2011), Thaler (2015) and/or Oliver (2017).

phenomena when marketing their products, generally to relatively poor people. These companies tend to emphasise the conveniences and joys of spending, hide the pain of repaying, and lend at barely explicit rates of interest that would have certainly been considered usury by Adam Smith. In short, one may reasonably contend that they manipulate people and, by doing so, cause harms. Therefore, along with asymmetries in information and power – and particularly as goods and services become more complex – knowledge of these psychological phenomena offer scope for the egoistically motivated to profit at the expense of others, throwing a spanner into the workings of the free market, a point well emphasised in Akerlof and Shiller's (2015) *Phishing for Phools*. Component 2, stated above, prescribes mutual benefit, but it does not ensure it. Although Mill (1859/1972) accepted that governments may act to prevent explicit harms to others, he perhaps did not recognise that people can be manipulated in their choices via the use of the behavioural economic phenomena to the extent that they are, in essence, harmed (see Berlin, 1969), and Sugden (2018) is also quiet on the legitimacy of regulating against such activities.[12] I shall return to this issue in Chapter 9.

Despite these dangers lurking within the modern market economy, the economist Guido Tabellini (2008), among others, suggests that liberal institutions serve to foster trust, and Samuel Bowles (2016) acknowledges that market-based societies have vibrant civic cultures due to, for instance, the geographic and social mobility, and the rule of law, that comes with them; that is, liberal market economies allow people to do things, and many of the things that they choose to do

---

[12] Sugden (2018) is quiet but not silent on the issue of one party manipulating another for their own ends, and refers to this as obfuscation. One example that he notes is when an airline imposes a penalty charge in excess of the corresponding costs for the reprinting of a boarding pass, with the charge stated in very small print when booking a ticket. He argues that the purpose of a contractarian analysis is to find transactions that are mutually advantageous, as viewed by those individuals who are party to them, but, to reiterate, if one is being manipulated then one might believe something is advantageous to oneself when, in fact, it is not, and therefore it is reasonable to contend that some (state) protections are warranted.

they do for the mutual benefit of themselves and others.[13] But Bowles also implies that attempts to design and presumably improve institutions by trying to channel egoistic self-interest are a fool's errand: 'it is safe to conclude that efforts to perfect the workings of markets may have collateral cultural effects that make people less likely to learn or retain the exchange-supporting norms and other values essential to good governance' (Bowles, 2016, p. 185); 'good incentives', he notes, 'are no substitute for good citizens' (p. 215), and egoism, if encouraged, can crowd out reciprocal tendencies.

A conclusion that can be reached regarding Smith, Mill and the liberal economic tradition is that reciprocity is yet again viewed as something that is broadly fundamental to human motivation. To view market exchanges as necessarily driven by selfish egoism is to have your telescope upside down (even if, admittedly, Smith believed that mutual indifference would lead to a broadly optimal market exchange over relatively simple goods). Moreover, we should not be encouraged to think of how much we can gain from exchange at the expense of others (which underlies the neoclassical assumption of an optimal exchange), but rather, what is a fair exchange between ourselves and others.[14] Of course, there will be those who will focus entirely upon themselves, and if the institutions do not guard against this then mutuality can be crowded out. Thus, we ought to strive to be fair, not exploitative, because, over the long term, that will better serve our enlightened self-interest, and on that I surmise that Smith and Mill

---

[13] Some believe that markets and economic exchange bring peace (e.g. Pinker, 2018). That is, when people are trading with each other they are not fighting, an argument used for awarding the European Union the 2012 Nobel Peace Prize. But there are, of course, counterarguments. For example, England and Germany were trading partners prior to World War I, and yet one can enter any church in England (and no doubt Germany also) and be shocked at the number of young local male parishioners killed in the French and Belgian countryside between 1914 and 1918.

[14] A personal example relates to me being offered a very good deal on a new car a couple of years ago, that came without a satnav. Normally, on such a large expense I would have expected the seller to provide the satnav for free, but because the car was (genuinely) being offered at not far off a breakeven price for the seller, we agreed to split the price on the satnav. I now have a good ongoing relationship (I like to think) with that car dealership.

would concur. Unfortunately, perhaps, the neoclassical assumption that markets, and indeed (because of the reach that neoclassical economic theory has had) humans generally, are driven necessarily by egoistic self-interest – and that we need not guard against this as it will produce optimum results – has become pervasive, and, in relation to public policy, has extended even to the realms of often complex social, and not just economic, exchange.

A FALSE DICHOTOMY

Although by now the reader will be aware that it is highly probable that reciprocity is a fundamental human motivation that evolved to benefit groups, and thus, ultimately, the individuals within those groups, the literature on how to motivate public sector performance improvements – i.e. improvements within public sector *groups* – has been relatively quiet on the specific concept and importance of reciprocity. Rather, since the 1990s, the debate has until very recently tended to focus on whether public sector workers are pure altruists or egoistic utility maximisers. The economist Julian Le Grand (1997; 2003), for instance, contends that democratic socialists, such as Richard Titmuss, adopted an altruistic view of human nature with which they heavily influenced the structure of the post–World-War-II British welfare state.[15] This view, Le Grand argues, led to British public sector services being organised collectively and managed without competitive incentives. Money was allocated to public sector professionals unconditionally, and they were allowed to get on with their jobs in the faith that they would altruistically deliver the best services that they could.[16] Le Grand, who in his role as a senior health and education policy advisor to Tony Blair was himself influential in

---

[15] Titmuss has been referred to above in relation to discussions of reciprocity, but he did occasionally seemingly confuse reciprocal altruism with pure altruism. However, he is not the only person who has been guilty of doing that. This is why he can be associated with different views of human motivation.

[16] I apologise for viewing this section through a predominantly British lens. This is done mainly for illustrative purposes. Readers can probably apply their own country's experiences because the strict dichotomy between pure altruism and selfish egoism as motivating forces of human behaviour has dominated discussions of welfare state

policy circles in the early-mid 2000s, argued that the post-war consensus that those who work within the British welfare state, or indeed any welfare state, are public spirited altruists ought no longer to hold, and should be replaced by the assumption that they are also often motivated by their own avaricious tendencies.

Le Grand (1997; 2003) categorised altruists as knights and egoists as knaves, and to be clear, he recognised that humans are motivated by both tendencies. He believes that undue faith has been placed on public sector workers being predominantly knightly. He thus essentially argued for the institutional environment to be framed such that the common tendency towards egoism among public sector professionals, when acted upon, serves society well. There are parallels here with Thaler and Sunstein's (2008) notion of a choice architecture guiding people's behaviours in a direction that might be optimal, either for themselves (in Thaler and Sunstein's argument), or for society in general (in Le Grand's argument); the main difference is that Le Grand believes that the environment should be designed to cater for economic rationality (i.e. selfish egoism) in human behaviours, whereas Thaler and Sunstein believe that it should instead cater for irrationality (i.e. the behavioural biases).

How one might temper or channel egoism for the common good is, of course, an old argument (see, for example., Hume, 1742/1975; Montesquieu, 1748/1989). Hume, for instance, from whom Le Grand borrowed his knight/knave terminology, wrote that every man ought to be supposed an avaricious knave. This, as we saw in Chapter 3, does not mean that Hume actually believed that every man is an avaricious knave, but rather that if those who are avaricious are not tempered or constrained then we are all in trouble. Hume therefore recommended a balancing of powers within a country, so that no one group could exploit all others, a viewpoint that was embraced by James Madison and Alexander Hamilton when they wrote the United States

governance in many countries over recent decades. Of course, not everyone accepts this dichotomous view, but it has been the dominant narrative.

Constitution, requiring a separation of powers between the two branches of the Legislature, the Executive and the Judiciary.

Le Grand's position is perhaps closer to that of Machiavelli than Hume or Montesquieu. Machiavelli (1532/1997), in *The Prince*, like Le Grand, urged leaders to pay attention to what motivates people so that an environment is created that drives people to act, seemingly automatically, in accordance with the leader's preferences, whereas Hume, for instance, proposed institutional arrangements that curtailed the opportunity for people to behave knavishly. Le Grand's position thus encourages egoism, essentially by arguing for demand-led competitive forces to be used within the public sector. Unless public sectors workers are incentivised as such, Le Grand posits, they will become lazy; if they have to compete for purchasers, contracts and clientele, they will knavishly be concerned with their revenues and will consequently provide a better quality service, assuming of course that the outcomes on which they are judged and measured are serving the public good (e.g. literacy standards in schools; waiting times in hospitals). À la Adam Smith's (1776/1999) butcher, baker and brewer in the *The Wealth of Nations*, Le Grand's notion of demand-led competition serving everyone's benefit may work in those public sector services that might be classified as simple; i.e. that are without significant asymmetries of information, and where the opportunities to use human psychological phenomena – such as the propensity for people to place an enormous weight upon the immediate moment (i.e. present bias) – to phish for contracts and clientele are absent (see Akerlof and Shiller, 2015; Oliver, 2017).

Public sector services are not analogous to, for example, restaurants, which can be forced out of business due to poor service and insufficient demand without too much societal suffering. If a hospital or a school performs badly and loses clientele – and thus suffers financially and is damaged further – it is still likely to be needed by much of the community that it serves. But perhaps there are categories of public services that are simple and thus, all else equal, are ripe for a socially beneficial application of demand-led competition;

for instance, arguably, infants' schooling, refuse collection, road repairs, many dental procedures, and perhaps even cataract and hernia operations. However, when things start getting complex (public university education; cardiovascular and cancer procedures, sometimes delivered to the same patient; constructing an IT system across a national health care system; building a tunnel between two nations), the opportunities for the selfish to act upon their egoism to the detriment of others multiply. They multiply further when the indicators of assessment are population rather than individual based; for example, for cardiovascular procedures, did the hospital, or others, adjust appropriately for case mix? Did it refuse difficult-to-treat patients in order to massage its outcomes? Unfortunately, those that succumb to their egoistic tendencies in the face of these opportunities may drive the otherwise public-spirited to do likewise, or face difficulties in securing revenues. When asymmetries in information are substantial, demand-led competition may lead, from a social benefit point of view, not to a race to the top, but to the bottom, and thus there is a risk of a race towards harms.[17]

Nonetheless, as intimated, we might conclude that there is a role for demand-led competition over simple services, *ceteris paribus*. Unfortunately, all else is not equal. It is sometimes said, for instance, that a constitution built for knaves will drive out knightly motivations, and there is a danger that encouraging egoism in one domain (e.g. over simple services) will cause people to also exercise egoism over others (i.e. more complex services), to the detriment of most. There are those who suggest that, with due care, embracing egoism can be valuable so long as countervailing measures are undertaken. Gintis et al. (2005, p. 4), for instance, write that 'Effective policies are those that support socially valued outcomes not only by harnessing selfish motives to socially valued ends, but also by evoking, cultivating, and empowering public-

---

[17] For a sporting analogy, in the Tour de France it was an open secret for many years that the egoism of perhaps initially just a few riders forced many others, in order to be able to compete on a level playing field, to cheat also, although cheating by Tour riders has limited potential to harm directly thousands of other people.

spirited motives.' But, to reiterate and with a nod to Hume, the safest way to harness egoism in the delivery of public services may be to refrain from encouraging it at all.

However, Le Grand is surely right to question whether public services ought to be designed on the assumption that the people who deliver them are pure altruists, given that pure altruism, as a basic motivation, is hardly ever evident.[18] People rarely give unconditionally, in any sustained sense. However, if one works with the dichotomy of selfish egoism versus pure altruism, then one reduces human motivations to caricatures rather than reality, and, in terms of institutional design, this may lead us from one damaging organisational structure to another. As the social policy analyst Robert Pinker (2006, p. 19) has noted, 'a model of human motivation based on a sharply drawn distinction between the qualities of egoism and altruism [bears] little or no relationship to what we know about human nature and the realities of the world in which we live.' Or to quote Gintis et al. (2005, p. 8) again, 'people are often neither self-regarding nor altruistic' – rather, they are reciprocators, both in the positive and negative sense, and are so for good reason, because it is in their enlightened long-term self-interest to be so. It is this – the natural tendency for people to behave reciprocally much of the time and the collective benefits thereof – that an institutional design informed by selfish egoism may crowd out. We should want to crowd in reciprocity; as argued earlier in this book, reciprocal tendencies, although having evolved over eons and often for good reason, still have to be nurtured. Some suggestions on how policy might be designed to be conducive to reciprocity will be offered in Chapters 7 and 8.

In relation to this chapter, we might reasonably conclude that a contestable assumption about human motivation in economic exchanges has had, over the last several decades, a profound influence on assumptions about what might drive human behaviours in social

---

[18] Although I am more sceptical of the merits of demand-led competition in public services than Le Grand, there is no doubt that he has been one of the leading progressive voices in public policy for over four decades (and counting).

exchanges (assuming that the areas that social policy deals with are taken to be within the domain of the social). In other words, the assumption that people are selfish egoists has been borrowed from neoclassical economic theory and applied to areas such as health and education – areas where this assumption was rarely previously thought to apply, even by those who embraced egoism in economic exchange.

A potted history is that Adam Smith believed that reciprocity underpinned social exchanges and that egoism could reasonably underpin simple economic exchanges (with his later fellow classical economist, John Stuart Mill, accepting that reciprocity was important to social and economic exchanges), neoclassical economists extended Smith's views on egoism to complex economic exchanges, and some of those sympathetic to the assumptions of neoclassical theory in turn applied egoism to some social exchanges (which may have caused Adam Smith to spin in his grave). It is reasonable to contend that the delivery of any good or service that is complex leaves too much scope for people to succumb to the egoism that lurks within our multifaceted natures, which, if followed, can have a malign impact on society, and can cause widespread harms. It may therefore be wise to design policies that appeal to the better angels of our nature, but before promulgating further the merits of reciprocity, we must acknowledge that this fundamental aspect of human motivation also, like oxytocin, has a dark side.

FOOD FOR THOUGHT

1. Do human motivations differ fundamentally between social and economic exchanges?
2. Is it acceptable to encourage egoism in the trade of simple goods or services that are not associated with substantial information asymmetries?
3. Should we aim to channel egoism for the public benefit, or should we instead attempt to constrain or punish egoistic actions?

6 The Dark Side of Reciprocity

In Mexico, criminal gangs – so-called pipesuckers – steal large amounts of petrol and diesel, costing the Mexican state the equivalent of hundreds of millions of US dollars each year that could otherwise be used to serve the public good. The gangs' success in these activities relies in part on the acquiescence and silence of local communities (including some of those who work for the state-run oil company and a number of gas stations), in facilitating the siphoning of the fuel, in providing the means of selling stolen fuel and indeed in the buying of it. Those who are supporting the gangs' illegal activities are benefiting financially from doing so; but their reciprocal relationship, although mutually beneficial, is imposing broader harms on Mexico's society. In short, acts that are essentially co-operative collusion between exchange partners can harm innocent third parties (i.e. they can cause negative externalities, in the parlance of standard economic theory), and the third parties need not be human.

Each year, the Natural History Museum in London exhibits a selection of entries to its Wildlife Photographer of the Year competition. The 2017 winner was a picture titled *Memorial to a Species*, taken by Ben Stirton, of a black rhinoceros killed by poachers for the sole purpose of harvesting its horn. It is a shocking image, with the mutilated yet still almost intact rhino lying close to a waterhole, made perhaps all the more shocking when one learns that there are now only about 5,000 black rhinos left in the wild.[1] One could argue that the reciprocal, albeit illegal, relationships between the poachers, the middlemen and the purchasers of rhino horn are, in this instance, causing

---

[1] At the time of writing, the photograph can be viewed at www.nhm.ac.uk/visit/wpy/gallery/2017/images/wildlife-photographer-of-the-year/5281/memorial-to-a-species.html

significant and possibly irrevocable harm to the planet's biodiversity. However, here one could also question whether the trading relationship that directly involves the final consumers of the rhino horn are truly reciprocal because the products for which the horn is used are medicines of dubious effectiveness. The suppliers of the rhino horn are thus offering false hope to people who are often desperate and guided inappropriately but without sufficient self-knowledge by their behavioural biases; one could say that the suppliers are, in the language of Akerlof and Shiller (2015), phishing for phools.

Even if that is the case, the trade between the poachers and the middlemen presumably confers genuine mutual benefits, and perhaps hope in and of itself is a valuable commodity (and maybe the rhino horn does occasionally offer real benefits). However, it is more likely that the hope that is driving the transactions is causing net harms to the consumers of the rhino horn, since they are paying money for something that is unlikely to work, and, of course, the rhinos themselves are being harmed, as are those of us who would prefer that these animals are not driven to extinction. Thus, reciprocity is in this case once again seemingly associated with significant specific and broader harms, (probably) with insufficient associated benefits to counter those harms.[2] Trading in stolen fuel in Mexico and poaching black rhino horn in South Africa are illegal of course, and one might conclude that those engaging in these transactions are egoists rather than co-operators, but one can contend that they are motivated to behave reciprocally with their exchange partners if not with society at large, and thus this most fundamental of human motivations causes these and many more illegal activities to occur anyway.

---

[2] Despite the title of Stirton's entry, the net harm is not dependent upon the black rhino being a critically endangered species. If an animal that is found in abundance – say chickens – were being harvested solely for manufacturing ineffective potions from their ground beaks then the harms there may well also outweigh the benefits, although, admittedly, phishing for phools while further endangering an already endangered species would probably strike most people emotionally as worse. Moreover, if the rhinos were being killed to feed starving people then some might conclude that the actions of all parties, although tragic, are on balance legitimate.

However, the problems associated with reciprocity are not limited to those where people fail to consider or care sufficiently about people (and other animals) who are not party to their exchanges; people often show active animosity towards those whom they feel are 'outsiders' – i.e. towards those with whom they do not regularly reciprocate and are not encouraged to co-operate with (see, for example, Tajfel (1982) on the dangers of dismissing outgroups). Antipathy towards those that we may classify as outsiders appears to develop quite early in our lives. For instance, the psychologists Frances Aboud (1988) and Andrew Baron and Mahzarin Banaji (2006) have demonstrated that by three to four years of age, with respect to race and gender, children have more negative views of outgroups than in-groups, and perceive the faces of people with racial backgrounds different from their own as angrier than those from their own race. We know from previous chapters that part of the reason that reciprocity evolved as a social norm was to help to fend off threats to the group, and that our biology is designed such that hormones are released to heighten our sense of danger when threats are present. Group selection theory, of which reciprocity is an integral part, tells us that our own group will work to outcompete other groups, even to the extent that it helps us to wage wars more effectively, and thus it is unsurprising that people are suspicious of and even hostile to those whom they view as outside their own kind. But this unfortunately does not detract from the fact that groups behaving co-operatively have been responsible for countless needless deaths and suffering.

In these opening paragraphs, I have served up a few starters on the harms that reciprocal actions might engender, but this often-beneficial aspect of human nature can offer up a rich menu of possible downsides, ranging from breeding resentment, to exploitation, to spiralling retribution, cronyism and nationalism, to name but five choice items. Let us move onto the main course.

RESENTMENT

Returning a gift that may be perceived as insufficient (intentionally or otherwise), or indeed failing or being unable to return a gift at all, may mean that some will be excluded from reciprocal exchanges and suffer social and material hardships as a consequence. However, as we learned in Chapter 3, they may face even harsher consequences as a lack of reciprocation can be viewed almost as an act of war in some premodern societies, and tends not to be looked upon too kindly in modern societies either (e.g. refusing to take one's turn in buying a round of drinks in a British pub is also often tantamount to an act of war). The initial giver may not have a monopoly on resentment in these circumstances, however. If the receiver feels that the giver is attempting to control (by, for example, the giver choosing a gift that she knows is beyond the receiver's ability to match like-for-like in the knowledge that the receiver will then be beholden to her in other ways), or if the receiver is simply not in a position to return a commensurable gift irrespective of the giver's desire to control, then this may breed resentment also. Moreover, a gift from a person that one does not like may sometimes strengthen rather than loosen the antipathy.[3]

Reciprocity can thus generate harmful feelings of moral indebtedness and inferiority. For many, the feeling that one is indebted to others is repugnant, and to assuage the debt, these people may be willing to do things that, to them, are almost as repugnant. Their first best position would be for there to never have been an exchange between the two parties at all, but given that they have been given something, they perhaps would rather reciprocate so as to avoid indebtedness and further strife. The psychologist Xiling Xiong and his colleagues (2018) have called the discomfort felt from the burden of obligation 'reciprocity anxiety', which they argue can damage self-esteem, sense of competence, and perception of independence. From a series of quasi-realistic vignette studies, Xiong et al. argue that retailers who offer small gifts to potential customers can cause discomfort for the customer, provoking dissatisfaction and a reluctance to visit the store.[4]

---

[3] I once gave a Christmas card to someone I didn't even know disliked me, and learned from a third party that my gesture angered him greatly.

[4] Sakare and Vine Vera, two shops on New Bond Street in London, employ people to thrust small bars of soap into the hands of unsuspecting passing pedestrians, and those who are not quick enough to refuse are pressurised into entering the stores. After reading

Such coercion conflicts with the spirit of reciprocal altruism, where both parties freely and willingly engage in exchange. At face value, the actions of coerced reciprocators seem similar to selfish egoists, since the latter may also prefer not to reciprocate yet will often do so rather than face punishment. The difference is that although the egoist is tempted by the potentially higher short-term rewards of transgressing, she will ultimately benefit from the exchange even if she reciprocates. In coerced reciprocation, the giver's gift serves only her own long-term benefit (an act of egoism, of sorts), which she offers in the knowledge that the receiver will feel compelled to reciprocate. In short, people can benefit themselves and impose harms if they are in a position to create an exchange situation that places a pressure on others to reciprocate, when those others would have preferred not to have been party to the exchange at all.[5,6]

Chapter 9, the reader may reach the conclusion that this practice should be outlawed. It is well known, of course, that reciprocity is also used by charitable organisations when they give small gifts, such as pens, when soliciting donations. Alpizar, Carlsson and Johansson-Stenman (2008) actually found that offering a small gift (a fridge magnet) to visitors to a national park to try to get them to offer additional money to support the park led to more people contributing compared to no gift being offered, but the overall average contribution fell. It is possible that people in general react against a perceived manipulation or coercion in this case. Robert Cialdini (2001) has written that small gifts can increase contributions over the short-term, but when people realise that it's a strategy to raise more money, the effect wears off.

[5] Hypothetically, in numerical terms, assume a selfish egoist will gain zero units of benefit if no attempted exchange at all occurs. If she is engaged in an exchange, she can gain twenty units of benefit if she fails to reciprocate and is not punished. If she is punished for transgressing, she loses the twenty units, but is still no worse off than she would be if she was not offered the initial gift. If she reciprocates, assume that her net gain will be fifteen units. Whatever happens, she will probably gain from the exchange, and at the very least will be no worse off. The coerced reciprocator also gains zero units if she is offered no initial gift. If she is offered a gift that she resents, she may lose ten units. If she fails to reciprocate, further strife might mean that she loses a total of twenty units, but if she reciprocates her loss might still increase a little to minus fifteen units, although she might feel a little better and have a net loss now of only five units – but in either case things will not be as bad as it would be if she fails to reciprocate. Nonetheless, whatever happens, she is at least five units of benefit down compared to the position of no initial gift.

[6] The notion that the pressure on a reciprocal altruist to reciprocate can seem to her beneficial or harmful depending on whether her response feels free or controlled has parallels with the postulates of self-determination theory developed by Deci and Ryan (1985; 2000), referred to earlier, which, to reiterate, implies that the satisfaction with, and effectiveness of, behaviour change interventions are more likely to be positive if

The issue of whether a person feels that they are being almost forced to respond reciprocally or whether their exchange feels more autonomous has also been the subject of biological analyses. For example, William Harbaugh and his colleagues (2007) report that respondents placed in brain scanners showed more dopaminergic activation – which is associated with greater pleasure – when they were asked to voluntarily donate to charity a proportion of an amount of money that they were given than when they were taxed the same amount. Although different to the issue of moral indebtedness and coerced reciprocity outlined in the previous paragraph, this does signal once again that attempts to control people (although in relation to taxation this is often admittedly unavoidable) can breed resentment and harms.

If a continuing reciprocal relationship is unwanted by the most recent receiving party to an initial or ongoing exchange, therefore, the resentment felt by either party – i.e. by the giver if they feel that the return is inadequate or by the receiver for feeling pressured into giving anything – can lead to a perilous situation, circumstances that are likely to be exacerbated if there is an imbalance of power (and thus the perception – accurate or otherwise – of an attempt to control) between the exchange partners. If one party to the exchange is considerably more powerful than the other, then she may implicitly force the weaker party to reciprocate irrespective of the latter's underlying reciprocal motivations or dislike of indebtedness – the fear of what may otherwise happen will be enough for a return to be made.[7] An example might be protection services 'offered' to shopkeepers by

---

people feel that the intervention is supporting them in what, ideally, they would really like to do, as opposed to in some sense controlling them. One possible (although admittedly not inevitable) policy implication might be that public sector workers may feel less controlled and thus more willing to engage reciprocally and co-operatively if the management of them is more localised and less state-centred, on which more will be written later.

[7] Of course, the powerful may use knowledge of intrinsic human behavioural biases to forge exchanges that are overwhelmingly more favourable to them than to others without the others realising it, thus avoiding resentment. This is related to Akerlof and Shiller's (2015) *Phishing for Phools* argument mentioned earlier, an argument that I will return to in Chapter 9.

organised criminal gangs, such as the mafia. Unfortunately for the weaker party, the offering in return, even if it is perceived to be adequate by the initial giver, will often fail to bring an end to the relationship – the powerful party may give once more, and thus perpetuate the cycle. This equilibrium – possibly optimal for the powerful but suboptimal for the weak who might impoverish themselves due to feelings of shame or fear – although difficult for the weak to break (particularly if the powerful manage to portray themselves to many as deserving of the fruits of their benevolence), is not as stable as the continuation of mutually beneficial actions based on genuine reciprocal fairness (Gouldner, 1960); in short, it imposes harms while it lasts, and creates perhaps even greater harms when it ends.[8]

A continuing exchange relationship that may be dressed up by some as beneficial to all parties in the exchange might in fact, therefore, be harmful to some, but this is not the only way in which reciprocal actions can cause harms. Indeed, they are harmful to all and not just some if the exchange is entirely negative – if it is driven by spiralling retaliation.

RETALIATION AND RETRIBUTION

If the weaker party in a coerced exchange eventually decides that enough is enough and refuses to reciprocate, she may be punished, causing her in turn to retaliate and then face further punishment, and so on and so forth. A negative continuing cycle of mutual retaliation is a possibility whenever one party decides, justly or unjustly (and irrespective of the relative balance of power), to punish another, a point similarly highlighted by Elinor Ostrom (1998), who contended that if punishment – i.e. negative reciprocity – leads to escalating retribution, then people may soon become demotivated, and relationships can become hostile and irreconcilable.[9] According to Kropotkin (1902/

---

[8] The French and Russian Revolutions might be stark examples.
[9] Spiralling retaliation can be potentially globally catastrophic, of course. At the time of writing this book, the British Foreign Secretary, Boris Johnson, justified the bombing of Syria by proclaiming 'enough is enough' on the use of chemical weapons, and that he hoped that it would deter further barbaric chemical attacks by the Syrian regime. I do

2014), this is why primitive legislatures often took care to see that the punishment fitted the crime (i.e. was neither insufficient nor excessive), so as to prevent inter-tribal or intra-clan conflict from escalating. It is also represented by less ancient religious codes; for example, the biblical notion of an eye for an eye and a tooth for a tooth, which in its imagery sounds a little barbaric but is arguably attempting to provide a standard of punishment that both sides to a transgression can accept.[10] Relatedly, but evidently opposed to the extraction of eyes and teeth as forms of punishment, Steven Pinker (2018, p. 12) writes:

> The reason that punishment should fit the crime ... is not to balance some mystical scale of justice but to ensure that a wrongdoer stops at a minor crime rather than escalating to a more harmful one. Cruel punishments, whether or not they are in some sense 'deserved', are no more effective at deterring harm than moderate but surer punishments, and they desensitize spectators and brutalize the society that implements them.

There is evidence from experiments of the sort discussed in Chapter 4 that shows that people are often willing to engage in costly retaliation of people who have punished them for antisocial behaviours (see, for example, Denant-Boemont, Masclet and Noussair, 2007; Herrmann, Thoni and Gächter, 2008; Nikiforakis, 2008), which can destabilise co-operative endeavours. The behavioural

---

[10] not wish to condemn or condone the air strikes here, but recent history suggests it is naïve to think that they won't be without further consequences. Johnson admitted himself that he did not know how Bashar al-Assad would respond, or how the British, French and Americans would respond in turn (www.bbc.co.uk/news/uk-43772719).
The saying, often attributed to Mahatma Ghandi, that an eye for an eye makes the whole world blind – assuming that everyone, including the transgressor, accepts that the punishment must fit the crime – therefore provides a somewhat misleading message. The hope would be that an eye for an eye deprives the transgressor of that which he has taken and no more, and that then would be an end to the matter. Or better still, the transgressor would be dissuaded from poking out eyes to begin with, metaphorically speaking. Two eyes for an eye might admittedly be even more of a deterrent, but may be more likely to lead to retribution. That said, Ghandi was trying to draw an end to existing cycles of retribution, which, when one has been the subject of punishment, takes tremendous courage. Therefore, we should perhaps not take everything that Ghandi may or may not have said too literally.

economist Anna Dreber, and her colleagues (including the previously mentioned Martin Nowak), undertook an experiment that exposed respondents to a repeated prisoner's dilemma (Dreber et al., 2008). In each prisoner's dilemma, each pair of respondents had the option to co-operate where they could pay one dollar in order for the other person to receive three dollars, to defect, where they could take a dollar from the other person, or to commit an act of altruistic punishment, where they could pay one dollar in order to take four dollars from the transgressor. Dreber et al. claimed that there was a clear negative association between a person's tendency to punish and his or her overall winnings: the best performing people never punished and the worst performing people were the ones who most often resorted to punishment. It may thus generally be the case that those who are quick to punish will be retaliated against more frequently, in turn provoking their own retaliation and ultimately harming themselves overall. This is not necessarily to argue that altruistic punishers are not important for sustaining group co-operation; it is simply to state that punishment, if used too freely and without due balance (perhaps particularly in dyadic exchanges), may lead to a downward spiral of retaliation that harms everyone.

Nowak (2011) tends to prefer offering rewards to meting out punishments as a means to discourage transgressions, particularly in societies where the rule of law is weak, circumstances, he argues, that are ripe for retaliation to spiral. He distinguishes between two types of punishment: first, there is peer punishment, which is normally a form of dyadic negative reciprocity of the sort observed vis-à-vis the mafia, for example, and which is susceptible to the potential problems discussed in this section. Second, there is hierarchical punishment, including that delivered by parents to their children, or in relation to the workings of the state judicial and penal systems. Echoing Kropotkin (1902/2014), formal judicial systems, which generally take decisions on whom and how to punish out of the hands of those who have been harmed directly by transgressors (with the intention of moving us closer to justice than revenge), may have evolved, in part, to prevent spiralling levels of retaliation that threaten the cohesion of the group. However, even where the rule of law is strong, there will be many circumstances where groups must rely on the threat of personal individual altruistic punishment to keep everyone in line, because it is impossible for the formal justice system to identify all transgressions.

As intimated earlier in relation to being pressured into returning a gift when one does not really want to, in addition to spiralling retaliation, the fear of retaliation can be bad for society. Of course, an altruistic punisher (strictly defined) is willing to incur some costs, otherwise her actions would not be altruistic, but the limits of acceptable costs may often be exceeded. Occasionally, the pressure to cooperate – i.e. reciprocal altruism – within a group can prevent altruistic punishers from acting for fear of retaliation, or to be ignored, with tragic consequences. For example, in the 1990s there was a high profile inquiry into the deaths of a relatively large number of paediatric patients – fifteen in total – undergoing cardiac surgery at Bristol Royal Infirmary in England (Department of Health, 2001; Klein, 2001). The inquiry found that two surgeons and the Chief Executive of the hospital had colluded in a cover-up. One might conclude that they reciprocated in this respect, to try to protect their own reputations and that of the hospital, and it is possible that lives were lost unnecessarily as a consequence. Eventually, an altruistic punisher – the whistle blower, Stephen Bolsin, who had spent years studying and attempting to redress the high death rate – brought the situation to wider attention; if extreme forms of retaliation were not an option here, then he or someone else might have alerted the media earlier, and less damage may well have been done.[11] Of course, acting cooperatively for mutual protection, even if this imposes significant wider harms, is not limited to clinical groups, and indeed clinicians and their managers are perhaps not the main cause of concern in this

---

[11] Bolsin was a consultant anaesthetist at the Bristol Royal Infirmary. Despite probably saving lives, influencing an improvement in clinical governance and holding senior positions, he was unable to obtain work in England after the incident. He was essentially punished by a group who thought that he had in some sense wronged.

respect. For instance, criminal gangs do likewise, imposing a code of silence regarding their colleagues' activities should they be questioned, the contravention of which is often considered generally within a criminal group as possibly the worst form of transgression. As such, a real prisoner's dilemma may tend not to be much of a dilemma at all, with their mutual co-operation generally pretty stable.[12]

Admittedly, these examples refer to antagonisms towards those who denounce members of the group (e.g. the criminal gang) to what may be perceived as other groups (e.g. the police), and thus the perception of the boundary of the group in these cases is much narrower than society as a whole. If, for instance, a gang member accurately denounced another gang member as an informer, she is unlikely to fear retaliation from other gang members and could perhaps look forward to some form of reward (even though she may have been willing to pay some cost in order to expose the transgressor). Nonetheless, people who engage in too much punishment, altruistic or otherwise, may be treated with a degree of opprobrium by the group to which they belong, partly because the decision on what a transgression is may sometimes be highly personal, and even when a particular act is widely viewed as unacceptable, there is often a degree of uncertainty as to whether the accused actually committed it. Trigger-happy accusations are likely to exacerbate the latter problem, and false accusations and unjustified punishment will, in some contexts (e.g. in circumstances of Nowak's

---

[12] Attacks perpetrated by criminals on mopeds, usually for the purpose of stealing, has been a growing (although now gradually declining) problem in London over recent years, and the number of moped-enabled crimes stands at more than 20,000 per annum in the city at the time of writing (www.bbc.co.uk/news/uk-england-london-44045128). These criminals steal the bikes that they use to commit their crimes. In March 2018, a young man was jailed for attacking a number of other riders with acid, in an attempt to take their bikes. A second criminal who was acting with this man was recorded on CCTV, but could not be identified because he was wearing a crash helmet. The jailed man refused to give up the name of his fellow perpetrator, which presumably would have been reciprocated if their roles were reversed, yet it would be better for society if he had (www.bbc.co.uk/news/uk-england-london-43373719).

notion of peer punishment), perhaps amplify the risk of spiralling retaliation.[13]

As implied in footnote 9, breaking a cycle of retaliation and retribution can be tremendously difficult. Alvin Gouldner (1960) writes on the potential usefulness of compensatory mechanisms, such as turning the other cheek, when one is harmed, but sometimes ending a cycle of retaliation requires the peaceful reconciliation between previous antagonists who have experienced the murder of friends and family members. Thus – unsurprisingly given that it requires those involved to suppress their most basic human instincts – the reciprocal harms can continue for decades. But as was observed in recent decades in South Africa, Rwanda and Northern Ireland, for example, with great courage, willpower and an ability to imagine that the benefits of long-term peace might outweigh the immediate urge for revenge, then it is possible to end a spiral of retaliation in even the most extreme circumstances.[14] That said, if we, to put it simply, turn the other cheek to all transgressions, the threat of negative reciprocity loses its power, which in itself will reward the egoist and harm the society, as reported by Edward Banfield in his study of the poor Italian rural community aforementioned in Chapter 3. Once again, when, where and how to reciprocate, if one's aim is to limit harms and serve the societal good, appears to be a contextual affair.

[13] Although it is likely that false accusation, punishment and retaliation may be more of an issue when the machinery of justice is not formalised in a hierarchical structure, the past, and probably the present, is littered with people wrongly accused and convicted of crimes they did not commit, such as the Birmingham Six and the Guildford Four in England, who each served about fifteen years in prison after being falsely pinpointed for their involvement in bomb attacks by the Provisional Irish Republican Army (IRA). Compared to peer punishment, however, the opportunity and therefore the tendency to retaliate in hierarchical punishment is probably lessened, but this underlines the fact that altruistic punishment – even when it is genuinely altruistic and not corrupt or part of some kind of vendetta – does have the capacity to cause great harm.

[14] In a recent BBC documentary, the comedian Patrick Kielty speaks of how he refused the IRA's offer to avenge the murder of his father, in a possible case of mistaken identity, by a loyalist paramilitary group. At the time of writing, the documentary can be viewed at www.bing.com/videos/search?q=patrick+kielty+documentary+youtube&view=detail&mid=187289B030AE217FF8BE187289B030AE217FF8BE&FORM=VIRE.

From the earlier discussion regarding clinical and criminal groups, an important feature of whether reciprocity within a group may serve the general social good will depend, in part, on where the group members' primary loyalties lie, in addition to the group's primary objectives. For instance, a very small and strictly defined group may serve the general social good very well if its objectives are indeed to serve or are aligned with the social good, as opposed to the good – however that is defined – of its own members. But the group's specific objectives will often dominate, which is a problem if the pursuit of these objectives harms other people. As postulated by group selection theory, people will often be loyal to their own group, and will act to compete with, and even show hostility towards, perceived outsiders. This can lead to cronyism, and worse.

CRONYISM, FUNDAMENTALISM, NATIONALISM AND OTHER ISMS

Ostrom (1998) noted that the tendency to reward favours with favours can lead to corruption. Anybody who has ever worked or studied in an organisation will have been aware of persons with influence who are, at face value, on friendly terms with each other, and thus offer mutual favours, often to the detriment of others who ostensibly belong to the same group. This is cronyism, and it can harm any group. Indeed, those who are not part of the influential clique may find their feeling of identity with the group irrevocably damaged, and thus withdraw their efforts of support, and yet had their reciprocal tendencies been nurtured, the group, as a whole, would have benefited. Such circumstances of enforced alienation that cause people to withdraw in on themselves may explain the sale of merchandise that display the kind of message printed on an apron available in my local café in South London (see Figure 6.1). People can be made to feel like outsiders in their own group.

On the human tendency, or instinct, to express hostility to outsiders, Pinker (2018, p. 26) writes:

FIGURE 6.1 A consequence of cronyism

People demonize those they disagree with, attributing differences of opinion to stupidity and dishonesty. For every misfortune they seek a scapegoat. They see morality as a source of grounds for condemning rivals and mobilizing indignation against them.

The grounds for condemnation may consist in the defendants' having harmed others, but they may also consist in their having flouted custom, questioned authority, undermined tribal solidarity, or engaged in unclean sexual or dietary practices. People see violence as moral, not immoral: across the world and throughout history, more people have been murdered to mete out justice than to satisfy greed.[15]

Differences in religious beliefs, or even subtle discrepancies in the same basic belief, have of course played a large part in generating hostility to perceived outsiders, as evidenced by the persecution of Catholics in Elizabethan England, or of protestant Huguenots in seventeenth century France, or the Sunni versus Shia conflict in modern day Iraq and Syria, to name just a few examples from the multitude that could be selected. Moreover, Sapolsky (2017, p. 624) notes that 'religiously based terrorism persists the longest and is least likely to subside due to fighters joining the political process'. These types of persecutions can be thought of as a form of religion-based group selection in that those who call for such actions are presumably motivated by the fear that transgressors will undermine the faith to which they adhere. Throughout history, the punishment for failing to believe in the dominant code has very often certainly exceeded the 'crime', and although much of the world has, over time, moved towards greater religious tolerance, in many parts this yet shows little sign of abating.

The reader will have no difficulty imagining that the tendency towards associating and reciprocating with those we consider insiders and the demonisation of outgroups can apply equally to ethnic and geographically defined groups as to religious groups, and thus can cause racism and nationalism.[16] Leaders of nationalist parties (and, indeed, other political parties) have used the innate desire for people to

---

[15] Pinker overlooks mosquito greed.
[16] Importantly, Pinker (2018) reminds us that nationalism should not be confused with social responsibility, civic values and cultural pride.

want to belong to a group and to behave reciprocally with other members of their group in order to strengthen their position and their ideology. The sociologist Gøsta Esping-Andersen (1990), for instance, points out that German and Italian fascist parties in the 1920s and 1930s granted an array of social rights that were conditional on loyalty and adherence to a prescribed morality, and another sociologist, Colin Crouch (1993), has written that corporatist give-and-take structures entered Italian and Portuguese fascism to demonstrate how the traditional conflicts between employees and employers in pre-fascist times could be ended – although, when in power, the fascists liquidated the labour movements, ending the need for the corporatist institutions. In more contemporary settings, there is currently a rise in nationalist sentiments, with Recep Tayyip Erdoğan, Vladimir Putin and Donald Trump, for example, using similar tactics in an attempt to create an us-and-them mentality in their own populations, and by appealing to populist opinions by offering a return to (perceived) past glories, wealth and opportunities to sectors of the population in return for political support.[17,18]

In addition to the old threats posed by reciprocal tendencies highlighted above, social and technological developments mean that new ones have emerged, in particular in relation to the use of social media. As noted in Chapter 2, Nowak (2011), for instance, contends that language, through communication and gossip, aids indirect reciprocity, which has many benefits but can also, intentionally or otherwise, serve to tarnish people unfairly. For example, some may choose to spread a false rumour, or they may have misinterpreted another person's actions, words

---

[17] Admittedly, for the global good the West could have perhaps done more to dissuade Erdoğan and Putin in the early years of their tenures from themselves feeling like outsiders.

[18] In an evolutionary sense, encountering outsiders may provoke a feeling of threat to one's own group, and to limited resources. If humans are biologically driven in this way, then to curb the risk of nationalism an immigration policy that allows a gradual introduction rather than a sudden large influx of immigrants is perhaps a wiser policy for any country to pursue (although humanitarian concerns, of course, complicate this picture).

or character, or they may resort to direct lying, the reach of all of which can be exacerbated through social media being used antisocially, with perpetrators protected by distance and a wall of virtual anonymity, with devastating potential effects.

All in all then, there is a dark side, or even many dark sides, to reciprocity that are probably unavoidable, but by drawing on the following ten lessons – or commandments (some of which may seem obvious, but all of which are informed by the concerns outlined in this chapter) – they can perhaps be to some degree ameliorated in public policy environments and elsewhere:

TEN LESSONS

Lesson 1: Be aware of potential harms to third parties from all reciprocal relationships.

Lesson 2: When nurturing co-operation and reciprocity within a group, try to ensure no emerging antagonism towards those outside the group.

Lesson 3: Ensure that all parties are co-operating under their own volition, and that no one is being obligated to reciprocate due to differential levels of power.

Lesson 4: When instituting and applying negative reciprocity, ensure that the punishment fits the crime, and that the sentences for transgressions are accepted by all parties in a reciprocating group before any misdeed occurs.

Lesson 5: If possible, provide anonymity for whistle-blowers if they observe and report instances of serious malpractice; at the very least, ensure that their careers are not negatively affected as a consequence. Relatedly, provide an open and non-punitive environment for people to report and address their own unintentional mistakes.[19]

---

[19] Recently, a UK doctor, Hadiza Bawa-Garba, who was convicted of manslaughter by gross negligence following the death of a boy from sepsis, won an appeal to practice medicine again. Her appeal was funded by fellow doctors who were concerned that the initial ruling to strike Dr Bawa-Garba off the medical register would discourage other doctors from being open in reporting mistakes. See https://bbc.co.uk/news/uk-england-leicestershire-45169589

Lesson 6: Discourage informal acts of negative reciprocity, because these may be perceived as arbitrary, excessive and/or unwarranted, and could lead to spiralling retaliation.

Lesson 7: If retaliation has spiralled, have in place procedures for reconciliation, which will require input from an influential and accepted arbitrator.

Lesson 8: Try to discourage the formation of cliques within larger groupings, particularly among those who hold influence, and attempt to create an environment of inclusivity among all members of the wider group to strengthen the general sense of identity.

Lesson 9: Cultivate tolerance from and towards all people with respect to religious, ethnic, national, gender etc. backgrounds, and punish any person within the group who transgresses significantly in this respect.

Lesson 10: Provide safeguards against the spreading of false rumours.

Despite in this chapter almost convincing myself that reciprocity is a bad thing, and although there will always be those who seek to take advantage of conditional co-operators, if institutions and public policies are designed carefully to bring forth the bright side of reciprocity, it can serve as a force for good. The next two chapters will offer some thoughts, based on what has been presented thus far in this book, on how this might be done.

FOOD FOR THOUGHT

1. Is it better to reciprocate or ignore an unwanted gift?
2. What is required to bring to an end a conflict where all relevant parties have been seriously harmed through repeated acts of retaliation?
3. When nurturing reciprocity within a group, is it inevitable that the group members will be suspicious and fearful of those outside the group?

7 Nurturing Reciprocity in Public Policy

Reciprocity is like a grape vine. Its fruit is sometimes sour, but if cared for properly and given the right environment, it can be succulent and sweet; if you do not prune it, it will become unwieldy, and if you fail to water it, it will wither and may die. As will have been learned from previous chapters, there is a vast multidisciplinary literature on reciprocity, and this is starting to filter through into the public policy discourse, with recent books related to the topic published by, for example, David Sloan Wilson (2015) and Samuel Bowles (2016). Yet in order for this fundamental aspect of human motivation to have a substantial impact on public policy, a sufficient number of people have yet to pass the Rubicon of considering how reciprocity may seriously and specifically inform policy design. This, I think, will happen; given the large literature on reciprocity, the surprise is that it hasn't happened yet.

This chapter will consider some general structural features of a policy environment that might support the human tendency towards behaving reciprocally, with hopefully positive effects. Chapter 8 will focus in a little more specifically on how the design of a selection of policy interventions might be usefully informed by our knowledge of reciprocity. These two chapters, which will inevitably overlap a little in terms of content, will not offer a definitive account of how reciprocity can inform the policy discourse. Rather, the intention is that they offer some indicative initial suggestions – i.e. some further food for thought. Although it is likely that humans will tend towards behaving reciprocally and co-operatively when the circumstances are correctly aligned for them to do so, an incorrect alignment may bring other motivations, such as selfish egoism, to the fore. The hope is that readers will consider the arguments and evidence presented in this chapter and the next, and then develop their own ideas on how policy contexts and interventions might be more appropriately designed.

It is perhaps worth emphasising at this point that structures and design that are intended to nurture and activate reciprocal actions will not always do so. To expect otherwise has been termed the Pollyanna Fallacy by Gouldner (1960, p. 164). The more modest and realistic aim is to provide circumstances that have the best chance of encouraging reciprocal altruism, and to avoid circumstances that undermine this motivation (so as to avoid displacing a social norm that underpins pro-sociality), and then, over time, to evaluate those policy interventions to discern whether or not they had the intended effect. To begin, however, possibly the most basic thing that policy makers can do to nurture reciprocity is to emphasise it as a motivation in the language that they use.

THE IMPORTANCE OF EMPHASIS

Unless we hold true to the unrealistic assumption that people are substantially motivated by pure altruism, for any collective effort to work participants must normally believe that if they are to contribute for others' benefit, then they will benefit also (even if the benefit amounts 'merely' to enhanced reputation or self-respect – for instance, when people choose to donate blood in countries where no material incentives are offered, beyond a cup of tea and a biscuit). Such arguments apply, of course, to social insurance. If we take health or social care insurance, for example, we might emphasise to relatively young, healthy people that they contribute towards the costs of people in need of these services now so that they themselves (and those they care about) will benefit in the future. The underlying messages to 'give so as to receive', or 'give to those who have given' are likely to be useful to policy makers, not only in gaining support for policies that they wish to introduce, but also to strengthen an aspect of human motivation that can underpin the collective good (although the caveats raised in Chapter 6 should not be overlooked).

To try to highlight the importance of using reciprocity to gain acceptance for one's policy proposals, let us consider *The Three Worlds of Welfare Capitalism*, in which Esping-Andersen (1990) contended that the ways in which different countries manage and finance their welfare sectors in contemporary capitalist societies is strongly dependent on the historical motivations for establishing those sectors.[1] Esping-Andersen identified three models of welfare capitalism, with the first – defined as the conservative tradition, often adopted to see off the threat of socialism in Central Europe in the nineteenth century – based around guilds and mutualities, sometimes seen as an extension of the family, (possibly) the original chief source of support in times of need. The conservative tradition can thus be considered a kinship model of welfare, perhaps fuelled by a combination of liking and continuation reciprocity.[2] Second, the liberal tradition, according to Esping-Andersen, is one that espouses freedom from any existing conservative and authoritative influences, and promotes public support, often through means testing, for groups that are considered, in some sense, deserving (e.g. the elderly, veterans of the armed forces, the deserving – i.e. blameless – poor).[3] Finally, there is the social democratic tradition, which aims to unite different social classes in support of the welfare state. In this tradition, contends Esping-Andersen, the government entices the middle classes with generous second-tier, earnings-related insurance schemes that supplement a flat-rate universal system. This is done to maintain

---

[1] To simplify his analysis, Esping-Andersen focused upon income replacement welfare payments, and did not include sectors such as health and education in his analysis. Nonetheless, not everyone accepts his categorisations of welfare systems, including many of my American political scientist friends, whose non-acceptance extends to vociferous opposition. However, this does not matter for my purposes, as I am not categorising the welfare system of any country in a particular way. Rather, I will claim that all categories, which might be taken as different caricatures of welfare systems, entail some notion of reciprocity.

[2] Kropotkin (1902/2014) similarly wrote that medieval guilds grew, like families, for mutual support.

[3] There are categories of people, such as children and the mentally compromised, who lack agency, and thus even in the liberal tradition, they might receive public assistance without any consideration as to whether they deserve it (Gouldner, 1960).

middle class support for the universal scheme, because it is their tax payments that are required to fund it.

Although Esping-Andersen did not acknowledge it explicitly, all three traditions summarised here are, to a considerable degree, informed by (albeit different notions of) reciprocity: the conservative tradition via pseudo-kinship, the liberal tradition via desert and the social democrat decision via *quid pro quo*.[4] All of these notions of reciprocity are, of course, malleable; for example, in who classifies as kin, in who deserves what, and on what might be sufficient to buy people into a system of welfare that benefits others.[5] As such, they might be used to try to justify systems of welfare that differ not only across the three traditions, but also within each tradition.

It is therefore possible to exercise this most basic human motivation towards different ends, but the key point is that reciprocity is being nurtured. It is not wise to appeal to pure altruism in order to construct and sustain a welfare system, since pure altruism is not, for most people, a sustained source of motivation, and it is imprudent to appeal to egoism, because egoism, if encouraged, may thrive and harm. If policy makers wish to create new and protect old institutions (particularly if welfare systems are so large that notions that all are kin are difficult to sustain), they might sensibly work hard to convince those who finance those systems – systems that substantially benefit 'others' – benefit them also. 'If some users get all of the benefits and pay few of the costs', wrote Elinor Ostrom (2000, p.150), 'others

---

[4] Sapolsky (2017) refers to evidence that suggests that Americans think that the most important reason for helping others is if they have helped them, whereas Chinese and Spanish people think that the principal determinant is, respectively, whether or not the persons who require help are of high rank, or whether they are friends or acquaintances. These findings suggest that the main reason for helping others is to some extent influenced by culture, which may be why different justifications are given for the design of different welfare systems.

[5] A stark example of how the notion of desert may be less than fixed is given in the footballer Ashley Cole's (2006) autobiography, *My Defence*. Cole tells how he was so outraged at the injustice of the club he played for, Arsenal, offering him £55,000 per week, rather than his demand of £60,000 per week, that he nearly drove his car off the road. Others of us might feel that in 2006, £55,000 per week for the tasks that Cole was charged with was quite enough.

become unwilling to follow rules over time'. Moreover, by appealing to this notion of give and take, policy makers are likely to strengthen, and certainly not weaken, the social norm of reciprocal altruism, which bodes well for the more widespread collective benefits that a group may accrue by holding true to this substantively prosocial sentiment.

Thus, those in positions of influence might usefully emphasise how their policies generate reciprocal benefits, and reciprocity also offers some clues pertaining to the most appropriate organisational level at which policy sectors ought to be managed.

THE CASE FOR DECENTRALISING

In *The Logic of Collective Action*, the economist Mancur Olson (1965), in supporting the notion that people are in essence rational egoists, argued that large groups will not be able to organise themselves voluntarily for coordinated and co-operative action, even if they have good reason for doing so. This is in part because the more people there are to share a collective benefit, the less that each individual can singularly gain, making the return on their co-operation less meaningful to them, and also in part because large groups may have substantial organisation costs that have to be subtracted from the expected benefits. Most importantly, however, Olson – synonymous with the typical predictions of the prisoner's dilemma – took the view that any rational egoist would choose to free ride on large group endeavours, and thus assuming that rational egoism is widespread, there would be insufficient effort within the group to generate the collective good. Olson's contention is known as the zero contribution thesis. Consistent with earlier arguments made in this book in relation to the move from tightly knit to more atomistic forms of social organisation, however, Olson acknowledged that relatively small groups might be able to sustain co-operation, because if a person tries to free ride in a small group, it is more noticeable, and it is thus easier to identify and punish the culprit. Olson concluded that the pursuit of individual self-interest – if perhaps more akin to enlightened than egoistic self-interest – is more likely to bring about, if by no means guarantee, group-oriented behaviour in relatively small groups.

Garrett Hardin, in his famous 1968 essay on the *Tragedy of the Commons*, argued something similar when he wrote that without the intervention of an influential third party, such as a strong central state, egoistic interests would dominate, destroying the commons. Hardin himself believed in a strong central state acting as an organ of negative reciprocity against egoistic transgressors, and others also see powerful enforcement agencies as necessary, in that people will then contribute voluntarily not only because they might be punished if they fail to do so – i.e. it will discourage egoism – but also because they believe that others will not be able to free ride on their own prosocial actions – i.e. it will encourage conditional co-operators (see, for example, Levi, 1988). Banfield (1958), in his study of the poor rural Italian community referred to in Chapter 3, concurred that the state exists to force men to be good, but perhaps, in relation to people behaving reciprocally to provide public goods and services, the state in this respect is only really needed if there is a general culture of egoistic self-interest, and that a culture of co-operation may lessen the need for this function of the state.

Elinor Ostrom's (1990) work provides some support for the above conjecture, where she finds that in common pool resource situations – for example, establishing local fishing rights, an example that one may hypothesise is ripe for the tragedy of the commons – quite tolerable and even collectively desirable outcomes arise when users are left to develop the rules and enforcement mechanisms themselves. In short, Ostrom contended that communities often develop their own co-operative rules without enforcement from the state and without imposing private property rights. She also believed that social norms play an important role in tackling common pool resource challenges (and therefore Banfield's Italian community may indeed not have been an ideal community in this respect). For instance, where there are strong shared norms against opportunistic behaviour, people will be less worried about the dangers of defection, and this can reduce the costs of monitoring and sanctioning activities. The shared norms are therefore a form of social capital.

Ostrom thus suggests that allowing regulation from the ground up, driven as it often is by mutual interest, may be more effective than trying to impose regulation from the top down, which is consistent with Deci and Ryan's (1985; 2000) views, noted in Chapters 3 and 6, on how measures that support intrinsic motivations, as opposed to those that seek to control, may be the wiser course of action. A cautionary note is, however, warranted, in that Ostrom pointed out that when a fishing community is large, and where there is significant heterogeneity of interests and different relevant time horizons within the community, there is sometimes a failure to organise group agreement in relation to fishing during spawning season and on the types of equipment used: 'Individuals who do not have similar images of the problems they face, who do not work out mechanisms to disaggregate complex problems into subparts, and who do not recognize the legitimacy of diverse interests are unlikely to solve their problems' (Ostrom, 1990, p. 149). Nonetheless:

> [I]t is possible that [people] learn whom to trust, what effects their actions will have on each other and on the CPR [common pool resource], and how to organize themselves to gain benefits and avoid harm. When individuals have lived in such situations for a substantial time and have developed shared norms and patterns of reciprocity, they possess social capital with which they can build institutional arrangements for resolving CPR dilemmas ... Public policies based on the notion that all CPR appropriators are helpless and must have rules imposed on them can destroy institutional capital that has been accumulated during years of experience in particular locations. (Ostrom, 1990, p. 184)

Ostrom therefore contends that local communities will often be best equipped to self-regulate and manage their collective goods and services; she also emphasised that the threat and application of a set of sanctions agreed by the local community to those who are tempted to, or do, transgress is a needed component of the regulations. Ostrom's common pool resource problems are the real world equivalents of the experimental public goods games reviewed in Chapter 4, and like the evidence gleaned from those games, she contends that negative reciprocity – which, she argues, should be graduated (i.e. mild for first offenders but more severe for repeat violators) – is required if co-operation within the group is to be sustained. Without the threat of punishment within the local community, to reiterate from earlier, selfish egoists, even if they are only small in number, may drive otherwise conditional co-operators to undertake less enlightened, short-sighted, actions.

In terms of what she believed to be the dominant, fundamental motivator of human behaviour, Ostrom thus appears to be at the opposite end of the spectrum to the rational egoist view held by Mancur Olson, and yet both recognised that the presence of egoistic tendencies, particularly in larger groups, can destroy group co-operation, and thus, conversely, that reciprocity has the best chance of being sustained if the group is not too large and its membership is not too fluid.[6] As noted earlier, it is, remarked Olson (1965), easier for smaller groups than for larger groups to be transparent and to hold their members to account, and social pressures are likely to be diminished in larger groupings; it is likely that coherence and the opportunity to engage in personal exchange are inversely correlated with group size. David Sloan Wilson (2015, p. 147) concurs: 'From an evolutionary perspective, we can say that large-scale human society needs to be multicellular. The more we participate in small groups that are

---

[6] As intimated earlier (e.g. Chapter 3, footnote 12), Nowak (2011) also contends that there will be an optimum amount of fluidity between groups: too little, and defectors may learn how to exploit co-operators; too much and the good feeling that takes time to build up between co-operators may not develop. There is some controlled experiment evidence that suggests that the impact of strong reciprocity on co-operation is better manifested when groups are coherent and permanent (Fehr and Gächter, 2000b) and where mutual commitments are exchanged (Ostrom, 1998). A policy lesson here is that it may not be the best idea to transfer civil servants or other public sector staff between different departments every couple of years.

appropriately structured, the happier we will be, the more our groups efforts will succeed, and the more we will contribute to the welfare of society at larger scales.'[7] Relatively small groups may be better able to develop innovative co-operative strategies that are beneficial to the collective, and consistent with group selection theory, may be further motivated to do so if there is in place a system of inter-group reputational competition.

The policy relevance of reputational concerns will be explored in some depth in the next chapter, but a good illustrative example is that of the Veterans Health Administration (VHA), the health care system that covers honourably discharged veterans of the United States armed forces. In the mid 1990s, the VHA introduced a system whereby the performance of its hospitals, in terms of quality indicators such as some cancer screening rates, patient cholesterol levels and the like, was disseminated throughout the system annually in the form of a league table. The intention was to get the hospitals competing with regards to their reputations, not for the purpose of attracting patients, but as an indicator of their standing with respect to their position in the league table. With this sort of mechanism, and with a nod to Chapter 6, policy makers need to guard against creating in-groups that are more concerned with beating outgroups than they are focused specifically on simply doing well (Sapolsky, 2017), which may lead to parochialism and a reluctance to share the messages of successful practices. But notwithstanding this concern, within five years of introducing this reputational mechanism the VHA, a system that was traditionally associated with poor quality care, demonstrated substantial performance improvements. Indeed, by 2005 it was outperforming all of the other sectors of US health care on almost all of the quality criteria over which a comparison was possible (Oliver, 2007). This example is instructive when one recalls from previous chapters that

---

[7] Of course, from an evolutionary perspective, traditional human cultures have been estimated to be rather small – about 150 people (Sapolsky, 2017) – and we probably cannot normally organise a whole public service at that level. But nonetheless, organisation at a regional level is, in theory, more likely to be conducive to reciprocal, co-operative tendencies than organisation at a superregional or national level.

a concern for reputation underpins the workings of indirect reciprocity, and these mechanisms may further benefit a whole policy sector (e.g. the VHA in general) if systems are in place for the relatively underperforming groups (in this example, hospitals) to learn from those who have discovered better, perhaps more co-operative, practices.[8] As the economists Rajiv Sethi and Eswaran Somanathan (2005, pp. 242–3) have noted, members 'of groups that exhibit efficient norms will enjoy higher material payoffs than members of groups that do not, and such norms may therefore spread through the population by the imitation of successful practices found in neighbouring groups' ... (and echoing Ostrom) 'norms of reciprocity are an important component of social capital.'

From the above, then, a plausible generally beneficial public policy lesson is for the organisation, management and financing of public sector services to be decentralised (perhaps subject to a nationally imposed minimum standard of service provision), with the caveat that the resources collected at the decentralised level would need to be risk-adjusted at the superregional level if equity of opportunity across all relevant groups is an objective.[9] The superregional or national level policy makers might usefully also take responsibility for encouraging and supporting experimentation within, and learning across, local areas in each policy sector (e.g. health, social care,

---

[8] Relatedly, on inter-group learning in relation to the management of ground water basins in California, Ostrom (1990, pp. 137–8) writes that 'because the appropriators from several neighbouring basins were all involved in similar problems, participants in one setting could learn from the experiences of those in similar settings. Sufficient overlap existed among participants across basins to ensure communication about results. Interbasin coordinating arenas were created at several junctures to enhance the ability to exchange information about agreements reached within and across basin boundaries'.

[9] If resources are collected by local-level bodies, they may feel more responsible for the revenue and this may strengthen their sense of reciprocity with those that finance the services. However, localities are likely to differ with respect to, for example, the age, gender and income mixes of their populations (among other things), and their populations will consequently have differential needs. Therefore, if equity of opportunity to access services is an objective at the superregional or national (or international) level, then it is inevitable that there has to be some reallocation of resources between the localities.

education, policing). The message from Ostrom (1990) regarding her study on the management of ground water basins is that cross-regional learning can be facilitated greatly if influential sectoral players – whether the sector be health, education or whatever – from across different regions meet regularly, perhaps at pan-regional discussion forums, to share ideas on how challenges to co-operative endeavours might best be addressed. The cross-regional sharing of ideas and experiences between professionals who have similar objectives would in part itself be an exercise in reciprocity, at least from and among those who have suggestions on what may or may not be worth replicating elsewhere while still retaining an openness to improve their own working environments.

In some countries, the national level organisation of certain services is almost sacred to many, epitomised by the National Health Service (NHS) in England, and it is likely that such an institutional structure is the most appropriate if one's goal is to secure national uniform standards of equity and quality at any particular moment in time. However, over time, imposing national standards might prove stultifying, and most people, including relatively deprived populations, may find that their public services work better for them if local experimentation and co-operation, and cross-regional learning, were allowed and encouraged. If the great scholars of human motivation – referred to throughout this book – are right, there is a strong intellectual, and even evolutionary, justification to argue that reciprocally driven co-operation in public sector services, and the quality and efficiency associated with co-operative actions, might be better secured if any faith in the national state as the principal organising and financing body was weakened.

This is not to argue that decentralised groupings should be disconnected from each other; indeed, quite the contrary, as previously argued in relation to the importance of cross-regional learning. Nor is it to argue that decentralisation is all that one requires to stir reciprocal actions. If one encourages egoism at the decentralised level, for example, then egoism is likely to prevail.[10] It is to contend that decentralising is a necessary, if not sufficient, condition in order for reciprocal co-operative arrangements to be given the best chance of thriving; but nor it is to argue that the central state has no role to play in the delivery of public services. Importantly, the central state sets the broad – and broadly agreed upon – policy objectives for each sector. Moreover, as suggested above, it remains best placed to set minimum standards and to regulate against and punish unacceptable performance at the local level, in some circumstances to arbitrate on what is the fair level of remuneration for particular services, to risk-adjust resources from relatively advantaged regions to those less advantaged in order to provide the conditions to ameliorate wide national inequities in opportunity if that is a paramount objective, and to encourage and support intra-regional experimentation and cross-regional learning. However, too much micro-management from the centre that underplays the extent to which local actors might be the best placed to manage local services and to meet the challenges therein dampens regional autonomy and is unlikely to fire the embers of creativity needed to improve public sector delivery as much as might otherwise be the case. Indeed, too much central state interference may even lead to those working at the local level to feel abjugated from due responsibility to improve public services, a point emphasised long ago by Peter Kropotkin (1902/2014).

We might then usefully emphasise the importance of reciprocity, and we might even work towards ensuring the necessary (although not sufficient) size and fluidity of groups for co-operative

---

[10] In the first decade of the twenty-first century, those responsible for NHS policy decided that it would be a good idea to create a new national system of electronic health records by decentralising its development to a number of regions. Different companies won the right to develop the system in different regions through a tendering process. In order to win the contracts, the companies made promises that they had no hope of delivering on, and there was insufficient joined-up thinking across the different companies on how the regionally constructed systems would deliver a coherent IT system for the whole of the NHS. This decentralised process, which paid little attention to how reciprocity ought to be fostered, did not deliver a nationally connected electronic health record system and wasted several billion UK pounds. For this, someone ought to have felt the full force of negative reciprocity.

endeavours to have the best chance of thriving. But perhaps none of this will work as well as it might unless we have a sense that 'we are all in this together'.

THE CASE FOR REDUCING INEQUALITY

Through a reciprocity-tinted lens, Chapter 4 touched upon the good sense often demonstrated by employers in offering a fair wage, and the next chapter will extend that discussion somewhat. But at a macro level, similar arguments may apply: none of us want to be locked in a cellar when the sun is shining.[11] As aforementioned in this chapter, the notion of desert – that people benefit disproportionately according to their efforts – is a concept to which many, perhaps most, people are not averse, but often have a somewhat distorted view of what their own efforts are worth (see footnote 5). Around the time that I was writing this book, Sir Martin Sorrell, the chief executive of WPP, the world's largest advertising agency, was pressured into quitting his position over claims of personal financial misconduct, claims that he nonetheless rejected. In 2015, there had been shareholder unrest over his annual pay package, which is not too surprising when one learns that the package equated to £70 million.[12]

Sorrell was admittedly the highest rewarded chief executive in the FTSE 100 group of companies, but there is evidence that the very rich in many countries have been awarding themselves indefensible increases in the shares of national income over recent decades. In this respect, reciprocity has perhaps gone awry. As an illustrative example, the share of national income in the United States that went to the richest 1 per cent of the population increased from 8 per cent in 1980 to

[11] Unless, of course, you are a duck-billed platypus. Or a mole. Or an academic.
[12] At the time of writing, the BBC's reporting of Sorrell's resignation can be viewed here: www.bbc.co.uk/news/business-43771974. Even if one believes that people deserve very high levels of remuneration for the jobs that they do, this does not rule out the notion that everyone should face an equitable start in life, which would suggest that high-income earners ought to be exposed to a substantial inheritance tax rate. Ways in which to address the possible consequent problems of capital flight, gifts, sign-overs to children and spouses and other means to avoid inheritance tax enforcement are beyond me here.

18 per cent in 2015 (Pinker, 2018);[13] others have estimated the share of net wealth, as opposed to income, enjoyed by the top 1 per cent at close to 40 per cent in the United States in 2014, and at 20–30 per cent in an array of other countries, including Japan, France, Canada, Greece, Germany, Denmark, Sweden and the United Kingdom (Credit Suisse, 2014). Even if more or less everyone in society saw their incomes and wealth increase over time, one can easily be made to feel poorer if others appear to have so much more. A person might be quite satisfied with a tangerine for Christmas if everyone else also receives a small piece of fruit, but might not be satisfied with a Nokia 3310 if everyone else is being gifted an iPhone X.[14] One might contest, *à la* Pinker in footnote 13, that a focus on relative rather than absolute income within particular peer groups can lead to a concern with the material position of those who really one should not be concerned about at all; for instance, this might have driven some (although hopefully not many) to sympathise with Ashley Cole's outrage at being offered 'only' £55,000 per week in 2006, noted earlier, and the outrage expressed by the recent disclosure of BBC salaries, when generously remunerated staff learned that their peers were being more than generously remunerated.[15] However, the general point remains that when a nation's income or wealth is being concentrated increasingly in the

---

[13] However, Pinker does not perceive income inequality in and of itself to be morally important, so long as everyone has enough. It seems, for him, it is absolute rather than relative income or wealth that matters, although I contend that the wide and possibly widening relative differences can undermine trust and a willingness to reciprocate (a view shared, it seems, by the WPP shareholders). There is abundant information on inequalities and the trends thereof across many different countries. Relatively recent sources that the interested reader might consult include those written by the economists Angus Deaton (2013), Thomas Piketty (2014) and Joseph Stiglitz (2012).

[14] Unless the person has particularly retro tastes, of course. By the time this book is published, even an iPhone X might seem retro.

[15] For example, see www.theguardian.com/media/live/2017/jul/19/bbc-publishes-salaries-of-highest-earning-stars-live-updates. Admittedly, many BBC staff are not remunerated at all generously, and the issue was further complicated by a gender wage imbalance. Incidentally, Sugden (2018) discusses another example of a footballer perhaps losing touch with prosocial norms, by contending that Lionel Messi's alleged tax avoidance attempts essentially potentially imposes harms on all those people, such a laundry staff, groundsmen, ticket collectors etc., who are, in part, responsible for him realising the extraordinary rewards for his talents at kicking a ball.

hands of a relatively small number of people, the majority, or at least a substantial minority, may have quite legitimate feelings that they are being left behind. A degree of inequality may be a driver of growth; it may be good for the group as a whole. But too much inequality may undermine motivation and other-regarding group-oriented social norms, and crowd in selfish egoism and its consequent long-term harms (cf. Banfield, 1958).

Widening income inequality is thus not conducive to sustaining a trusting, reciprocal, co-operative society. As Sapolsky (2017, p. 292) notes: 'Trust requires reciprocity, and reciprocity requires equality, whereas hierarchy is about domination and asymmetry'. But we must remember that reciprocity is a two-way street. Redistributive mechanisms may be easier to sustain if those who are in receipt of welfare benefits, for instance, are, if they are able, seen to contribute to the fabric of society. For example, streets, parks and rivers can be tidied, and loneliness, which is a significant problem, particularly among the elderly, can be alleviated. Tasks that help to address these issues, and many others that might also serve to improve skills, could be performed on a part-time basis by many of those in receipt of welfare benefits. Although it may be unpalatable to some, we have learned that humans are not naturally pure altruists. If we have a situation where the non-poor feel that the poor are doing little to alleviate their situation or are offering little in return for assistance, then the non-poor will perhaps feel less inclined to help them. It might well be that in such circumstances the working poor and those in the middle of the income distribution feel squeezed the most, seeing the very rich, sometimes literally, sail away from them, and yet feeling that they are subsidising those who choose welfare over work. As argued earlier in relation to Esping-Anderson's (1990) thesis, in order to sustain effectively the support for a public policy or an adequate system of welfare, it is wise to emphasise to those who are paying for it what they are getting out of it, and requiring those who benefit to offer something tangible in return (assuming that they are mentally and physically able to do so) would be one way of doing that.

In this chapter, I have endeavoured to offer big-picture messages on some conditions that may need to be established for reciprocity to have the best chance of flourishing. First, there is the importance of emphasising how one's policies are informed by and promote reciprocal relationships, so as to go with the grain of this fundamental group-orientated motivator of human behaviour. The alternative strategies of emphasising selfish egoism, as one might do in, for example, demand-led choice policies, may ultimately harm the groups that one is attempting to inspire, and in the long run and in general, emphasising pure altruism is likely to be counterproductive. Second, selfish egoism has more scope to flourish the larger the group, and the imposition of too much micromanagement by a central state is also likely to undermine the capability, autonomy and thus motivation of local actors, who are often most appropriately placed to organise and manage themselves to deal with the challenges that they face. Therefore, the decentralisation of much of the management and financing of public services, subject to an adequate nationwide risk-adjusted reallocation of funds, is perhaps the sensible path to pursue, coupled with processes that encourage successful practices to be learned and shared across regions. Third, at the general societal level and thus not specifically in relation to the delivery of public services, too much concentration of income and wealth in the hands of a small percentage of the population is inconducive to fostering trust and reciprocity among their fellow citizens. We cannot have a completely flat playing field, but, to extend my use of metaphors, to leave most with the impression that they are limited to gruel while a select few are dining regularly on oysters may damage the prosocial norms on which successful societies rely. It would be wise for politicians to recognise that relative income and wealth matters.

These three recommendations are not, of course, original. Libraries have been written on them, particularly the latter two. But a point that is less often made is that, despite people's ideological predispositions, all three are justified intellectually by a concern with fostering reciprocity, the social norm that has evolved to aid group survival. Societies in general, and public sectors specifically, are collections of groups. It makes sense to try to provide general conditions for the flourishing, and certainly not the undermining, of this fundamental human motivator. Admittedly, the suggestions in this chapter, other than perhaps those relating to reputational competition as a driver of improvement, are at the very general level, but then that was the stated objective here. Chapter 8 considers not only reputational competition, but also other ways in which the design of public policy interventions might be informed a little more specifically by the tendency to reciprocate.

FOOD FOR THOUGHT

1. If people are encouraged to be selfish, are they more likely to be so?
2. Are co-operative endeavours in large groups doomed?
3. So long as the poor are getting richer, does inequality matter?

8 Reciprocity-Informed Policy Design

In 2011, the psychologist Shai Daziger and his colleagues, published a study where they examined 1,100 judicial rulings and found that prisoners were granted parole about 60 per cent of the time when the judges had recently eaten, but when making their rulings just before they were about to eat, the judges' rate of parole granting was precisely zero per cent. In a different study by social psychologist Joshua Ackerman and colleagues (2010), respondents were split between those who sat in soft chairs and those who sat in hard chairs, and it was discovered that those in the latter were more likely to perceive partners in economic games as unemotional, and were less willing to be flexible in their dealings with them, rendering reciprocal compromises more difficult. It has also been reported that people tend to be less generous to strangers if they are carrying a heavy cognitive load (Sapolsky, 2017) and when they are hurried (Darley and Batson, 1973).[1] The above studies all appear to suggest that people are likely to be more generous, and thus more prone to reciprocal and co-operative (and, admittedly, perhaps purely altruistic) actions if they feel physically and mentally comfortable than if they are in some discomfort, which is presumably not a trivial consideration for policy makers and managers.

However, when public policy makers are considering the conditions that may motivate reciprocal and co-operative tendencies in others with the intention of serving their overall policy objectives, they need also to ensure that those that they are targeting have the same objectives in mind. This point can be illustrated with a famous

---

[1] Darley and Batson's study is the rather famous one that demonstrated that people are less likely to assist a person seemingly in distress if they are running to attend a class than if they are not in a rush, even if the class that they are hurrying to is a teaching on the Parable of the Good Samaritan.

study undertaken by the economists Uri Gneezy and Aldo Rustichini (2000) on a group of Israeli childcare nurseries. To the inconvenience of the nursery staff, many of the parents in Gneezy and Rusticini's study had got into the habit of arriving late to pick up their children. It was thought that a straightforward financial disincentive, in the form of a fine for lateness, would curtail this habit, but the consequence of the fine was actually a significant increase in the incidence of lateness, which was sustained after the fine was removed. In essence, it was a tool of negative reciprocity that apparently did not work. Those imposing the fine had thought that the parents would interpret it as a punishment for lateness, but it was interpreted by many as a reasonable fee for additional childcare. The stories people tell themselves gives meaning to the incentives. Sandel (2013) contends that the medium of exchange should be determined by the norm that you are trying to encourage. The use of money (i.e. the fine), which he argues is inextricably linked to the notion of the market exchange, dampened moral and civic commitment.

At first glance, then, the evidence uncovered by the Israeli day care study conflicts with the assumptions of standard economic theory, where, via a simple application of the relative price mechanism, a fine for doing something undesired would be expected to reduce the incidence of that activity. However, the parents tended to reframe the fine as a payment for something that they were willing to pay for, and they apparently did not conceive of the possibility that the nursery staff would rather go home than receive the additional money. Thus, from the parents' perspective their behaviour was perfectly consistent with standard economic theory. There are important circumstances, though, where the standard theory predictions less ambiguously falter, including at least sometimes, and perhaps often, with respect to the wages offered to those whose effort levels are not possible to measure accurately (i.e. where there are incomplete contracts). The standard theory prediction is that with incomplete contracts, the rational egoistic employee will minimise her effort levels, and knowing this, the rational egoistic employer will minimise the offered wage. There are, however, arguments and evidence that suggest that both employees and employers are often somewhat more enlightened than standard theory predicts.

FAIR EFFORT FOR FAIR PAY, AND TRUST BETWEEN BUYERS AND SELLERS

In Chapter 4, it was mentioned that George Akerlof (1982) speculated that a higher-than-necessary wage is often offered by employers in the expectation that employees would perceive this as a gift, and thus reciprocate by working harder than egoistic self-interest dictates. It was also noted that Fehr et al. (1997) reported some empirical support for Akerlof's conjecture, albeit with quite a large amount of selfish egoism intact. Indeed, Fehr et al. reported that 83 per cent of their respondents still shirked on their agreed effort levels to some extent, although only about 10 per cent shirked fully. Shirking declined to 26 per cent of the respondents when employers could punish shirkers and offer rewards for non-shirking and anti-shirking (so to speak). However, caution is advised when considering these additional incentives. Fehr and Gächter (2000b), for instance, found that if one limits oneself to fining shirking (without including the positive incentives for non-shirking), then this can substantially harm effort levels, perhaps because employees now feel they are being controlled in a hostile environment.[2] Nonetheless, the notion that employees respond reciprocally to what they perceive as fair actions has parallels with the arguments presented in Chapter 7 on curtailing extreme concentrations of income and wealth. It may also suggest that any reliance on the public spirit of public sector staff to work hard will only take you so far; in order to secure and sustain good public sector services, it

---

[2] We will return to the possible dangers of pejorative forms of performance incentive later in the chapter, but they mirror Ostrom's (2000) concern that co-operation forced by externally imposed rules will have little staying power in that they relate to the counterproductive effects of attempts to control, discussed in previous chapters. It may also suggest that people have a preference for evolved Humean forms of co-operation over imposed Hobbesian forms (see Chapter 3).

might be wise to take note that those who provide them need to be offered a decent basic wage.

There is much earlier evidence that is consistent with Akerlof's conjecture. For instance, in 1964 the psychologists J. Stacy Adams and Patricia Jacobsen reported an experiment where they hired students to read galley proofs. They divided the students into three groups. The first group were told that they were unqualified to earn the then-standard proof readers' fee of thirty cents per page but would be paid that rate anyway. The second group were also told that they were unqualified and were paid twenty cents per page, and the third group were told that they were qualified and were paid thirty cents per page. It was found that the first group worked harder and produced better quality work than either of the other two groups. This lends further support to the notion that a high wage strategy, particularly in the face of an incomplete contract, is rational, because it helps to sustain higher effort levels and profits than paying low wages (Fehr and Falk, 1999), although there is the possibility that this could lower overall employment levels (Fehr and Gächter, 2000a).

Similar in structure to the principal–agent problem between employer and employee where effort is not easily observed is the relationship between buyer and seller, where the quality of the good or service is not easy to discern – i.e. for so-called complex goods and services, riven with asymmetries of information, discussed in relation to public services in Chapter 5. In his classic article on the market for lemons, George Akerlof (1970), using the example of used cars, postulated that buyers will not be willing to buy a used car at a high price due to a lack of trust in the seller to disclose any or all of the things that could be wrong with it, which will motivate sellers to offer only the proverbial lemons, a state of affairs that harms both the buyer and the seller. Akerlof's example – used cars – assumes a one-off purchase, where, in general, there is insufficient time, experience and inclination for the parties in the exchange to build a bond of trust. The sociologist Peter Kollock (1994) investigated whether this supposed lack of trust is endemic also to circumstances where there are repeated transactions.

Kollock used rubber and rice as examples of a complex and a simple good, respectively.[3] As suggested in Chapter 5, simple goods are what Adam Smith (1776/1999) had in mind when he argued that trust, other-regarding preferences and mutual love were not necessary for society to subsist. Over simple goods, assuming no substantively differential power relationships between the exchange partners and little opportunity for psychological phishing, the level of trust is not high because it does not need to be for there to be a generally satisfactory outcome.

However, over complex goods, trust and mutual regard are beneficial to buyers and sellers when repeat transactions are desired; Kollock (1994, p. 316) wrote that 'If actors are not required to trade "in good faith", the interaction can have the structure of a social dilemma in that (like the rubber market) individuals gain by being deceitful, but all are hurt if all choose this course of action.' Many publicly financed services are complex, and it is thus plausible that encouraging egoism via, for example, demand-led competition will create a race to the bottom if providers are able to conceal, due to imperfect information, the real quality of their services. This is not to argue that reciprocal and other prosocial tendencies will be entirely absent when demand-led competition is encouraged, or that egoism will evaporate when institutional arrangements are designed to support reciprocity. But to encourage egoism in the trade of complex goods and services when there are grounds to believe that this motivational force can lead to highly suboptimal outcomes for buyers and sellers – and where some otherwise enlightened sellers might be forced to act egoistically in order to survive – seems unfortunate.

How might sellers gain the trust of buyers when the quality of what they are selling is not readily observable? This leads us back to the notion of reputation, discussed briefly in Chapter 7 in relation to

---

[3] It is apparently impossible to determine the quality of rubber at the point of sale by a plantation, and it is only after extensive processing that one can discern whether a grower took the time to ensure a high quality crop.

how it might inform policy design and considered in a little more depth later in this chapter. As emphasised at the beginning of this book, a concern for one's reputation probably evolved because a good reputation serves to signal that one is a good person with whom to co-operate. This fundamental aspect of our character extends to sellers who are attempting to maintain, attain and sustain prices and customers by guaranteeing good quality, and, to reiterate, might be expected to be more prominent when dealing with complex than with simple goods. In a laboratory setting, this is exactly what Kollock (1994) observed: sellers were very concerned about their own reputations over complex and simple goods,[4] but more so over complex goods (cf. again, eBay, Amazon, Airbnb, and most other trading websites you can think of); buyers, who bear the risk of the information asymmetry, also focussed upon sellers' reputations over complex goods; people rated the trustworthiness of their exchange partners higher over complex goods than simple goods; and they were more likely to remain with their trading partners over complex goods, even when others were attempting to entice them elsewhere. That sellers in these experiments focus upon their reputation and buyers respond in turn lends itself to enlightened self-interest – or continuation reciprocity according to Kolm's (2008) definitions (see Chapter 1) – that serves everybody well. Motivating shorter-term egoism in its stead, and in particular in public sector services, is only likely to widen the reality of Akerlof's (1970) somewhat depressing vision.

Thus, appealing to egoism, principally in the form of demand-led competition, even with the intention of serving the public good, may well be detrimental to this objective. In terms of our public services, many of us could be left with lemons, with little hope of making lemonade. But this does not imply that the broad notion of trade is necessarily bad for public policy; exchange, after all, in the essence of reciprocity.

---

[4] And the quality of both types of good increased over trading cycles.

NON-COMPETITIVE TRADE

Pay-for-performance, in which providers are given additional remuneration for meeting particular pre-set quality criteria, has become an increasingly prevalent public policy tool internationally over the past two decades. In theory, the mechanism is a simple exchange with neither payer nor provider seeking services or payment from other parties, and with both sides presumably keen to 'trade' with each other repeatedly. With specific reference to the mechanism, providers therefore have no fear that a service rival will unfairly undermine them or be tempted to do likewise to others. The general structure of the mechanism appears conducive to reciprocal actions and thus one might usefully consider how these actions could be reinforced. To do that, we must consider some of the potential problems of paying for performance improvements.

Of course, in relation to complex goods and services, there remain incentives for payers to try to underpay for performance improvements and for providers to produce less than what might be deemed objectively fair. The latter possibility may be exacerbated if pay-for-performance methods are imposed on public sector providers, in part because they may then be seen as controlling rather than supportive, which might undermine morale, but also if they are perceived as offering unfair remuneration. Relatedly, if the quality indicators are ill thought-out, or if they are measures that are divorced from the providers' notions of genuine quality of service, they might either distort more fundamental priorities or be ignored entirely. After all, those who provide public services have expertise, often acquired over many years and even decades, on what might be best delivered to the users of their services, and thus placing too much weight on feeding the wants of the demand-side – whether this be in health care, education or any other public service – runs the danger of allowing the (sightless) tail to lead the dog. Moreover, if the remuneration is too generous, then this is problematic for those who ultimately pay for public sector services (i.e. tax payers). In all of the above, the fundamental notion of reciprocity – a mutually agreed fair exchange – would have been lost. If pay-for-performance is to have a chance of working as intended, then it would appear that the providers and the payers have to be involved jointly in determining fair prices and indicators of quality that are broadly perceived as appropriate. Furthermore, given the potential for disagreements, the negotiations are likely to benefit from input from a knowledgeable arbitrator that all parties accept and even respect, who would monitor the exchange relationship and the forthcoming provider outcomes. Creating these conditions for reciprocity may optimise the chance that the policy will benefit those it is meant to serve.[5]

Even if the above conditions are met, however, many remain sceptical of pay-for-performance mechanisms. For instance, the legal scholar and psychologist Dan Kahan (2005) contends that performance incentives of this kind may undermine co-operative tendencies by introducing the expectation that one must get paid for everything that one does, and thus might consequently erode any motivation to undertake voluntary beneficial actions.[6] If many professionals rely on

---

[5] As an aside, Kropotkin (1902/2014, p. 116) notes that in medieval times, perhaps at a time when societies and economic systems were somewhat less atomistic than they are in the developed world today, prices were often set by trusted third persons: 'The merchants and the sailors ... were to state on oath the first cost of the goods and the expenses of transportation. Then the mayor of the town and two discreet men were to name the price at which the wares were to be sold ... This way of "naming the price" so well answers to the very conceptions of trade which were current in medieval times that it must have been all but universal. To have the price established by a third party was a very old custom; and for all interchange within the city it certainly was a widely-spread habit to leave the establishment of prices to "discreet men" – to a third party – and not to the vendor or the buyer'.

[6] Relating to the arguments for decentralisation in Chapter 7, Ostrom (2005) has written that many policies that have been developed in modern democracies serve to crowd out trust, reciprocity, co-operation, knowledge of local circumstances and experimentation. The possibility of an insufficiently thought through performance incentive mechanism crowding out those who are intrinsically motivated to provide public sector services, and crowding in those who are not intrinsically motivated, cannot be discounted. Given that people often give unforeseen meaning to incentives, as discussed earlier in relation to the Israeli nursery, it might be worth considering reframing the fees that are sometimes offered in performance management mechanisms as prizes (or something along those lines – on this, see also Bowles, 2016; Frey, 2013), so that they remain, in some sense, special, and thus do not form an expectation.

each other to deliver a defined outcome (in health care or education, for example), the near certainty that the performance mechanism will not encapsulate every process that is important to the successful delivery of that outcome renders it plausible that the overall objective will indeed be undermined by the introduction of pay-for-performance mechanisms. Perhaps informed by the natural inclination towards negative reciprocity, Kahan intimates that credible penalties are likely to be more beneficial than performance-linked rewards, because people who resent fraud, corruption or cheating, for example, might see penalties against such activities as supportive of their own belief system, which may strengthen their identity with the organisation in which they operate and detract from the temptation to commit an injustice – indeed, as earlier intimated, Ostrom (1990; 2000) notes that monitoring and graduated sanctions are typical in common pool resource institutions. In this sense, penalties and fines may have a moral dimension (Sandel, 2013), but the notion that the penalties must be credible and possibly graduated is instructive, as we have learned that those that are interpreted as excessive and/or controlling might prove counterproductive.

One must be a little cautious in interpreting the arguments against performance-related pay, however, because some may use this as justification for offering only low remuneration levels to public sector workers, bringing forth the rather spurious argument that higher pay will undermine their intrinsic motivation to work hard. The intrinsically motivated still have to support themselves and their families, and as suggested earlier in this chapter, a decent basic wage may well be rewarded with higher effort levels. It is therefore perhaps sensible to incentivise general working behaviours via wages and use pay-for-performance only to motivate the undertaking of particular specific tasks that are generally felt in need of highlighting. If a decent basic wage is paid, and, through negotiations, performance-assessed quality criteria are chosen that providers support, then any positive financial incentives in the mechanism might not need to be large in order to be effective, because they may be perceived not as a material inducement but more like a reminder that certain activities should not be overlooked. In essence, the incentives would serve as prompts – a kindly all-seeing eye – for the providers to ensure that practices that are consistent with their autonomous preferences are being followed.[7] That said, there are forms of performance management that do not necessitate the use of money at all.

REPUTATION ONCE MORE

In the nineteenth century, the Welsh utopian socialist and manager at the New Lanark cotton mill in Scotland, Robert Owen, provided superior conditions for his workers and noticed productivity increase as a consequence, again demonstrating the power of reciprocity. Moreover, he arranged for a piece of wood to be hung near to each of his worker's stations, with the colour of the wood indicating the conduct of the worker on the previous day: black for bad, blue for passable, yellow for good and white for excellent. Each day, Owen walked through the mill, looking at the pieces of wood but not saying anything and not admonishing anyone. This reputational motivator, it was reported, greatly improved the workers' performance (Wolff, 2003), and was perhaps an early example of the priming phenomenon discussed in Chapter 1. In a Churchillian flourish, the historian A. L. Morton (1969/1978, pp. 98–9) commented that: 'Never perhaps in the history of the human race has so simple a device created in so short a period so much order, virtue, goodness and happiness, out of such ignorance, error and misery'.

Akerlof and Shiller (2015) also refer to historical attempts at harnessing the power of reputation. For instance, they mention The Society for the Protection of Trade against Swindlers and Sharpers, established in London in 1776, who expelled members who were deemed to have unethical business practices, and provided printed certificates that members could display that indicated that

---

[7] There are parallels here with the small (and effective) charges that have been introduced in supermarkets for plastic bag use in several countries: see, for example, Disney, Le Grand and Atkinson (2013).

they were of good credit and reputation. Moreover, The National Consumers League, founded in the United States by Florence Kelley in 1899, held that consumers are the indirect employers of the factory workers that produce the things they buy, and therefore they have a moral responsibility for the welfare of the workers.[8] The League thus inspected working conditions and awarded a white label to factories that passed the inspection, which vouched also for the safety of the products that they produced.

It has therefore been known for a long time that reputational effects can be used to affect behaviour, which, given that a concern for reputation lies so deep in human psychology – linked, as it is, with the desire to indicate that one is trustworthy – is perhaps unsurprising. What is a little surprising, though, is that discussions on how to use reputation and trust specifically, and reciprocity more generally, as motivations for improving the design of public policy have, until recently, been quite limited. The political scientist Oliver Treib and his colleagues (2007) have written on the benefits of networks, conceptually sitting between hierarchies and markets, based on actors identifying complementary interests, and with relationships built on trust, loyalty and reciprocity. Networks are based on horizontal patterns of interactions as opposed to power asymmetries, although contracts will be incomplete due to bounded rationality and asymmetries of information (Héritier and Lehmkuhl, 2008). The public policy analysts Vivien Lowndes and Chris Skelcher (1998) contend that any conflicts that arise within networks are resolved on the basis of the members' reputational concerns, which mirrors the notion that trust and reciprocity resolve the problems of incomplete contracts, discussed earlier. As a general mode of governance, networks thus appear preferable to hierarchies and markets if one accepts that reciprocity is fundamental to human nature, but it may equally be reasonably contended that, in terms of specific policy prescriptions to bring about

---

[8] Cf. the argument in footnote 7 in Chapter 5, in relation to paying Uber drivers a fair fare.

performance improvements, the discussion of networks is a little amorphous.⁹

Building on the discussion in relation to the Veterans Health Administration in Chapter 7, however, disseminating reputational indicators can be a powerful reciprocity-related method by which to drive performance improvements in public sector services. Instituting the reputational model is not a means to motivate egoism; as has been earlier argued, demand-led competition appeals to egoistic motivations, which are risky motivations to encourage over complex goods and services. Rather than using egoism to motivate people, the intention with using reputation as a driver is to foster a concern among suppliers for gaining the trust of their users by demonstrating that they are offering acceptable quality in the face of information asymmetries. The notion is that even without the threat of losing clientele, suppliers will want to try to demonstrate that they are providing a good service.

Regarding the health and education sectors in the United Kingdom and some parts of the United States, operational researcher Gwyn Bevan and behavioural scientist Barbara Fasolo (2013) provide further evidence that the reputational model of governance – namely, the public reporting of performance – works. For example, at the beginning of the twenty-first century, a mechanism known as the hospital star rating system was introduced in the National Health Service (NHS) in England, with which hospitals were assessed annually on a number of quality and financial indicators. The most notable indicator was how well each hospital was performing against waiting times targets for elective inpatient procedures, an aspect of performance over which the NHS had traditionally been much criticised. Following assessment, the hospitals were each awarded from

---

9   Admittedly, although Lowndes and Skelcher (1998) extoll the benefits of collaborative, inter-agency partnerships and emphasise these as an alternative to the market, they take care to state that the creation of partnerships does not imply that relations between the relevant actors will always be based on mutual benefit, trust and reciprocity, but that partnerships are associations with a variety of forms of social organisation, including hierarchy, the market and networks.

zero to three stars, with more stars indicating better performance. Moreover, the number of stars that each hospital was awarded was publicised widely in the national and local media, and thus the policy clearly impacted upon reputations. The star rating system may have motivated hospital managers to pay more attention to the performance of their own hospital in absolute terms, with, for example, anything less than two stars being viewed as disappointing (to say the least). Or they may have been more motivated to consider the relative performance of their own hospital compared to, for instance, the performance of a similar-sized hospital in a neighbouring town or city. Whether motivating absolute or relative concerns (or both), the star rating system appeared to work, in that it was associated with substantial reductions in NHS waiting times (Besley, Bevan and Burchardi, 2009).

In a controlled experiment in the United States, the health policy scholar Judith Hibbard and her colleagues (2003; 2005) also attempted to discern how hospitals could be motivated to better perform. In the experiment, one set of hospitals were given no information about their quality, a second set were given information on their quality through private feedback, and for a third set the quality was publicly reported. It was only in the third set that attempts were made to substantially improve performance, and this was again driven by reputational concerns rather than concerns pertaining to market share.[10] Tuscany in Italy has quite recently adopted and developed these ideas on reputational motivation to attempt to improve health care performance, and to positive effect (for example, see Bevan, Evans and Nuti, 2019). Academics and local policy leaders in Tuscany have designed diagrammatic targets that resemble dartboards at a sub-regional level, which indicate how well each area is performing against multiple criteria. To illustrate, the diagrammatic target for the Careggi area of Tuscany is reproduced in Figure 8.1.[11]

---

[10] Similarly, Chassin (2002) reported improvements in risk-adjusted mortality rates in poor performing New York hospitals following the pubic reporting of their rates.

[11] I am grateful to Sabina Nuti for sending me the diagram in Figure 8.1. Further examples of these diagrammatic targets can be viewed in Bevan et al. (2019). The website for the

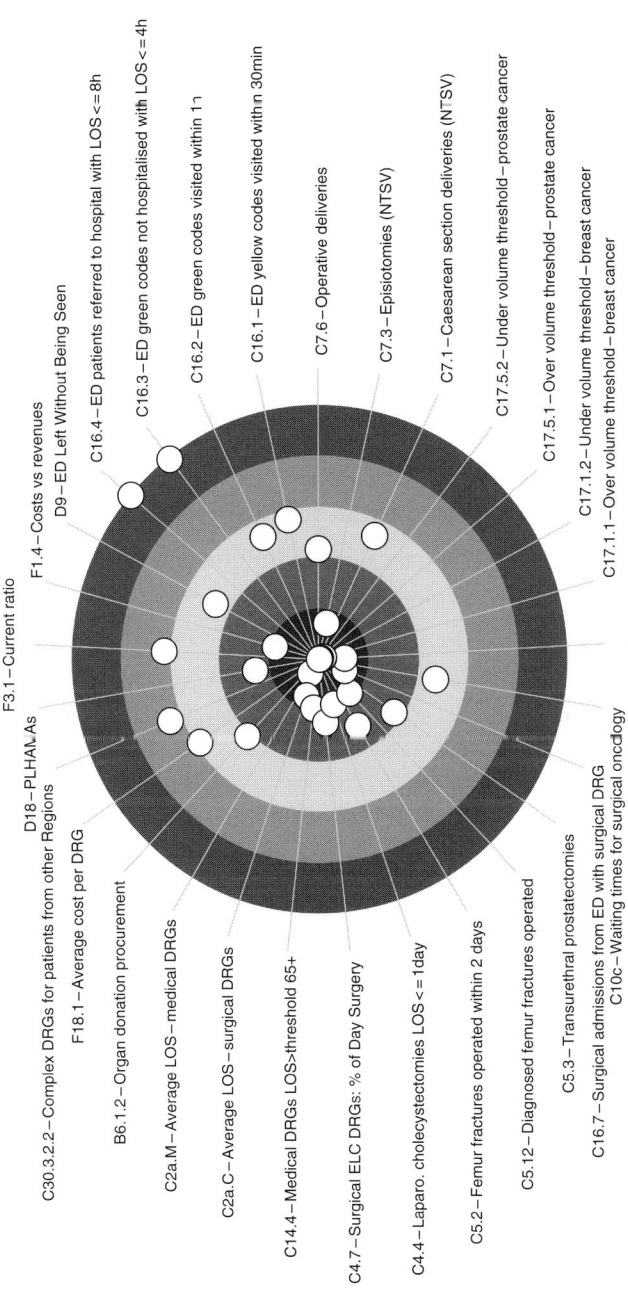

FIGURE 8.1 The Careggi performance target

The area is given a score of between one and five – ranging from poor to excellent performance – on each criterion. The target has five rings, with the poorest level of performance represented by the outer ring, and the best possible performance (a level five performance) scoring a bullseye. Visually, therefore, the closer the small white circles sit to the centre of the target in Figure 8.1, the better the area's health care sector is performing (at least on the criteria on which it is assessed). Relating to the discussion introduced in Chapter 7, the performance of each area within Tuscany, which is quite easily visualised by these dartboard diagrams, is reported publicly, which in turn creates an element of reputational competition across the different areas (cf. group selection theory once again).[1] The areas can quickly identify the specific criteria where they apparently underperform in relative terms, and can strive to learn from those areas that seem to be performing better. Nobody wants to be perceived as a poor relative performer for the fundamental reasons pertaining to trust, co-operation and reciprocity highlighted earlier; the diagrams have served as an apparently effective motivational driver of improvements in Tuscan health care services.

In arguing the case for the reputational model, Bevan and Fasolo (2013, p. 56) contend that reputation 'could work out of fear of having betrayed the public's trust and provides an urgent reason for acting before the public reacts and "punishes" this betrayal ... shocks of this kind are an integral part of generating the high powered incentives necessary for improvement'. However, caution is needed around the notions of fear, betrayal and punishment when using reputation as a motivational driver, principally because poor relative performance may not be poor in any absolute sense. In circumstances where providers are perhaps not doing as well as other similar organisations – which may even in some circumstances be for reasons that are beyond their control – but are nonetheless performing acceptably in an objective sense, the looming threat of punishment may be demoralising and

[1] Tuscan performance mechanism (in Italian; and at the time of writing) is http://performance.sssup.it/netval/

demotivating; in short, it might prove counterproductive to the aims that one is trying to achieve. It may therefore be wise to articulate clearly that the threat of punishment – i.e. the threat of negative reciprocity – will be restricted to those cases where clear incompetence or objectively unacceptable performance that is within the control of the responsible public sector personnel has been identified. Those organisations that do not fall into these categories but that are nonetheless performing relatively poorly might be better motivated with support than control. By publicly reporting their performance and that of those whom they consider to be their peers, they may be autonomously driven to identify the areas of delivery that merit their particular attention and to learn from others. As argued in Chapter 7, a role for the national or superregional government is to provide the structures for such cross-regional policy learning. But so as to minimise the risk of damaging my own reputation by repeating myself (too much), let us consider a further way in which reciprocity might usefully inform policy design, this time at a more micro, individualistic level.

MESSAGING RECIPROCITY

The interventions discussed above are principally focused upon motivating public sector professionals. Many policy interventions are directed alternatively towards the behaviours of citizens and service users – indeed, this has thus far been the primary objective in the burgeoning field of behavioural public policy (for example, see Oliver, 2017) – and reciprocity can usefully also inform this strategy. As long ago as 1972, Kenneth Arrow hypothesised that one motivation for donating blood was that of indirect reciprocity when he wrote that 'perhaps, one gives good things, such as blood, in exchange for a generalized obligation on the part of fellow men to help in other circumstances if needed' (Arrow, 1972, p. 349).[12]

---

[12]   Consistent with what has been argued throughout this book, Kropotkin (1902/2014) believed that that one might give in the vague expectation that one or those one cares for might receive help when in need in the future is an evolved, hard-wired human trait.

More recently, the Behavioural Insights Team (2013), in one of the largest behavioural-related randomised controlled trials ever conducted in the United Kingdom, set about testing whether emphasising indirect reciprocity, as well as other human motivations, could induce more people to register as organ donors.[13] They ran their trial over five weeks, which does raise the familiar question regarding the evaluation of behavioural interventions pertaining to whether short-term effects are sustainable over the long term. But leaving that concern aside, over one million people were enrolled in the trial, with the respondents randomly exposed to one of eight messages, with each message framed according to a particular behavioural motivation. Thus, about 135,000 people were exposed to each message when they renewed their driving licence or paid their annual vehicle tax. The authors reported that the most effective message, which they estimated would lead to an additional 96,000 organ donor registrations each year compared to the control message of 'Please join the NHS Organ Donor Register', was that which they argued was informed by reciprocity (which read: 'If you needed an organ transplant, would you have one? If so please help others').[14]

There has not, as yet, been much experimentation with using reciprocity-informed messages to (perhaps) improve people's behaviour, but there is clearly scope to try this type of intervention in areas beyond organ donor registration. For instance, the Behavioural Insights Team, through Michael Hallsworth and his colleagues (2016), have reported that missed hospital appointments, which are costly to most health care systems, could be reduced by up to one-quarter in the

---

[13] A point relevant to the discussion in Chapter 9 is that these messages are intended principally to address externalities.

[14] One of the other messages was informed by loss aversion: i.e. the general observation that people respond more to losses than they do to gains of an equivalent magnitude. The message was: 'Three people die every day because there are not enough organ donors'. The reciprocity frame did better, but not statistically significantly better, than the loss aversion frame. The reciprocity frame significantly outperformed all other frames. It is perhaps also worth noting that since next of kin consent is invariably required to actually use organs, getting people onto the register does not mean that their organs will be used in the event of their death. But getting them to sign up to the register is a good start.

United Kingdom by simply sending patients a message that informs them how much their appointment, if missed, would cost the health service. It is plausible that the effectiveness of the reminder could be strengthened even further if patients were told that the cost, if incurred, could have been used for the benefit of their family and friends, and/or ask the patients how they would feel if someone else imposed a similar cost on the health service. Moreover, we do not have to limit reciprocity-informed messages to the demand-side; it is possible that they could be used to good effect, for instance, to improve doctors' prescribing patterns or feedback efforts by teachers, to name just two possible, if thus far hypothetical, examples.

Overall with respect to this chapter, then, and informed by the literature on reciprocity, it seems reasonable to conclude that the use of performance incentives at the decentralised level might serve as a positive force for improving the benefits offered by public services so long as certain conditions are met. Namely, that salaries are the predominant component of remuneration for public sector employees, that all relevant parties recognise and accept that the chosen indicators of good performance in any pay-for-performance mechanism are appropriate in relation to achieving an overall objective (e.g. good health or education outcomes), and that all parties accept the compensation offered for meeting performance targets as fair. Credible and perhaps graduated financial penalties for prior agreed poor performance are also worth considering, although caution is advised to ensure that these serve only as a disincentive for incompetence, negligence and egoistic temptations, because if the observed poor performance is beyond the control or capabilities of the providers of public services, financially penalising them may only cause more harm. Further, the literature on reciprocity suggests that a careful implementation of something akin to the reputational model of governance, that threatens to punish indisputably bad absolute performance and that supports and aims to widen the implementation of innovative good practice, is worthy of serious consideration. And finally, when trying to encourage people to act in ways that are consistent with shared objectives, it makes sense to remind them that if others were to act in those very same ways, then they, and their friends and family members, may well feel the benefits.

As noted by Sethi and Somanathan (2001, p. 295), reciprocity 'has increasingly come to be recognised as an important aspect of human decision making with significant social and economic implications such as the downward rigidity of real wages, the private provision of certain public goods, the sustainable management of natural resources in local commons, voluntary donations of time and effort, and the decentralized enforcement of cooperative social norms'. Having to some extent considered how reciprocity might inform the design of public policy interventions, Chapter 9 will discuss how, from my preferred perspective, this fundamental motivator of human behaviour sits within a broad conceptual framework – a political economy if you will – of behavioural public policy.

FOOD FOR THOUGHT

1. Will workers respond to employer generosity by working harder than necessary?
2. With respect to performance assessment mechanisms, should policy makers consider rewards, penalties, both or neither?
3. Are public sector workers more likely to strive to improve or feel demotivated if their performance is compared openly to that of others?

9 Towards a Political Economy of Behavioural Public Policy

The application of behavioural insights to public policy design – defined here as behavioural public policy – is, in any specific and substantive sense, a relatively recent endeavour, although decades of social science scholarship underpins the approach.[1] Several conceptual frameworks have been developed within the field of behavioural public policy – some, for example, retain the notion of liberty while others allow heavy regulation and even bans; some focus on reducing harms to, and improving benefits for, those that the interventions target specifically while others focus more on reducing harms to other parties; and some aim to influence automatic, reflexive choices while others seek to encourage people to engage in more reflective deliberation. Whichever framework one adopts, however, reciprocity, as a fundamental motivator of individual behaviour, has an important role to play.

In this chapter, I will argue that the dominant framework in behavioural public policy to date is that which focuses upon internalities – i.e. that which aims to change the behaviour of those targeted for their own benefit – and where the normative goal is to improve welfare, utility or happiness, epitomised by the libertarian paternalism, or nudge, approach (Thaler and Sunstein, 2003; 2008). Some of the people whom I respect the most in the areas in which I work, including Luc Bovens, Gus O'Donnell and Cass Sunstein, adhere to this approach,[2] but for me, this is not the principal normative approach – the political economic framework – that should shape the field. In short, and in general, I am sceptical as to whether policy makers

---

[1] My take on the history and development of behavioural public policy can be read within the pages of Oliver (2017). To reiterate from Chapter 5, footnote 11, other quite recent related book-length surveys include those by Nobel Laureates Daniel Kahneman (2011) and Richard Thaler (2015).

[2] Admittedly, some people for whom I have little respect adhere to the approach also.

ought to be interfering in personal lifestyle behaviours for paternalistic ends (that is to say, for the good of those persons targeted for behaviour change), and I am unconvinced that welfare or utility maximisation ought to be the policy maker's normative goal.

There may of course be an evolutionary drive to be paternalistic;[3] children, for instance, would perhaps much of the time not survive too well without the paternalistic interference of their parents (even Brussels sprouts are good for you, apparently), principally because children often – and, up to a certain age, always – lack the capacity to do what is good for them. Like reciprocity, therefore, we may be paternalistically hard-wired. However, to my mind, this paternalistic urge should not, as a general rule, be acted upon in the form of coercion or manipulation of responsible adults by politicians and other policy makers, although this of course does not preclude attempts to educate people about the possible self-harm-inflicting consequences of some of their activities.

My favoured political economy of behavioural public policy fits within the liberal economic tradition of, for example, John Stuart Mill and, more contemporaneously, Robert Sugden, although compared to others within this tradition the approach detailed here perceives the possibility of more elaborately constructed externalities, or harms, that policy makers may legitimately seek to guard against.

ADDRESSING INTERNALITIES

As noted, libertarian paternalism has thus far been the most prominent framework in the behavioural public policy discourse – nudges are policy applications of this conceptual framework. Like its close cousin, asymmetric paternalism (published in 2003 by a prominent group of behavioural economists, led by Colin Camerer, although asymmetric paternalism is more open to the idea of regulation), libertarian paternalism is a soft form of paternalism – a form of means

---

[3] I consider paternalism as an approach that is focused on addressing internalities, not externalities.

paternalism. That is, the approach seeks to guide people's behaviour in particular directions without the use of force or mandates; people are free to continue with existing behaviours if they wish, with Thaler and Sunstein (2008) contending that retaining the freedom to choose is the best safeguard against a misguided policy intervention. Underpinning libertarian paternalism is the assumption that, of the many decisions that each of us makes quickly and almost automatically each day by being guided by various innate behavioural influences, a few will lead us to act in ways that, if we deliberated a little more, we would not follow.[4] The basic idea in libertarian paternalism is that with knowledge of these behavioural influences, the context or environment (or what Thaler and Sunstein term the choice architecture) that people face can be redesigned such that their automatic choices better align with their deliberative preferences. In short, then, for an intervention to be a nudge it has to be liberty-preserving, target internalities and be informed by behavioural science. Each of these three requirements is represented by an axis in Figure 9.1.

In the figure, moving towards the origin on the vertical axis, the horizontal axis and the diagonal axis respectively indicates that a policy is increasingly liberty-preserving rather than regulatory, increasingly addressing internalities rather than externalities, and increasingly informed by behavioural science rather than standard economic theory or rational choice theory. Consequently, a pure nudge must lie at the point where the axes intersect. Examples of pure nudges might include placing apples at the front and cheesecake at the back of canteen shelves, painting green footsteps that lead up to rubbish bins on pedestrian pavements, and allowing people to deposit money into accounts when they attempt to quit smoking on the understanding that the money will be returned to them if their abstinence is maintained beyond, say, six months.

[4] Most of these behavioural influences are the findings of behavioural economics or, more broadly, behavioural science that conflict with the assumptions of standard economic theory, including, for example, loss aversion mentioned in Chapter 8, present bias mentioned in Chapter 5, and, indeed, reciprocity, deviating as it does from the assumption of egoistic motivations.

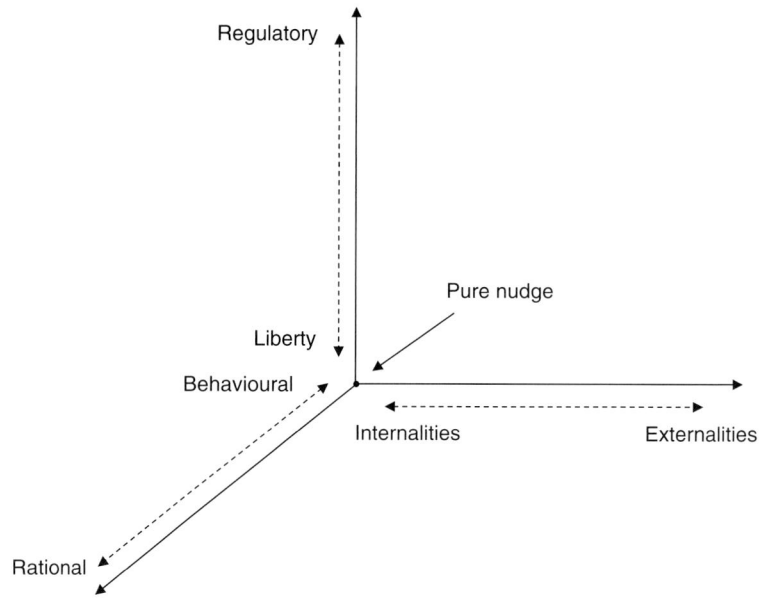

FIGURE 9.1 The requirements of libertarian paternalism

It has been argued that soft forms of paternalism do not go far enough; that respecting liberty will ultimately mean that these policy interventions will be insufficiently effective at addressing the actions of those who threaten their own health and financial security, for example (on this, see Conly, 2013). Those who follow this line of reasoning call instead for hard paternalism – or coercive paternalism or ends paternalism; that is, although they also contend that activities, such as smoking, may be driven by behavioural phenomena (e.g. present bias), they call for these activities to be banned on the demand-side.

However, as intimated at the beginning of this chapter, paternalism – soft or hard – is open to the critique that it unreasonably infantilises the adults it targets, and that policy makers ought to have no role in influencing the behaviours of those of sound mind if their activities impose no harms on others, a view akin to John Stuart Mill's (1859/1972) harm principle. The counterargument, given by libertarian paternalists and those who may more broadly be defined as behavioural welfare economists (Sugden, 2018), is predicated on retaining the normative postulate of utility maximisation, assumed under rational choice theory. That is, libertarian paternalists believe that due to the behavioural influences that contravene rational choice theory (and its inbuilt assumption of utility maximisation), people will sometimes fail to act and choose in their own best interests (i.e. to maximise utility) – and thus it is legitimate for policy makers to steer them in that normative direction. But one can question this normative assumption.

THE VIEW FROM NOWHERE

As noted, rational choice theory, standard economic theory and behavioural welfare economics all postulate that people ought to maximise utility (for simplicity and to reiterate, hereby treated as synonymous with welfare and happiness). All therefore have utilitarianism as a part of their intellectual origins, the founding father of which was the philosopher Jeremy Bentham. Bentham (1781/1988) believed that mankind was governed by what he referred to as the sovereign masters of pain, which we seek to minimise, and pleasure, which we seek to maximise. He viewed pain and pleasure as experienced feelings that are on a continuum and can thus be compared; and that they guide us on what we ought to do, and what we shall do. From this he derived his famous dictum: that the societal objective ought to be the greatest happiness for the greatest number.

Although by the beginning of the twentieth century, measures of Benthamite utility – i.e. numerical interpersonally comparable indicators of how much pain and pleasure individuals experience in the moment – were thought to be impossible to uncover, modern neoclassical economic theory, which is based upon decisions over future experiences rather than experiences in the moment, retained the notion that people ought to, and will want to, maximise their utility. Therefore, aside from allowing for random errors, we can infer from this that the decisions that people make over future episodes, and their retrospective assessments of their previous courses of action, will be consistent with them maximising the amount of utility that they experience. There is now evidence to suggest that this inference is sometimes incorrect.

This evidence began to emerge at the beginning of the 1990s, and shows that when people are asked to offer a retrospective preference over different events, there is a tendency for their relative preferences to differ systematically – i.e. non-randomly – from that guided by the greatest total moment-to-moment instant utilities that they experienced as they lived through each event (see Kahneman, Walker and Sarin [1997] for a review). Similar observations have been made with respect to prospective evaluations and expected experienced utility, and the cause of these systematic discrepancies are factors known as the gestalt characteristics (Ariely and Carmon, 2000). These characteristics are aspects of an event that respondents perceive as salient, to which they attach a particularly high weight, and include the tendency over relatively short episodes for people to prefer worse outcomes to precede better outcomes rather than vice-versa (Loewenstein and Prelic, 1993), an aversion to sudden, steep rates of change in outcomes (Hsee and Abelson, 1991), and, perhaps most significantly, the tendency for people to place a heavy emphasis on the peak and end moments of an episode (Fredrickson and Kahneman, 1993). This last gestalt characteristic is called peak-end evaluation, and can cause people to underemphasise the duration of the event.[5]

To illustrate peak-end evaluation with two prominent empirical studies of the effect, consider first evidence reported in 1996 by Daniel Kahneman and the clinician Donald Redelmeier. In their study, sigmoidoscopy and lithotripsy patients, during their procedures, recorded every sixty seconds their feelings of discomfort.[6] These

---

[5] As with reciprocity, there is likely to be an evolutionary explanation for the tendency to be influenced by the gestalt characteristics, which may have something to do with the urge to survive (e.g. avoid troughs), or the drive to flourish or to seek fulfilment as one sees fit (e.g. to prefer things to get better and to end well).

[6] Sigmoidoscopy procedures require a flexible tube to be inserted in a patient's rectum to examine their colon, and lithotripsy is a procedure where kidney stones are broken into

were measures of their moments of instant disutility, and by aggregating these at the end of the procedures a measure of total experienced disutility of the procedure for each patient could be calculated. Following their procedures, the patients' retrospective evaluations of the total discomfort that they experienced was also recorded on a ten-point scale. The authors reported that the peak-end effect and duration neglect were observed strongly in the retrospective evaluations. Redelmeier and colleagues (2003), again including Kahneman, followed up on this experiment by dividing a further 682 sigmoidoscopy patients into two groups. Unbeknownst to the patients, the tube was left inserted inside those in one of the groups for an additional short period at the end of the procedure for no clinical reason. This would have been physically uncomfortable, but would not generally have been as painful as when the procedure was ongoing. Instant disutility and retrospective assessment were recorded similarly to the first study, but here, in addition to peak-end evaluation and duration neglect being again observed, it was found that the group for whom the instrument was left inserted generally tended to remember the procedure as less painful than those for whom it was removed as soon as the clinically necessary procedure was over. That the former group must have experienced greater total experienced disutility as a consequence of having the procedure duration extended unnecessarily means that the authors recorded a violation of temporal monotonicity (or, in other words, dominance): the unambiguously worst experience tended to be remembered as less bad than an experience that caused less aggregate pain.

Thus, the gestalt characteristics can cause people to choose options that conflict with the assumption of experienced utility maximisation. This begs the question of whether people who succumb to the gestalts are making errors of judgment, or whether these characteristics are legitimate influences on their preferences that ought to be

small pieces with ultrasound waves. The duration of these procedures varied considerably across patients from just a few minutes to about an hour.

respected. Given that standard economic theory and behavioural welfare economics assume that people's choices ought to be consistent with utility maximisation, then one could make the case that the adherents of both of these schools of thought would see the gestalt influences as errors if they believe that utility maximisation equates to the simple aggregation of the moments of instant utility, *à la* Bentham. Perhaps the most prominent neo-Benthamite in the modern discourse is the British economist Richard Layard (2005), who expresses the view that in order to avoid inconsistency across policy actions, all laws and all rules of morality must be based on a single underlying principle, which he, following his intellectual hero, believes ought to be to secure the greatest overall happiness within any population. Since they are unreliable indicators of experienced utility, Layard and his acolytes thus distrust retrospective and prospective preferences, proposing instead a variety of experienced utility elicitation methods, including sliding scales and knobs that people can move to record their continuous mood, asking respondents to record their mood every minute or so, and the so-called day reconstruction method, where participants are required to record their current mood and their activities periodically during the day. This neo-Benthamite approach, notes the philosopher Daniel Hausman (2015), has drawn serious interest from several governments.

Nonetheless, Hausman identifies some problems with the neo-Benthamite approach, not least in relation to the way in which its advocates measure experienced utility and their claims that these measures have policy relevance. For example, he contends that the evidential connection between a person's mood in the moment and how well their life is going in relation to their health, educational achievements, financial security or any other policy consideration is weak. For example, adaptation to a poor state of affairs – for instance, to objectively defined harms imposed on a person by another party – implies that this state will not impact substantially on mood, and yet if the poor state falls within the purview of public policy then presumably policy makers would want to address it. The view that adaptation undermines subjective assessment as a means to inform public policy is associated with Amartya Sen's (1999) notion of a happy slave. That is, few would choose to be a slave even if it was known and accepted that one would adapt well to that state, because the opportunity to flourish as oneself sees fit would be substantively curtailed as a consequence.[7]

A possibly even stronger criticism of the neo-Benthamites, however, focuses on their proposal to maximise the sum of happiness and consequently to inform policy with a simple aggregation of the moments of instant utility. To return to Hausman (2015, p. 114), 'a good life is not a sum of the net goodness of its moments ... The same sum of momentary experiences can add up to a wonderful life or an incoherent and mediocre one, depending on how the experiences are ordered and what overall narrative they sustain.' Much earlier, David Hume (1777/1983) made a similar point in relation to the value of a life with an analogy of how a building cannot be valued by summing independently the values that one would place upon, for example, its roof, windows, doorway and portico without considering how these components fit together, and earlier still Aristotle (350BC/1998) noted that happiness cannot be assessed by a feeling or sensation in the moment, but can only be seen through the quality of a whole life. Therefore, when we look forward to an episode, or reflect back on it, whether it be a quite fleeting experience (e.g. watching a film), a more extended one (e.g. a summer holiday), a more extended one still (e.g. our university years), or even our whole life (or, if looking forward, what remains of it), the gestalts may matter because they give meaning to the story. In remembering, a focus on these characteristics helps us to identify where and when the peaks occurred, how severe the troughs were (perhaps many of us would wish to trade off some total utility in order to avoid volatility), whether the experience ended well

---

[7] The flipside of underestimating one's plight is exaggerating it, which can happen, according to Hausman, when transitory states seem more important to people in the moment than following a more dispassionate reflective assessment. Incidentally, we will shortly return to the importance of providing opportunities to flourish.

or badly, whether things improved or got worse, and how quickly they got better or worse etc.[8] In short, particular experiences in an event and how certain experiences fit together, and not the simple aggregation of everything, gives the event (or a life) its meaning. They in part determine how fulfilling the event was to a person, and whether the person feels they had the opportunity, or will have the opportunity, to flourish.

Prospective and retrospective evaluations might therefore give a more accurate assessment of the impact that an experience has on a person than aggregating the momentary instant utilities because they allow the person to step out of the experience and they offer a better view of how good or bad it really was in terms of its positive or negative contribution to a flourishing and fulfilling life. To give a concrete example, perhaps people tend to remember the peak moments of rearing children because an integral of all of the moments of instant utility might make the proposition of repeating the experience somewhat unattractive. Hausman (2015) himself writes that he hardly remembers the tedious moments of rearing his children, but does vividly remember the joy of reading to them and thus implicitly aligns wellbeing to fulfilment, not to moment-by-moment happiness.

Of course, many economists, such as Binmore (2005) cited in Chapters 1 and 4, would contend that the effects of the gestalts, and the concern with how the moments of an experience fit together, can be encapsulated by additional arguments in the utility function. Therefore, following this line of reasoning, when making retrospective and prospective evaluations, although neo-Benthamite utility maximisation may be violated, people may be perfectly consistent with a broader definition of utility maximisation. As noted in Chapter 4, however, there is a risk that by placing anything in the utility function, then utility maximisation can justify everything, and thus no predictions or policy advice are forthcoming – i.e. whatever a person does could be attributed to her

---

[8] For prospective assessments of expected events, the tense in this sentence can be altered accordingly.

maximising utility, which is what she ought to do, so let's leave it at that. It is of course possible that a focus on the gestalts maximises overall utility for some people; for others this focus, as well as other choices, actions and behaviours that they undertake in life, could be driven by other considerations. They trade off utility, for instance, to feel that their life has meaning or fulfilment of some kind, as I am doing right now as I write this – and as you are doing by reading it – when, as insinuated in Chapter 5, we could both be doing something more enjoyable instead.

This is not to conclude that utility, welfare and happiness are not important. Most people might well strive to maximise utility some of the time, and some may do this through a hedonistic drive for pure pleasure. I myself occasionally prioritise happiness above all else. However, we cannot know what generally drives human decisions and behaviour. As has been noted in this section, even among economists there are different views in this respect. People probably have various and varied legitimate reasons for their actions, both interpersonally and, across contexts, intrapersonally, and to assume that utility (or welfare or happiness) maximisation is the appropriate universal normative requirement is, as proclaimed by Sugden (2018), the view from nowhere.[9] I contend here, therefore, that the role of policy makers ought to be to provide opportunities for people to flourish – for them (i.e. the people) to pursue meaning and fulfilment to and in their lives (which can include striving to maximise utility) – as they see fit, subject to public resource constraints and distributional concerns.[10] Encouraging reciprocity and co-operation is likely to help people to achieve the goals that they pursue, irrespective of what those goals happen to be, unless, of course, one's goal is to be a short-sighted isolated selfish egoist.[11]

---

[9] Strictly speaking, as indicated in footnote 10 of Chapter 5, it is the view of someone (i.e. Bentham) imposed everywhere, but I will stick with Sugden's description here.

[10] That is, that the goal is to provide equitable opportunities to flourish. Incidentally, I have encountered reviewers in the past who contend that the realm of the ought is that of the preacher, not the social scientist. But since I am here attempting to provide a normative framework for behavioural public policy, I feel I ought to ought.

[11] Technically, libertarian paternalism, discussed above, does not impinge upon the target population's liberty to pursue other goals if they so wish, although some

RECIPROCITY AND FLOURISHING

Therefore, if the purpose of policy makers is to help create the conditions for people to flourish as they and the communities in which they live see fit, then encouraging reciprocity, as an aspect of behavioural public policy, is potentially an important arm of this effort. Of course, policy makers would have to guard against the possible negative consequences of reciprocity discussed in Chapter 6 – i.e. its potential to breed resentment, retaliation, retribution, cronyism, fundamentalism, nationalism and the like. But with care and through enlightened self-interest, reciprocal actions can serve as a force for groups of people to more effectively reach their preferred destinations. Some initial suggestions for how policy makers might encourage reciprocity were offered in Chapter 7, from simply emphasising the importance of this motivator of human behaviour in their rhetoric, to decentralising decision making, to ensuring that income and wealth are not concentrated excessively in the hands of a small proportion of the population.

Although this approach does not aim to instil a view from nowhere onto targeted populations – allowing people in their local communities to pursue their own goals and giving them the freedom to be innovative in designing ways in which to achieve their objectives – Chapter 8 highlighted that in most public policy settings – e.g. health, social care, education etc. – many of the objectives have already been broadly decided upon at the national or super-regional level (e.g. the production of health, the reduction of health inequalities, the reduction of hospital waiting times, the safe and compassionate care of elderly people, literacy levels at particular

> worry that since nudges often produce unreflective behaviour change, their influence is invariably unavoidable. In his recent book, the political scientist Peter John (2018) proposes that people ought to be nudged to think. For example, a description of the intention of each nudge intervention may be given alongside the nudge to see if people agree with the underlying intentions of the intervention. If so, or if not, this may be consistent with respecting what those targeted want to do with their own lives. This being said, and as also already discussed, behavioural welfare economists generally retain utility maximisation as the normative goal, which, as will now be clear, is, at the very least, contestable.

ages, school examination pass rates etc.), presumably with the acquiescence of local communities. This does not disallow the pursuit also of local-specific preferred goals or experimentation in the ways in which the goals might be achieved, so long as the general national policy sector-specific objectives remain an important focus, but it is worth noting that, unlike utility maximisation, the national objectives do not constitute a view from nowhere. They are goals specific to the policy sector in question, and were generally and broadly agreed upon following a period of open debate. Indeed, the pursuit of many of these prevailing goals was the principal reason that their associated public policy sector was established in the first place (e.g. health care sectors were established to improve – although not necessarily maximise – levels of health within populations).

Outside of the responsibility of public sector services, this framework postulates that local communities organise themselves in the ways they see fit to achieve any objectives that they wish to pursue (subject to a constraint that will be discussed in the next section). This does not necessarily require the members of the community to share the same goals – they may still reciprocate and collaborate to mutual satisfaction in their pursuit of different personal conceptions of a flourishing life. If the conditions for mutually supportive efforts towards meeting the personal goals are strengthened then the contention here is that it is reasonable to expect that their goals are more likely to be realised. One might see the pursuit of the broad objectives of public sector services – health, education etc. – as consistent with Amartya Sen's capability approach (e.g. see Sen, 1999), in that these are fundamental prerequisites for people to be able to flourish in the private sphere, whatever their private objectives may be.[12] In the private sphere, however, the argument here is that people decide for themselves on the goals that they wish to pursue, without strong input from public policy makers, who generally do not have the

---

[12] This is also the reason why basic freedoms would be protected.

capability to discern what people ought to want (i.e. although public health care services must pursue health, people in their private decisions do not have to).[13] This latter view is consistent with the liberal economic tradition, which, as earlier intimated, is exemplified most recently by Sugden (2018).[14]

With great autonomy over choice, however, there will always be opportunities for egoists to act upon their instincts. They will seek to benefit themselves without regard for, and at the expense of, others. Some versions of the liberal economic tradition recognise this, and, as starkly represented by Mill's harm principle (1859/1972), allow the regulation of private actions if those actions are imposing harms – i.e. negative externalities – on others. Mill did not seem to recognise very explicitly that an actor or organisation could use the behavioural influences such as present bias (etc.) to essentially, and often covertly,

---

[13]   If the pursuit of health (for example) at the expense of other considerations were imposed on the private sphere, then we might have a legitimate argument to force people to run for half an hour each day and to feed them mainly vegetables. But I suspect that few would want to live in such a society.

[14]   To reiterate, Sugden (2018) supports the notion of reciprocity through mutual interest, but his normative goal is to maximise opportunity without explicit reference to people's preferences partly because peoples' choices, although they might not maximise their utility, are *their* choices and are part of their identity. This resonates with Bowles's (2016, p. 192) statement, linked to the notion of reputation, that: 'When people engage in trade, produce goods and services, save and invest, vote and advocate policies, they are attempting not only to *get* things, but also to *be* someone, both in their own eyes and in the eyes of others'. That said, although Sugden and Bowles both appeal to reciprocity, their perspectives differ somewhat. Specifically, Sugden believes that people are reciprocators and that since they are the best judges of what they want, we just need to give them more opportunities. Through this lens, a well-ordered society/economy is to be understood as a co-operative venture among people who have different ideas about the constituents of wellbeing. Bowles, on the other hand, focuses on a hypothetical legislator, whose job is to create more goodness in people, resonating with Sugden's view from nowhere. According to Bowles, more reciprocity leads to more co-operation, which will in turn lead to more good being done for individuals and for society; he thus believes that laws and incentives should be shaped to crowd in social preferences. The position that I have taken aligns with Bowles in the public sphere, in that public sectors each have broadly agreed upon objectives vis-à-vis the 'good', but perhaps more closely aligns with Sugden in the private sphere, where it is not the legislator's role to determine or intervene in relation what is good for people (so long as people are not harming others). However, perhaps more Bowles-like than Sugden-like, I suggest that, in both spheres, there is the potential for reciprocity to be crowded out by other motivations, and therefore policy makers have a role to play in shaping society to guard against this possibility.

impose harms on others, and although, as noted in Chapter 5, Sugden (2018) acknowledges that such practices exist – terming them acts of obfuscation – he is seemingly ambivalent towards any government attempt to ameliorate them. Those who follow the liberal economic tradition thus appear to accept, in the main, the assumption of *caveat emptor* – let the buyer beware.

It is perhaps the case that many adherents to the liberal economic tradition place (too) much faith in the idea that the market, by fostering reciprocity, can render mute the biasing potential of the behavioural influences, but for more than a century the private marketing industry has shown that this is not the case. Akerlof and Shiller (2015), in *Phishing for Phools*, reveal that in certain sectors these activities remain rife, and can undermine mutual self-interest.[15,16] Moreover, if the products and services being sold to consumers impose potential harms on them (for example, cigarettes, high sugar content breakfast cereals, short-term loans), particularly when consumers are being manipulated into buying more of these offerings than they might otherwise choose, a strong case can be made that these behaviourally informed efforts – or harms – ought to be regulated against.

BUDGING PHISHING

There is an alternative conceptual behavioural public policy framework to the forms of paternalism discussed earlier in this chapter: behavioural regulation, applications of which are called budges (Oliver, 2013; 2015; 2017). A budge is a regulation against an activity that relies

---

[15] In previous chapters it was suggested that, over simple goods (and services), universal egoism can force what is, for all intents and purposes, a fair exchange, and that over complex goods, suppliers may often work to build trust with their consumers by demonstrating other-regarding behaviours. But none of this precludes the fact that over both types of goods, suppliers may use behavioural insights to generate increases in sales – to wit, to phish – particularly if phishing is standard practice in their industry.

[16] In addition to manipulating people with behavioural influences, Akerlof and Shiller (2015) include the exploitation of information asymmetries as a further type of phishing.

on its effectiveness by being informed by behavioural insights, and where its effectiveness imposes potential harms on others. For example, the marketing arms of confectionary companies are well aware that salience and immediacy (i.e. present-ness) can have a large effect on consumer buying patterns. This is why they have traditionally paid supermarkets substantial amounts of money to have their products displayed near to checkout counters. If we were to conclude that consumers were purchasing more confectionary than they otherwise would – and indeed, more than is good for them (and their children) – due to this particular form of product placement, then policy makers would have an intellectual justification to regulate against this activity.[17,18]

Like nudges, budges can be placed within a three dimensional diagram, which is depicted as Figure 9.2. Compared to Figure 9.1, the vertical and horizontal axes have been inverted, such that a policy placed at the origin would now be a regulation, justified by knowledge of behavioural economics, to tackle a negative externality: a pure budge.

---

[17] In the summer of 2018, the Secretary of State for Health in England announced plans to ban the sale of confectionary and fatty snacks near supermarket checkout counters (as well as introducing tighter regulations on television and online advertising of junk food and mandatory calorie count labelling in restaurants), in an effort to reduce the rate of obesity in children. See www.bbc.co.uk/news/health-44574477. Public authorities might be wise to take note that for food labelling to be effective, it probably needs to be uncomplicated. The Chilean government has mandated that unhealthy foods be labelled with a simple black warning symbol (and for foods with such a symbol, they cannot include toys and there are restrictions on the advertising of them to children). The symbol may serve as both a warning to the consumer, and as a reputational driver for the manufacturer, keen to avoid having to place it on their products. See www.npr.org/sections/thesalt/2016/08/12/486898630/chile-battles-obesity-with-stop-signs-on-packaged-foods.

[18] There is another class of budges where instead of regulating to reduce negative externalities, a policy maker may regulate to increase positive externalities. For instance, sometimes human inertia imposes harms on others. An example is where people do not opt-in to be an organ donor in countries that require such action, not because they do not want to but because they are too lazy or busy to do so. The budge here then may be to regulate so as to move the country to either presumed consent or prompted choice (where people have to choose whether to register or not when renewing their vehicle tax, for instance) for organ donor registration. For the purposes of my arguments in this chapter, however, I will stick to reducing negative externalities.

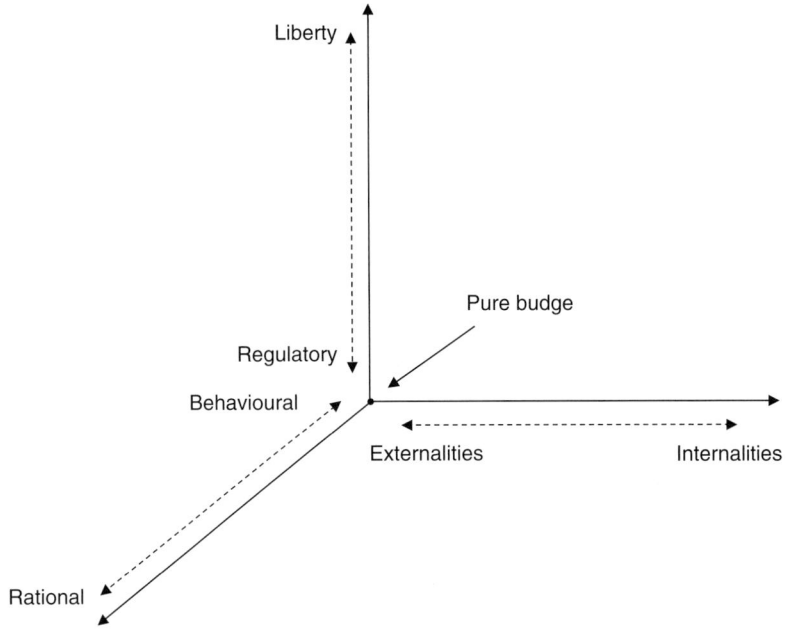

FIGURE 9.2 The requirements of behavioural regulation

There are countless examples of potentially beneficial budges, but to offer a flavour of the approach, similar to the aforementioned issue of putting confectionary close to checkout counters, supermarkets are often financially induced to place alcoholic beverages at the end of shopping aisles, in the knowledge that this salient positioning increases sales. Indeed, it has been estimated that this practice increases the sale of alcohol by as much as would be realised by dropping the price of these products by the admittedly wide margin of 4–9 per cent, which, if accurate, is clearly beneficial to alcohol suppliers (Nakamura et al., 2014). If it was broadly concluded that the end-of-aisle placement of alcoholic products was manipulating people's choices such that egoistic self-interest was imposing harms on consumers – i.e. that given the price point, it had undermined a mutually beneficial reciprocal exchange – then there would be grounds for regulating against – for budging – this practice.

In addition to food consumption (see footnote 17), at the time of writing, public authorities in England also appear to be embracing the concept of budging (even if they are not defining it as such) with respect to the gambling industry. People often gamble due to behavioural influences: for instance, they overweight the probability of winning, and anchor on the jackpot. While recognising that responsible gambling may enrich the lives of some people, the exploitation of these behavioural patterns has the potential to inflict serious harms, particularly on financially vulnerable people who are susceptible to these influences with respect to the use of fixed-odds betting terminals (e.g. roulette machines) that are readily accessible in betting shops on high streets. The gambling industry is aware of these behavioural patterns, and allow people to bet up to £100 every twenty seconds on these machines. The government has now woken up to the harms that this can cause, and has decided to regulate – to budge – to the extent that the maximum stake that the machines will be allowed to accept will be reduced to £2, to the considerable chagrin of the industry.[19]

Optimistically, regulatory authorities might not always have to do battle with industry in order for the latter to alter their practices. In the spirit of reciprocity, it may sometimes prove fruitful for public policy makers to attempt to work with those they wish to budge, by emphasising that there may be reputational, and hence commercial, benefits for those who agree more readily to be regulated, although history suggests that extending this goodwill all the way towards agreeing to industry self-regulation might best be avoided. The government could play a role here in publicising those that agree to supress their egoistic tendencies as examples of outstanding corporate responsibility, and, of course, there is always recourse to using acts of negative reciprocity against those who do not contain their egoism.

[19] See www.bbc.co.uk/news/business-44148285. It ought to be noted that evaluations will need to be undertaken to identify whether the budges mentioned here work as intended; these examples are included merely to illustrate the concept.

To conclude this chapter, it is postulated here that the principal overarching normative goal of behavioural public policy should not be to focus on moving internalities towards some conception of utility maximisation, but rather, in the spirit of the liberal economic tradition, to foster reciprocity and co-operation so that people are better equipped to flourish and give meaning and fulfilment to their lives in the ways that they see fit. But the approach goes further than liberal economics in recognising that allowing people greater freedoms affords more opportunities for the egoistically inclined to manipulate – to phish – to impose further harms on others. It is therefore suggested that when the behavioural influences – present bias, loss aversion, probability weighting and the like – are being used towards self-serving, harmful ends, then there is a legitimate intellectual justification for regulating against those harms. In one sentence, the framework proposed here is for policy makers to provide behavioural-informed opportunities for people to flourish on their own terms, and to regulate against behavioural-informed harms. No claim is made here that this approach will liberate all untapped potential or solve all of society's ills, but in contributing towards advancing the former and limiting the latter, this, to me, offers the most promising political economy of behavioural public policy.

FOOD FOR THOUGHT

1. Should policy makers interfere in personal lifestyle choices that impose no harms on others?
2. Is utility maximisation a view from nowhere?
3. Is phishing a legitimate business activity that should be of no concern to policy makers?

10 Summing Up

My contention throughout this book is that most of us, much of the time, are, in the words of Howard Becker (1956), *homo reciprocus*. Irrespective of whether or not one accepts this argument, the topic is rich – indeed, possibly the richest in all of social science and beyond. It pervades multiple disciplines and is a core feature of some of them, and yet has not until recently received substantial attention in the literature on public policy design. Given that policy design essentially concerns human behaviour in groups, the relative lack of attention paid to reciprocity seems remiss.

After considering the notion of reciprocity, the position taken in this book is aligned closely with at least some conception of the liberal economic tradition. I am not, by and large, a paternalist, if paternalism is defined by a concern with addressing internalities, although I am, of course, strongly in favour of educating people on the risks that pervade contemporary societies. Whether people then act on that information, and how they act on it, is up to them, assuming that they are imposing no harms on others. There is cause then for scepticism in relation to arguments for manipulating or coercing people in their private decisions towards goals that are not necessarily their own, because they might prefer to pursue objectives that neither I nor anyone else (other than the person concerned) can imagine.

However, in terms of ameliorating negative externalities, I would go further than, for instance, John Stuart Mill (1859/1972) and his famous harm principle, in that he did not explicitly recognise that innate influences on human behaviour, such as present bias, inertia (or status quo bias) and loss aversion, could be used for nefarious purposes. In this sense, some of the recommendations that I ultimately reach are in the spirit of Akerlof and Shiller's (2015)

Phishing for Phools. Thus, overall, although I have made a case for liberty and autonomy as opposed to too much control, some level of control, in the form of policy recommendations – such as the appropriate regulation of egoistic tendencies and the amelioration of excessive concentrations of income and wealth – that may be viewed as tinged with socialism, are necessary for there to be equitable opportunities to flourish.

It is, I feel, important to emphasise that the conclusions that I have presented did not drive the agenda of this book, at least not consciously. That is to say, I did not hold a generally anti-paternalistic point of view and then decide to commit myself to justifying it.[1] Rather, I spent several years studying the topic of reciprocity across several different disciplines, and that reading drove my conclusions. I was previously more sympathetic towards paternalism, some form of welfare maximisation and a more powerful role for the central state, for example. But I found those views dissipating the more I learned about the potential that reciprocal actions could unleash, and how policy might best be designed to harness that potential. So, in summary, what did I learn?

PRINCIPAL ARGUMENTS

Acts of reciprocity, of one sort or another, can be found everywhere. I began the book with a consideration of the different forms of reciprocity, driven variously, as they are, by purported fairness, liking and/or enlightened self-interest. Reciprocity can be direct, indirect and negative, and there is in general a concern both for the intentions of others and for the final distribution of outcomes. Reciprocity can be all of these things because its expression is highly contextual – the meaning that people attach to the way the context is framed drives behavioural responses, and if care is not taken, reciprocity can certainly be crowded out for what many may perceive as our baser instincts. In an evolutionary sense, perhaps the most fundamental

---

[1] I will allude a little to confirmation bias later in this chapter.

reason for acting reciprocally is that it can bring about benefits and protection to the group. Via the enlightened form of self-interest, many, perhaps most, people know innately that if the group of which they are a member does well, then they as individuals are likely to do well also, and over the long term will do better than if they act egoistically in the moment. Out of this evolutionary process developed a social norm, a norm that links perceptions of kindness and unkindness by others as attempts to create, sustain and undermine (intentionally or otherwise) group co-operation, and practices developed to punish, through acts of negative reciprocity, those who are inclined towards the latter.

Reciprocity has roots that predate human kind, which suggests that it is something that is quite fundamental to the animal kingdom. Much of this behaviour is seemingly instinctive – e.g. cats licking each other – but actions that can be defined as attitudinal may have served as the kernel for the development of more complex forms of reciprocity. By common consent, however – although there are some examples of non-human primates and even other species arguably demonstrating a deliberative form of reciprocity that goes beyond the mere attitudinal, and although we have much to learn about animal behaviours – a tendency towards more sophisticated forms of reciprocity that rely on memory and a sense of obligation is predominantly human. Indeed, the human talent for deliberative reciprocity and hence co-operation is probably an important reason why humans have been so successful at populating the planet and dominating other species. The urge to act reciprocally lies very deep within the human psyche. There is some evidence that very young children, for instance, sometimes even before they have developed the ability to talk, show tendencies towards reciprocal altruism and altruistic punishment (although language and gossip greatly facilitate these phenomena), and demonstrate some concern for a person's reputation, which is crucial for the effective operation of indirect reciprocity.

To gain some indication of how deep reciprocity lies in humans, we can also attempt to gather evidence on how our ancestors may have lived. Although extant tribal communities have invariably been touched by the modern world, they probably offer a reasonable approximation of the practices conducted in human societies for tens of thousands of years. Reciprocity – in both its positive and negative forms – is of fundamental importance to the functioning of tribal communities. Here, people reciprocate all the time – e.g. through sharing meat, childcare responsibilities, wisdom etc. – and within and between communities, gifts are used to bind and obligate; moreover, the threat of negative reciprocity discourages the transgression of social norms and attempts to exert power. In tribal communities, it is likely that reciprocity evolved organically for the good of the group, but as societies became larger and more atomised, creating opportunities for people to act on egoistic motivations with less fear of detection, a form of social contract was perhaps needed to nurture and sustain the socially beneficial norm of reciprocity. In short, as implied by Darwin (1879/2004), the normative postulate of the golden rule was emphasised in most of the world's religious and quasi-religious codes because it was already known implicitly that reciprocal actions are beneficial to the operation of human societies.

The study of reciprocity within some disciplines – e.g. animal behaviouralism, anthropology, philosophy, political economy, psychology and sociology – is thus longstanding. It has also attracted the interest of some of those working in the relatively new field of behavioural economics, which is apt, since behavioural economics is essentially the study of systematic patterns in human behaviour. Behavioural economists, often in collaboration with psychologists, typically study reciprocity in controlled laboratory experiments using economic games. These experiments demonstrate once again that the extent to which reciprocity is observed and sustained is dependent heavily on context, with repetition of the game, the inclusion or not of the opportunity to punish, anonymity between partners, whether the money on offer is windfall or earned, and a host of other possible factors all having an influence. The evidence on the whole also supports the notion that while intentions certainly matter, for reciprocity to be sustained over an extended period, outcomes matter too. Indeed, at least for continuation reciprocity, intentions probably matter because of the expected impact that they will ultimately have on outcomes.

As noted above, in the specific design of public policy interventions, however, reciprocity, somewhat mystifyingly, has until relatively recently been largely overlooked as a key motivator of human behaviour. Rather, the debate on public sector governance and human motivation has tended to focus on the dichotomy of pure altruism and selfish egoism, with the latter generally winning out over recent decades, possibly due to the increase in the influence of neoclassical economists on the public policy discourse in several countries since the 1970s. And yet when we examine the writings of the classical economists we find that over complex goods, the assumption that people either should be or are selfish egoists is not necessary to the efficient functioning of the market exchange, let alone the social exchange. The modern supporters of using egoism to inform the design of public policy may contend that this admittedly ever-present aspect of human behaviour can be harnessed to positive ends, but by legitimising egoism we will perhaps crowd out the aspect of human behaviour – i.e. reciprocal altruism – that is essential for generating and sustaining co-operation within groups. It would be better, I contend, to suppress egoism by harnessing reciprocity, the better angel of our natures.

That said, unless we are cautious, reciprocity can be devilish too, and can be used for malign purposes. Thus, for instance, policy makers, and others, ought to be on their guard against the potential harms that reciprocal actions can impose on third parties, and to try to ensure that fostering reciprocity and co-operation within a group does not generate or intensify any animosity that group members may feel towards outsiders. Indeed, one ought to guard against mutually reinforcing cliques forming and treating others who are ostensibly within the same broader group as outsiders, as this may create suspicion and hostility from both sides that can only damage the wider collective.

Moreover, one ought to keep an eye on whether some are being obligated to reciprocate due to differential power relationships, which potentially undermines the very notion of a fair exchange, and in relation to negative reciprocity, in order to minimise feelings of injustice, one ought to ensure that the punishment is accepted generally by all potential partners as befitting the crime. Punishment should not be informal or arbitrary, as this will risk spiralling retaliation; if this risk has been realised, then procedures for reconciliation ought to be laid down.

Notwithstanding these potential negative implications of reciprocity (and there are of course others, some of which were elaborated on in Chapter 6, including seismic issues relating to fundamentalism, and religious, ethnic and gender tolerance), reciprocity, if harnessed in the right way, can, as aforementioned, serve substantively as a force for good. Many of the extraordinary achievements of mankind – including the development of public policy sectors – would not, after all, have been possible without reciprocation and co-operation. We must create and sustain the conditions for reciprocity to flourish, some of which have been eroded in many places over time. A primary condition for reciprocity to flourish, I have argued, is for it to be emphasised and reinforced in the political discourse. In order for there to be a policy infrastructure to support reciprocal actions, the importance of reciprocity needs to be emphasised in the political rhetoric, just as an emphasis on language associated with egoism led to structures being put in place to support demand-led competition in public services. The language of reciprocity can be misused, of course (e.g. 'Lionel Messi deserves £350,000 per week'), but if we want social structures that support the basic human motivation to reciprocate and hence co-operate, then how they do so ought to be explained clearly. Relatedly, the policy discourse should not confuse reciprocal altruism with pure altruism, because the latter is not a widely held fundamental human motivation, and any policy design that is informed by it is unlikely to retain public support over the long term (giving scope for selfish egoism to gain influence).

The political scientist Michael Taylor (1987, p. 168) wrote that 'voluntary cooperative behaviors atrophy in the presence of the state and grow in its absence ... the state exacerbates the conditions which are supposed to make it necessary'.[2] Elinor Ostrom (2000), referred to throughout this book, made similar arguments. I have maintained in this book that the decentralisation of more of the management of public services to local planners, purchasers and providers, while in many countries still part of the state, would be a wise strategy to pursue, partly because securing reciprocal motivations and actions and abating egoistical ones is more difficult the larger the group, partly because this would afford greater local level innovation, which, if good results were shown, could be disseminated cross-regionally, and partly because local level actors will be more in tune with the objectives and priorities of the people they serve. In addition to a rhetorical emphasis on reciprocity and a greater decentralisation of public sector service decision-making, a general condition for fostering this motivational force is, I have contended, policy action on reducing the high concentrations of income and wealth within small percentages of the population. If one wants people to give and take it makes sense to create conditions where they do not feel that others are merely taking.

Suggestions were also offered in this book on how reciprocity may justify some slightly more specific policy directions. For instance, it was argued that so long as salaries are the predominant form of remuneration for public sector employees, performance incentives – both positive and negative – might be generally beneficial so long as all relevant parties accept that the chosen indicators of good and bad performance are appropriate and deem the corresponding performance-related compensation and penalties as fair. Moreover, insofar as reciprocity is entwined with reputational concerns, there is support here for a reputational model of governance that threatens

[2] See Montgomery and Bean (1999) for further argument and evidence that the state can frustrate rather than aid the private provision of public goods.

to punish indisputably bad absolute performance and that supports and aims to widen the implementation of innovative good practice. Relatedly, group selection theory implies that providing the conditions for reputational competition across regions in relation to a particular public sector service may incentivise greater co-operation and more innovation within each region, generating lessons and practices that could then be shared across regions. Unfortunately, although group selection theory predicts that more co-operative groups will outcompete less co-operative groups, it also predicts that selfish egoists will outcompete reciprocal altruists within each group, leading it to predict that those who gravitate to the top of each organisation are, more often than not, objectionable.[3]

As we have seen, the study of reciprocal behaviour is a focus within behavioural economics, and thus we may ask ourselves of the role it plays within behavioural public policy. In fact, it can play many roles. It is, for instance, a potentially powerful tool for the effective framing of behavioural change messages, as we saw in Chapter 8 in relation to organ donor registrations. Reciprocity may be embraced and used in whichever conceptual behavioural public policy framework one prefers and is central to the political economy of behavioural public policy postulated in Chapter 9. That is, that conditions be created that nurture reciprocal behaviours, which, if carefully designed, will help people to flourish in both meeting the already predetermined broadly defined objectives of our public sector services and in relation to their privately held goals, where they may find fulfilment in any way they wish (which includes maximising utility or happiness). In any way they wish, that is, so long as they are not imposing harms on others. The second arm of this framework is that any harms that are consequent on behaviourally informed actions are potentially fair game for regulatory control. So, promote flourishing and curtail harms: for me, that is how to frame behavioural public policy.

[3] I will leave it to the reader to reflect on whether this prediction is borne out in practice. From personal observation, if asked whether it is or not, I am rather inclined to say yes, it definitely is.

ENCORE

Typically, an encore is requested by the audience rather than the player. I am aware that my readers have not made such a request, and, figuratively speaking, they may have already left the building, but I'll offer forth a few final thoughts in any case.

Descriptively, reciprocity, at least in humans, is often deliberative and not merely attitudinal, and is fundamental to fostering co-operation; thus, assuming that co-operation is predominantly a good thing, then reciprocity is a normative requirement also. However, nobody, as far as I know, would suggest that other motivations, particularly selfish egoism, are not also common. The other principle motivations that are discussed in the literature tend to be individualistic in nature, in that they assume that we take from *or* give to others. Reciprocity differs in that it recognises implicitly that humans are, perhaps above all else, social creatures – we take from *and* give to each other. Ostrom (1998) contends that of all the motivations of human behaviour, it is this one that is key to solving problems that require collective action. Moreover, in the negative sense, reciprocity guards against the egoistical and protects those who are inclined towards altruism, pure or otherwise.

It seems almost paradoxical, then, that the demand-led competitive market, underpinned by the notion of egoism, has been embraced in social policy in many countries over the past twenty-five years, an apparently reductionist move that would have been rejected by many of the great figures in intellectual thought, across disciplines, including economics.[4] Many of the services delivered by public sectors are too complex to expect competitive markets that encourage egoism to deliver them efficiently or justly. Planned public sector services often arose, after all, because the competitive market was not an efficient or just means of delivery, and the planning and organisation of those services must encourage, rather than

---

[4] Admittedly, some great figures in the history of intellectual thought may have supported the use of competitive markets in social policy.

undermine, the obligations that the relevant members of any group ought to feel – and naturally, to a significant extent, do feel – towards each other.

Serge-Christophe Kolm (2008) contended that with regards to securing the overall quality of a society, reciprocity is the only alternative to oppressive command, although given the misery that excessive control can inflict upon people, it is questionable that oppressive command can secure much overall quality. Peter Kropotkin (1902/2014) believed that a society that was not controlled too heavily by central government would flourish through the co-operative activities within communities, and Edward Banfield (1958) argued that the ability for everyone to keep a better watch on each other at a decentralised level would reduce corruption. These points have already been emphasised earlier of course, but they provide further longstanding intellectual support for substantive autonomy at the local level and the consequent positive effect upon reciprocity and co-operation that this may have.

As noted at the beginning of this chapter, I did not hold particular policy positions – such as decentralised decision-making – close to my heart and then endeavour to justify them with a study of reciprocity.[5] Rather, the policy aims that I have argued for are, I maintain, informed by reciprocity as a basic and generally beneficial motivator of human behaviour. Therefore, I do not think I am guilty of confirmation bias in relation to seeking to emphasise an aspect of human behaviour that justifies particular policies that I *ex ante* believed in. Where I perhaps may more legitimately be accused of confirmation bias is believing that reciprocity is widespread and more powerfully beneficial than other motivations in human behaviours. As I have readily conveyed, people are motivated by different factors, such as enlightened and egoistic self-interest – and even altruism – and although most people are at various times

---

[5] Incidentally, before studying reciprocity I was more favourably inclined towards central state authority over the management of public sector services, principally in relation to securing national standards of equity in opportunities and outcomes.

influenced by all of these factors, the degree to which each individual is influenced predominantly by any one of them is probably, at least partly, biologically determined.[6] The extent to which someone finds my arguments convincing is likely to be determined by how that person herself is motivated – for instance, one might expect that a predominantly egoistical person is going to find many points of contention within the pages of this book.[7]

Complicating the matter of choosing a position to hold – and attempting to convince others of the merits of that position – is the fact that reciprocity, and indeed all other aspects of human behaviour, is highly contextual and malleable. It may be the case that there will be circumstances where reciprocal motivations are not to the fore, but as I have tried to argue in this book, it is harmful to undermine the natural inclination for people to reciprocate because, although malleable, once the urge to reciprocate has been lost to egoism, it might prove difficult to restore at the general societal level. As Banfield (1958, p. 166) wrote in relation to the poor rural Italian community that he lived among in the 1950s, 'Under the most favorable conditions it might take two or three or four generations for nature to restore and reinvigorate the social bonds which have been withered

---

[6] The positions that many people often hold are also likely to be influenced heavily by the times in which they live. For instance, Hobbes, in his proclamation of the natural state being a war of each against all, was writing at the time of the English Civil War, Mill saw co-operative endeavour in the relative peace and unprecedented global reach of nineteenth century Britain, a heavy dose of altruism in shaping public policy arose following the devastation of World War II, egoists ascended when public services (and much else) were widely believed to be failing, and – perhaps – reciprocity will benefit from a behaviourally informed scepticism that egoism is an appropriate assumption on which to shape public services.

[7] Egoists who interpret Adam Smith and Charles Darwin in their own image tend to be highly selective of the text to which they refer and suffer from a quite extreme form of confirmation bias. In my own defence, I hope I have demonstrated in this book that I have read extensively across many disciplines (although I might be chastised for not referencing von Mises, Hayek and Friedman, among others) and have become quite convinced that reciprocity is indeed a foundational motivator of human behaviour; that it evolved principally for the good of the group, and, hence, the long-term interests of the individuals within the group. But I cannot of course rule out the possibility that I suffer from confirmation bias, either in this book or more generally. It is human nature to do so, after all.

and desiccated for a century or more'. It is important that the social bonds that are still observed in most contemporary societies are not allowed to wither to the extent that Banfield observed in the society that he studied.

I have argued that autonomy can bring out the best in people. Unfortunately, it can also bring out the worst in them, which is why negative reciprocity, and the threat thereof, is needed. It is why instituting some concept of an all-seeing eye (so long as care is taken to avoid the perception of a Big Brother state), why motivating people through a concern for their own reputations, and why budging those who would otherwise impose harms on others, might all be needed to protect those who are not egoistically motivated, and to inspire people irrespective of their core motivations. Martin Nowak (2011) maintains that we ought to look beyond the idea that punishment and threat can enforce co-operation and argues that creative co-operation is better forged through friendship and reward. That is an optimistic picture and I fear that it is wrong; we will always need the threat and use of punishment to deter, or at least temper, egoistic temptations.

But let us not finish on a sour note. That we should, and often do, act reciprocally is, I contend, an idea that most people can accept. There is certainly a dark side to reciprocity, but perhaps more often than not it appeals to the better angels of our nature, and in the process generates significant individual and group benefits. Consequently, policies, institutions, organisations and sectors should be designed to encourage and sustain this most fundamental motivator of human behaviour. In short, my message is simple: don't be an egoist; be a reciprocator.

SOME FINAL FOOD FOR THOUGHT

1. Will the egoistic tend to succeed within groups, and if so, how can this be tackled?
2. Will the positions that people hold on human motivation be influenced by the times in which they live?
3. Should pure altruism, reciprocity *and* egoism be used to inform the design of public policies?

References

Aboud, F. E. 1988. *Children and Prejudice*. New York: Blackwell.

Ackerman, J. M., Nocera, C. C., and Bargh, J. A. 2010. Incidental Haptic Sensations Influence Social Judgments and Decisions. *Science* 328: 1712–15.

Adams, J. S., and Jacobsen, P. R. 1964. Effects of Wage Inequities on Work Quality. *Journal of Abnormal and Social Psychology* 69: 19–25.

Ainslie, G. 2005. You Can't Give Permission To Be a Bastard: Empathy and Self-Signaling as Uncontrollable Independent Variables in Bargaining Games. *Behavioural and Brain Sciences* 28: 815–16.

Akerlof, G. A. 1970. The Market for 'Lemons': Quality, Uncertainty and the Market Mechanism. *Quarterly Journal of Economics* 84: 488–500.

Akerlof, G. 1982. Labor Contracts as Partial Gift Exchange. *Quarterly Journal of Economics* 97: 543–69.

Akerlof, G. A., and Shiller, R. J. 2015. *Phishing for Phools: The Economics of Manipulation and Deception*. Princeton: Princeton University Press.

Alpizar, F., Carlsson, F., and Johansson-Stenman, O. 2008. Anonymity, Reciprocity, and Conformity: Evidence from Voluntary Contributions to a National Park in Costa Rica. *Journal of Public Economics* 92, 1047–60.

Ardrey, R. 1966. *The Territorial Imperative: A Personal Inquiry into the Animal Origins of Property and Nations*. New York: Atheneum Books.

Ariely, D., and Carmon, Z. 2000. Gestalt Characteristics of Experiences: The Defining Features of Summarized Events. *Journal of Behavioral Decision Making* 13: 191–201.

Aristotle. 350BC/1998. *The Nicomachean Ethics*. Oxford: Oxford University Press.

Arrow, K. 1972. Gifts and Exchanges. *Philosophy and Public Affairs* 1: 343–62.

Axelrod, R. 1984. *The Evolution of Cooperation*. New York: Basic Books.

Axelrod R., and Hamilton W. D. 1981. The Evolution of Cooperation. *Science* 211: 1390–96.

Banfield, E. C. 1958. *The Moral Basis of a Backward Society*. New York: The Free Press.

Bardsley, N. 2008. Dictator Game Giving: Altruism or Artefact? *Experimental Economics* 11: 122–33.

Bardsley, N., and Moffatt, P. 2007. The Experimetrics of Public Goods: Inferring Motivations from Contributions. *Theory and Decision* 62: 161–93.

Baron, A. S., and Banaji, M. R. 2006. The Development of Implicit Attitudes: Evidence of Race Evaluations from Ages 6, 10 and Adulthood. *Psychological Science* 17: 53–8.

Bateson, M., Nettle, D., and Roberts, G. 2006. Cues of Being Watched Enhance Cooperation in a Real-World Setting. *Biology Letters* 2: 412–14.

Becker, H. 1956. *Man in Reciprocity*. New York: Prager.

Behavioural Insights Team. 2013. *Applying Behavioural Insights to Organ Donation: Preliminary Results from a Randomised Controlled Trial*. London: Behavioural Insights Team.

Bentham, J. 1781/1988. *The Principles of Morals and Legislation*. New York: Prometheus Books.

Berlin, I. 1969. *Four Essays on Liberty*. Oxford: Oxford University Press.

Besley, T., Bevan, G., and Burchardi, K. 2009. *Naming and Shaming: The Impacts of Different Regimes on Hospital Waiting Times in England and Wales*. London: Centre for Economic Policy Research Discussion Paper 7306, London School of Economics and Political Science.

Bevan, G., and Fasolo, B. 2013. Models of Governance of Public Services: Empirical and Behavioural Analysis of Econs and Humans. In Oliver, A. (Ed.), *Behavioural Public Policy*. Cambridge University Press, Cambridge, pp. 38–62.

Bevan, G., Evans, A., and Nuti, S. 2019. Reputations Count: Why Benchmarking Performance is Improving Health Care Across the World. *Health Economics, Policy and Law* 14: Forthcoming.

Bewley, T. 1999. *Why Wages Don't Fall During a Recession*. Cambridge, MA: Harvard University Press.

Bicchieri, C. 2006. *The Grammar of Society: The Nature and Dynamics of Social Norms*. Cambridge: Cambridge University Press.

Binmore, K. 1999. Why Experiment in Economics? *The Economic Journal* 109: F16–F24.

Binmore, K. 2005. Economic Man – Or Straw Man? *Behavioral and Brain Sciences* 28: 817–18.

Blau, P. M. 1964. *Exchange and Power in Social Life*. New York: Wiley.

Boehm, C. 2012. *Moral Origins: The Evolution of Virtue, Altruism, and Shame*. New York: Basic Books.

Bowles, S. 2016. *The Moral Economy: Why Good Incentives Are No Substitute for Good Citizens*. New Haven: Yale University Press.

Boyd, R. 1989. Mistakes Allow Evolutionary Stability in the Repeated Prisoner's Dilemma Game. *Journal of Theoretical Biology* 136: 47–56.

Brosnan, S. F., and de Waal, F. B. M. 2003. Monkeys Reject Unequal Pay. *Nature* 425: 297–99.

Bruni, L., and Sugden, R. 2008. Fraternity: Why the Market Need Not Be a Morally Free Zone. *Economics and Philosophy* 24: 35–64.

Bruni, L., and Sugden, R. 2013. Reclaiming Virtue Ethics for Economics. *Journal of Economic Perspectives* 27: 141–64.

Camerer, C., and Thaler, R. 1995. Ultimatums, Dictators, and Manners. *Journal of Economic Perspectives* 9: 209–19.

Camerer, C., Issacharoff, S., Loewenstein, G., O'Donoghue, T., and Rabin, M. 2003. Regulation for Conservatives: Behavioral Economics and the Case for 'Asymmetric Paternalism'. *University of Pennsylvania Law Review* 1151: 1211–54.

Cameron, L. 1999. Raising the Stakes in the Ultimatum Game: Experimental Evidence from Indonesia. *Economic Inquiry* 37: 47–59.

Carpenter, J. P., and Matthews, P. H. 2012. Norm Enforcement: Anger, Indignation, or Reciprocity? *Journal of the European Economic Association* 10: 555–72.

Carter, G. G., and Wilkinson, G. S. 2013. Food Sharing in Vampire Bats: Reciprocal Help Predicts Donations More Than Relatedness or Harassment. *Proceedings of the Royal Society B* 280: 20122573.

Chapais, B. 1995. Alliances as a Means of Competition in Primates: Evolutionary, Developmental, and Cognitive Aspects. *Yearbook of Physical Anthropology* 38: 115–36.

Charness, G., and Rabin, M. 2002. Understanding Social Preferences With Simple Tests. *The Quarterly Journal of Economics* 117: 817–69.

Chassin, M. R. 2002. Achieving and Sustaining Improved Quality: Lessons from New York State and Cardiac Surgery. *Health Affairs* 21: 40–51.

Cherry, T. L., Frykblom, P., and Shogren, J. F. 2002. Hardnose the Dictator. *American Economic Review* 92: 1218–21.

Cialdini, R. 2001. *Influence, Science and Practice*. Boston: Allyn and Bacon.

Cohn, A., Fehr, E., and Maréchal, M. E. 2014. Business Culture and Dishonesty in the Banking Industry. *Nature* 516: 86–9.

Cole, A. 2006. *My Defence*. London: Headline Publishing Group.

Conly, S. 2013. *Against Autonomy: Justifying Coercive Paternalism*. Cambridge: Cambridge University Press.

Couch, C. 1993. *Industrial Relations and European State Traditions*. Oxford: Oxford University Press.

Credit Suisse. 2014. *Global Wealth Databook 2014*. Zurich: Credit Suisse Research Institute.

Darley, J. M., and Batson, C. D. 1973. A Study of Situational and Dispositional Variables in Helping Behavior. *Journal of Personality and Social Psychology* 27: 100–8.

Darwin, C. 1879/2004. *The Descent of Man*. London: Penguin Classics.

Dawkins, R. 1976. *The Selfish Gene*. Oxford: Oxford University Press.

Danziger, S., Levav, J., and Avnaim-Pesso, L. 2011. Extraneous Factors in Judicial Decisions. Proceedings of The National Academy of Sciences of the United States of America 108: 6889–92.

Deaton, A. 2013. *The Great Escape: Health, Wealth, and the Origins of Inequality*. Princeton: Princeton University Press.

Deci, E. L., and Ryan, R. M. 1985. *Intrinsic Motivation and Self-Determination in Human Behavior*. New York: Plenum.

Deci, E., and Ryan, R. 2000. The 'What' and 'Why' of Goal Pursuits: Human Needs and the Self-Determination of Behavior. *Psychological Enquiry* 11: 227–68.

de Dreu, C. K. W., Greer, L. L., Handgraaf, M. J. J., Shalvi, S., van Kleef, G. A., Baas, M., ten Velden, F. S., van Dijk, E., and Feith, S. W. W. 2010. The Neuropeptide Oxytocin Regulates Parochial Altruism in Intergroup Conflict Among Humans. *Science* 11: 1408–11.

Denant-Boemont, L., Masclet, D., and Noussair, C. 2007. Punishment, Counter-Punishment and Sanction Enforcement in a Social Dilemma Experiment. *Economic Theory* 33: 145–67.

Department of Health. 2001. *Learning From Bristol: Report of the Public Inquiry Into Children's Heart Surgery at the Bristol Royal Infirmary (The Kennedy Report)*. London: The Stationery Office.

de Waal, F. 2010. *The Age of Empathy: Nature's Lessons for a Kinder Society*. London: Souvenir Press.

Diamond, J. 1997. *Guns, Germs, and Steel: The Fates of Human Societies*. New York: W. W. Norton.

Disney, K., Le Grand, J., and Atkinson, G. 2013. From Irresponsible Knaves to Responsible Knights for Just 5p: Behavioural Public Policy and the Environment. In Oliver, A. (Ed.), *Behavioural Public Policy*. Cambridge: Cambridge University Press, pp.69–87.

Dolan, P., and Galizzi, M. M. 2015. Like Ripples On a Pond: Behavioral Spillovers and Their Implications for Research and Policy. *Journal of Economic Psychology* 47: 1–16.

Dreber, A., Rand D. G., Fudenberg, D., and Nowak, M. A. 2008. Winners Don't Punish. *Nature* 452: 348–51.

Dufwenberg, M., and Kirchsteiger, G. 2004. A Theory of Sequential Reciprocity. *Games and Economic Behavior* 47: 268–98.

Eisenegger, C., Naef, M., Snozzi, R., Heinrichs, M., and Fehr, E. 2010. Prejudice and Truth About the Effect of Testosterone on Human Bargaining Behaviour. *Nature* 463: 356–9.

Esping-Andersen, G. 1990. *The Three Worlds of Welfare Capitalism*. Cambridge: Polity Press.

Falk, A., and Fischbacher, U. 2006. A Theory of Reciprocity. *Games and Economic Behavior* 54: 293–315.

Falk, A., Fehr, E., and Fischbacher, U. 2003. On the Nature of Fair Behavior. *Economic Inquiry* 41: 20–6.

Falk, A., Fehr, E., and Fischbacher, U. 2008. Testing Theories of Fairness – Intentions Matter. *Games and Economic Behavior* 62: 287–303.

Fehr, E., and Falk, A. 1999. Wage Rigidity in a Competitive Incomplete Contract Market. *Journal of Political Economy* 107: 106–34.

Fehr, E., and Fischbacher, U. 2004. Third Party Punishment and Social Norms. *Evolution and Human Behavior* 25: 63–87.

Fehr, E., and Fischbacher, U. 2005. The Economics of Strong Reciprocity. In Gintis, H., Bowles, S., Boyd, R., and Fehr, E. (Eds.), *Moral Sentiments and Material Interest: The Foundation of Cooperation in Economic Life*. Cambridge, MA: MIT Press, pp.151–92.

Fehr, E., and Gächter, S. 2000a. Fairness and Retaliation: The Economics of Reciprocity. *Journal of Economic Perspectives* 14: 159–81.

Fehr, E., and Gächter, S. 2000b. Cooperation and Punishment in Public Goods Experiments. *American Economic Review* 90: 980–94.

Fehr, E., and Leibbrandt, A. 2011. A Field Study of Cooperativeness and Impatience in the Tragedy of the Commons. *Journal of Public Economics* 95: 1144–55.

Fehr, E., Gächter, S., and Kirchsteiger, G. 1997. Reciprocity as a Contract Enforcement Device: Experimental Evidence. *Econometrica* 65: 833–60.

Fischbacher, U., and Gächter, S. 2010. Social Preferences, Beliefs, and the Dynamics of Free Riding in Public Goods Experiments. *American Economics Review* 100: 541–56.

Fong, C. M., Bowles, S., and Gintis, H. 2005. Reciprocity and the Welfare State. In Gintis, H., Bowles, S., Boyd, R., and Fehr, E. (Eds.), *Moral Sentiments and Material Interest: The Foundation of Cooperation in Economic Life*. Cambridge, MA: MIT Press, pp. 277–302.

Forsythe, R., Horowitz, J., Savin, E., and Sefton, M. 1994. Replicability, Fairness and Pay in Experiments with Simple Bargaining Games. *Games and Economics Behavior* 6: 347–69.

Fredrickson, B. L., and Kahneman, D. 1993. Duration Neglect in Retrospective Evaluations of Affective Episodes. *Journal of Personality and Social Psychology* 65: 44–55.

Frey, B. 2013. How Should People Be Rewarded For Their Work? In Oliver, A. (Ed.), *Behavioural Public Policy*. Cambridge: Cambridge University Press, pp. 165–183.

Gächter, S., Kölle, F., and Quercia, S. 2017. Reciprocity and the Tragedies of Maintaining and Providing the Commons. *Nature Human Behaviour* 1: 650–656.

Galizzi, M. M., and Navarro-Martínez, D. Forthcoming. On the External Validity of Social Preference Games: A Systematic Lab-Field Study. *Management Science*.

Genovesi, A. 1765–67/2005. *Delle Lezioni di Commercio o sia di Economia Civile*. Napoli: Instituto Italiano per gli Studi Filofící.

Gintis, H., Bowles, S., Boyd, R., and Fehr, E. 2005. Moral Sentiments and Material Interests: Origins, Evidence, and Consequences. In Gintis, H., Bowles, S., Boyd, R., and Fehr, E. (Eds.), *Moral Sentiments and Material Interest: The Foundation of Cooperation in Economic Life*. Cambridge, MA: MIT Press, pp.3–40.

Gneezy, U., and Rustichini, A. 2000. A Fine is a Price. *The Journal of Legal Studies* 29: 1–17.

Gospic, K., Mohlin, E., Fransson, P., Petrovic, P., Johannesson, M., and Ingvar, M. 2011. Limbic Justice: Amygdala Involvement in Immediate Rejections in the Ultimatum Game. *PloSOne* 9: e1001054.

Gouldner, A. W. 1960. The Norm of Reciprocity: A Preliminary Statement. *American Sociological Review* 25: 161–78.

Güth, W., Schmittberger, R., and Schwarze, B. 1982. An Experimental Analysis of Ultimatum Bargaining. *Journal of Economic Behavior & Organization* 3: 367–88.

Haidt, J. 2012. *The Righteous Mind: Why Good People Are Divided by Politics and Religion*. London: Penguin.

Hallsworth, M., Snijders, V., Burd, H., Prestt, J., Judah, G., Huf, S., and Halpern, D. 2016. *Applying Behavioural Insights: Simple Ways to Improve Health Outcomes*. London: Behavioural Insights Team.

Harbaugh, W. T., and Krause, K. 2000. Children's Altruism in Public Goods and Dictator Experiments. *Economic Inquiry* 38: 95–109.

Harbaugh, W. T., Mayr, U., and Burghart, T. R. 2007. Neural Responses to Taxation and Voluntary Giving Reveal Motives for Charitable Donations. *Science* 316: 1622–5.

Hardin, G. 1968. The Tragedy of the Commons. *Science* 162: 1243–8.

Hausman, D. M. 2015. *Valuing Health: Well-Being, Freedom and Suffering.* Oxford: Oxford University Press.

Heath, A. 1976. *Rational Choice and Exchange: A Critique of Exchange Theory.* Cambridge: Cambridge University Press.

Helanterä, H. 2009. Do Unicolonial Wood Ants Favor Kin? *Journal of Biology* 8: 56, https://doi.org/10.1186/jbiol154.

Henrich, J. 2000. Does Culture Matter in Economic Behaviour: Ultimatum Game Bargaining among the Machiguenga of the Peruvian Amazon. *American Economic Review* 90: 973–979.

Henrich, J. 2016. *The Secret of our Success: How Culture is Driving Human Evolution, Domesticating Our Species and Making us Smarter.* Princeton: Princeton University Press.

Henrich, N., and Henrich, J. 2007. *Why Humans Cooperate: A Cultural and Evolutionary Explanation.* Oxford: Oxford University Press.

Henrich, J., Boyd, R., Bowles, S., Camerer, C., Fehr, E., Gintis, H., McElreath, R., Alvard, M., Barr, A., Ensminger, J., Smith Henrich, N., Hill, K., Gil-White, F., Gurven, M., Marlowe, F. W., Patton, J. Q., and Tracer, D. 2005. 'Economic Man' in Cross-Cultural Perspective: Behavioral Experiments in 15 Small-Scale Societies. *Behavioral and Brain Sciences* 28: 795–855.

Héritier, A., and Lehmkuhl, D. 2008. The Shadow of Hierarchy and New Modes of Governance. *Journal of Public Policy* 28: 1–17.

Herrmann, B., Thoni, C., and Gächter, S. 2008. Antisocial Punishment Across Societies. *Science* 319: 1362–7.

Hibbard, J. H., Stockard, J., and Tusler, M. 2003. Does Publicizing Hospital Performance Stimulate Quality Improvement Efforts? *Health Affairs* 22, 84–94.

Hibbard, J. H., Stockard, J., and Tusler, M. 2005. Hospital Performance Reports: Impact on Quality, Market Share, and Reputation. *Health Affairs* 24, 1150–60.

Hobbes, T. 1651/1962. *Leviathan.* London: Macmillan.

Honeyman, G. 2017. *Eleanor Oliphant Is Completely Fine.* London: HarperCollins, 2017.

Hsee, C. K., and Abelson, R. P. 1991. Velocity Relation: Satisfaction as a Function of the First Derivative of Outcome Over Time. *Journal of Personality and Social Psychology* 60: 341–7.

Hume, D. 1739–40/1978. *A Treatise of Human Nature.* Oxford: Oxford University Press.

Hume, D. 1742/1975. Of the Independency of Parliament. In Green, T.H. and Gross, T.H. (Eds.) *Essays, Moral, Political and Literary*, Volume 1. London: Longmans.

Hume, D. 1777/1983. *An Enquiry Concerning the Principles of Morals.* Indianapolis: Hackett Publishing Company.

Isaac, R. M., Walker, J., and Williams, A. W. 1994. Group Size and the Voluntary Provision of Public Goods: Experimental Evidence Utilizing Large Groups. *Journal of Public Economics* 54: 1–36.

John, P. 2018. *How Far to Nudge? Assessing Behavioural Public Policy.* Cheltenham: Edward Elgar Publishing.

Kahan, D. M. 2005. The Logic of Reciprocity: Trust, Collective Action, and Law. In Gintis, H., Bowles, S., Boyd, R. and Fehr, E. (Eds.), *Moral Sentiments and Material Interest: The Foundation of Cooperation in Economic Life.* Cambridge, MA: MIT Press.

Kahneman, D. 2011. *Thinking, Fast and Slow.* London: Allen Lane.

Kahneman, D., Knetsch, J. L., and Thaler, R. H. 1986. Fairness and the Assumptions of Economics. *Journal of Business* 59: s285–s300.

Kahneman, D., Wakker, P. P., and Sarin, R. 1997. Back to Bentham? Explorations of Expected Utility. *The Quarterly Journal of Economics* 112: 375–405.

Kim, R., Hill, R. S., Walker, M. B., Eder, J., Headland, T., Hewlett, B., Hurtado, A. M., Marlowe, F., Wiessner, P., and Wood, B. 2011. Co-Residence Patterns in Hunter-Gatherer Societies Show Unique Human Social Structure. *Science* 11: 1286–9.

Klein, R. 2001. *The New Politics of the NHS.* Fourth Edition. Harlow: Pearson Education.

Kollock, P. 1994. The Emergence of Exchange Structures: An Experimental Study of Uncertainty, Commitment, and Trust. *American Journal of Sociology* 100: 313–45.

Kolm, S.-C. 2008. *Reciprocity: An Economics of Social Relations.* Cambridge: Cambridge University Press.

Kropotkin, P. 1902/2014. *Mutual Aid: A Factor in Evolution.* Seattle: Createspace Independent Publishing Platform.

Kurzban, R., DeScioli, P., and O'Brien, E. 2007. Audience Effects on Moralistic Punishment. *Evolution and Human Behavior* 28: 75–84.

Layard, R. 2005. *Happiness: Lessons From a New Science.* London: Allen Lane.

Legg, P. 2017. *Crime in the Second World War: Spivs, Scoundrels, Rogues and Worse.* Wiltshire: Sabrestorm Publishing.

Le Grand, J. 1997. Knights, Knaves or Pawns? Human Behaviour and Social Policy. *Journal of Social Policy* 26: 149–69.

Le Grand, J. 2003. *Motivation, Agency, and Public Policy: Of Knights & Knaves, Pawns & Queens.* Oxford: Oxford University Press.

Leimar, O., and Hammerstein, P. 2001 Evolution of Cooperation through Indirect Reciprocity. *Proceedings of the Royal Society B* 268: 745–753.

Levi, M. 1988. *Of Rule and Revenue*. Berkeley: University of California Press.

Loewenstein, G., and Prelec, D. 1993. Preferences For Sequences of Outcomes. *Psychological Review* 100: 91–8.

Lorenz, K. 191966/2002. *On Aggression*. London: Routledge Classics.

Lowndes, V., and Skelcher, C. 1998. The Dynamics of Multi-Organizational Partnerships: An Analysis of Changing Modes of Governance. *Public Administration* 76: 313–33.

Lucas, M. M., Wagner, L., and Chow, C. 2008. Fair Game: The Intuitive Economics of Resource Exchange in Four-Year Olds. *Journal of Social, Evolutionary, and Cultural Psychology* 2: 74–88.

Machiavelli, N. 1532/1997. *The Prince*. New Haven: Yale University Press.

Malinowski, B. 1932. *Crime and Custom in Savage Society*. London: Paul, Trench, Trubner.

Martin, C. F., Bhui, R., Bossaerts, P., Matsuzawa, T., and Camerer, C. F. 2014. Experienced Chimpanzees Are More Strategic Than Humans in Competitive Games. *Scientific Reports* 4: 5182.

Mauss, M. 1954. *The Gift: Forms and Functions of Exchange in Archaic Societies*. Glencoe, IL: The Free Press.

McKelvey, R., and Palfrey, T. 1992. An Experimental Study of the Centipede Game. *Econometrica* 60: 803–36.

Mill, J. S. 1871/1909. *Principles of Political Economy*. First edition 1848. London: Longmans.

Mill, J. S. 1859/1972. *On Liberty*. London: Dent.

Mill, J. S. 1861/1972. *Utilitarianism*. London: Dent.

Mill, J. S. 1869/1988. *The Subjection of Women*. Indianapolis, IN: Hackett.

Montesquieu. 1748/1989. *The Spirit of the Laws*. Cambridge: Cambridge University Press.

Montgomery, M. R., and Bean, R. 1999. Market Failure, Government Failure, and the Private Supply of Public Goods: The Case of Climate-Controlled Walkway Networks. *Public Choice* 99: 403–37.

Morton, A. L. 191969/1978. *The Life and Ideas of Robert Owen*. New York: International Publishers.

Murnighan, J. K., and Saxon, M. S. 1998. Ultimatum Bargaining by Children and Adults. *Journal of Economic Psychology* 19: 415–45.

Nagel, T. 1986. *The View from Nowhere*. Oxford: Oxford University Press.

Nakamura, R., Pechey, R., Suhrcke, M., Jebb, S. A., and Marteau, T. M. 2014. Sales Impact of Displaying Alcoholic and Non-Alcoholic Beverages in End-of-Aisle Locations: An Observational Study. *Social Science & Medicine* 108: 68–73.

Nikiforakis, N. 2008. Punishment and Counter-Punishment in Public Good Games: Can We Really Govern Ourselves? *Journal of Public Economics* 92: 91–112.

Nowak, M. 2011. *Super Cooperators: Beyond the Survival of the Fittest. Why Cooperation, not Competition, is the Key to Life.* Edinburgh: Canongate Books.

Nowak, M., and Sigmund, K. 1992. Tit for Tat in Heterogeneous Populations. *Nature* 355: 250–3.

Oliver, A. 2007. The Veterans Health Administration: An American Success Story? *Milbank Quarterly* 85: 5–35.

Oliver, A. 2013. From Nudging to Budging: Using Behavioural Economics to Inform Public Sector Policy. *Journal of Social Policy* 42: 685–700.

Oliver, A. 2015. Nudging, Shoving and Budging: Behavioural Economic-Informed Policy. *Public Administration* 93: 700–14.

Oliver, A. 2017. *The Origins of Behavioural Public Policy.* Cambridge: Cambridge University Press.

Oliver, A. 2018. Do Unto Others: On the Importance of Reciprocity in Public Administration. *American Review of Public Administration* 48: 279–90.

Olson, M. 1965. *The Logic of Collective Action: Public Goods and the Theory of Groups.* Cambridge, MA: Harvard University Press.

Ostrom, E. 1990. *Governing the Commons. The Evolution of Institutions for Collective Action.* New York: Cambridge University Press.

Ostrom, E. 1998. A Behavioural Approach to the Rational Choice Theory of Collective Action: Presidential Address, American Political Science Association, 1997. *The American Political Science Review* 92: 1–22.

Ostrom, E. 2000. Collective Action and the Evolution of Social Norms. *Journal of Economic Perspectives* 14: 137–58.

Ostrom, E. 2005. Policies that Crowd Out Reciprocity and Collective Action. In Gintis, H., Bowles, S., Boyd, R., and Fehr, E. (Eds.), *Moral Sentiments and Material Interest: The Foundation of Cooperation in Economic Life.* Cambridge, MA: MIT Press.

Parsons, T. 1951. *The Social System.* Glencoe, IL: Free Press.

Piketty, T. 2014. *Capital in the Twenty-First Century.* Cambridge, MA: Harvard University Press.

Pinker, R. 2006. From Gift Relationships to Quasi-Markets: An Odyssey along the Policy Paths of Altruism and Egoism. *Social Policy & Administration* 40: 10–25.

Pinker, S. 2011. *The Better Angels of Our Nature: Why Violence Has Declined.* New York: Penguin.

Pinker, S. 2018. *Enlightenment Now: The Case for Reason, Science, Humanism and Progress.* London: Allen Lane.

Rabin, M. 1993. Incorporating Fairness into Game Theory and Economics. *The American Economic Review* 83: 1281–1302.

Rand, D. G., Yoeli, E., and Hoffman, M. 2014. Harnessing Reciprocity to Promote Cooperation and the Provisioning of Public Goods. *Policy Insights from the Behavioral and Brain Sciences*, 1: 263–9.

Redelmeier, D. A., and Kahneman, D. 1996. Patient's Memories of Painful Medical Treatments: Real-Time and Retrospective Evaluations of Two Minimally Invasive Procedures. *Pain* 66: 3–8.

Redelmeier, D., Katz, J., and Kahneman, D. 2003. Memories of Colonoscopy: A Randomized Trial. *Pain* 104: 187–94.

Roth, A. 1995. Bargaining Experiments. In Kagel, J., and Roth, A. (Eds.), *Handbook of Experimental Economics*. Princeton: Princeton University Press, pp. 254–348.

Rousseau, J.-J. 1755/2009. *Discourse on the Origin of Inequality*. Oxford: Oxford University Press.

Rustagi, D., Engel, S., and Kosfeld, M. 2010. Conditional Cooperation and Costly Monitoring Explain Success in Forest Commons Management. *Science* 330: 961–5.

Sandel, M. J. 2013. *What Money Can't Buy: The Moral Limits of Markets*. London: Penguin Books.

Sapolsky, R. 2017. *Behave: The Biology of Humans at Our Best and Worst*. London: Bodley Head.

Sen, A. 1999. *Development as Freedom*. New York: Random House.

Sethi, R., and Somanathan, E. 2001. Preference Evolution and Reciprocity. *Journal of Economic Theory* 97: 273–97.

Sethi, R., and Somanathan, E. 2005. Norm Compliance and Strong Reciprocity. In Gintis, H., Bowles, S., Boyd, R., and Fehr, E. (Eds.), *Moral Sentiments and Material Interest: The Foundation of Cooperation in Economic Life*. Cambridge, MA: MIT Press, pp. 229–50.

Silk, J. B. 2005. The Evolution of Cooperation in Primate Groups. In Gintis, H., Bowles, S., Boyd, R., and Fehr, E. (Eds.), *Moral Sentiments and Material Interest: The Foundation of Cooperation in Economic Life*. Cambridge, MA: MIT Press, pp. 43–74.

Smith, A. 1759/2009. *The Theory of Moral Sentiments*. London: Penguin Classics.

Smith, A. 1776/1999. *The Wealth of Nations*, Book 1. London: Penguin Classics.

Smith, E. A., and Bird, R. B. 2005. Costly Signalling and Cooperative Behavior. In Gintis, H., Bowles, S., Boyd, R., and Fehr, E. (Eds.), *Moral Sentiments and Material Interest: The Foundation of Cooperation in Economic Life*. Cambridge, MA: MIT Press, pp. 115–48.

Steinbeck, J. 1963. *East of Eden*. London: Pan Books.

Stiglitz, J. E. 2012. *The Price of Inequality*. London: Penguin Books.

Strobel, A., Zimmermann, J., Schmitz, A., Reuter, M., Lis, S., Windmann, S., and Kirsch, P. 2011. Beyond Revenge: Neural and Genetic Bases of Altruistic Punishment. *NeuroImage* 54: 671–80.

Sugden, R. 1986. *The Economics of Rights, Cooperation and Welfare*. Oxford: Basil Blackwell.

Sugden, R. 2018. *The Community of Advantage: A Behavioural Defence of the Liberal Tradition of Economics*. Oxford: Oxford University Press.

Tabellini, G. 2008. Institutions and Culture. *Journal of the European Economic Association* 6: 255–94.

Tajfel, H. 1982. Social Psychology of Intergroup Relations. *Annual Review of Psychology* 33: 1–39.

Taylor, M. 1987. *The Possibility of Cooperation*. Cambridge: Cambridge University Press.

Thaler, R. H. 2015. *Misbehaving: The Making of Behavioural Economics*. New York: Penguin Random House.

Thaler, R. H., and Sunstein, C. R. 2003. Libertarian Paternalism. *The American Economic Review* 93: 175–9.

Thaler, R. H., and Sunstein, C. R. 2008. *Nudge: Improving Decisions About Health, Wealth and Happiness*. New Haven: Yale University Press.

Thurnwald, R. 1932. *Economics in Primitive Communities*. London: Oxford University Press.

Titmuss, R. M. 191970/1997. *The Gift Relationship: From Human Blood to Social Policy*. New York: The New Press.

Tomasello, M. 2009. *Why We Cooperate*. Cambridge, MA: MIT Press.

Tomasello, M., Carpenter, M., Call, J., Behne, T., and Moll, H. 2005. Understanding and Sharing Intentions: The Origins of Cultural Cognition. *Behavioral and Brain Sciences* 28: 675–91.

Treib, O., Bähr, H., and Falkner, G. 2007. Modes of Governance: Towards a Conceptual Clarification. *Journal of European Public Policy* 14: 1–20.

Trivers, R. L. 1971. The Evolution of Reciprocal Altruism. *The Quarterly Review of Biology* 46: 35–57.

Wilkinson, G. S. 1984. Reciprocal Food Sharing in the Vampire Bat. *Nature* 308: 181–4.

Wilson, D. S. 2015. *Does Altruism Exist? Culture, Genes, and the Welfare of Others*. New Haven: Yale University Press.

Wilson, D. S., and Wilson, E. O. 2007. Rethinking the Theoretical Foundation of Sociobiology. *Quarterly Review of Biology* 82: 327–48.

Wilson, E. O. 1971. *The Insect Societies*. Cambridge, MA: Harvard University Press.

Wolff. J. 2003. *Why Read Marx Today?* Oxford: Oxford University Press.

Wynne-Edwards, V.C. 1986. *Evolution through Group Selection*. London: Blackwell Science.

Xiong, X., Guo, S., Gu, L., Huang, R., and Zhou, X. 2018. Reciprocity Anxiety: Individual Differences in Feeling Discomfort in Reciprocity Situations. *Journal of Economic Psychology* 67: 149–61.

Yamagishi, T. 1986. The Provision of a Sanctioning System as a Public Good. *Journal of Personality and Social Psychology* 51: 110–16.

Zak, P. J. 2012. *The Moral Molecule: The New Science of What Makes Us Good or Evil*. London: Bantam Press.

Index

Absolute income, 124
Ackerman, Joshua, 128
Adams, J. Stacy, 131
Adaptation, 154
Agriculture, 22
Ainslie, George, 57
Akerlof, George, 32, 72, 85, 94, 130, 131, 137, 161, 166
All-seeing eye, 177
Altruistic punishment, 4, 12, 13, 14, 17, 71, 79, 101, 102, 104, 168
Amoral familists, 53
Anonymity, 28
Antisocial punishment, 49
Ants, 22
Aristotle, 155
Arrow, Kenneth, 83, 143
Asch, Solomon, 36
Asymmetric paternalism, 148
Attenborough, David, 27
Attitudinal reciprocity, 2, 12, 168
Autonomy, 98, 117, 137, 149, 158, 160, 167, 177
Axelrod, Robert, 2

Balance reciprocity, 4, 9
Banfield, Edward, 52, 53, 54, 175, 176
Bardsley, Nick, 66
Becker, Howard, 166
Behavioural Insights Team, 144
Behavioural public policy, 143, 147, 148, 157, 158, 161, 165, 173
Behavioural welfare economics, 151, 154
Bentham, Jeremy, 83, 151, 157
Bevan, Gwyn, 139, 142
Bicchieri, Cristina, 14
Binmore, Kenneth, 8, 57
Bird, Rebecca Bliege, 17
Blair, Tony, 87
Blau, Peter, 78
Bowles, Samuel, 35, 44, 69, 85, 111, 160

Bruni, Luigino, 79
Budge, 161, 162, 163, 164, 177

Camerer, Colin, 148
Capability approach, 159
Capuchins, 27, 73
Centipede game, 66
Chapais, Bernard, 29
Chickens, 43, 94
Chimpanzees, 29, 30, 31
Choice architecture, 88, 149
Cialdini, Robert, 97
Coercion, 97, 148
Coercive hierarchy, 3
Coercive paternalism, 150
Co-evolutionary theory, 43
Common pool resources, 116, 118, 136
Competition, 89, 90, 91
Confirmation bias, 167, 175, 176
Confucius, 1
Continuation reciprocity, 4, 9, 113, 133, 170
Contractarianism, 84, 169
Cronyism, 105
Crouch, Colin, 108
Crowding, 15, 18, 86, 91, 125, 135, 160, 167, 170
Culture, 13

Darwin, Charles, 14, 21, 39, 169, 176
Dawkins, Richard, 24, 43
Day reconstruction method, 154
Daziger, Shai, 128
de Dreu, Carsten, 63
de Waal, Frans, 27, 28, 32
Decentralisation, 120, 121, 126, 135, 172, 175
Deci, Edward, 49, 117
Desert, 113, 123
Diamond, Jared, 42
Dictator game, 64
Direct reciprocity, 2, 12, 167
Dreber, Anna, 101

Dufwenberg, Martin, 59
Duration neglect, 153
Dyadic exchange, 2

Egoism, xiv, 3, 4, 8, 13, 17, 30, 31, 36, 38, 58, 60, 67, 72, 76, 79, 86, 87, 88, 90, 91, 92, 97, 114, 115, 118, 125, 129, 132, 133, 149, 160, 161, 164, 167, 168, 169, 170, 171, 172, 174, 175, 176, 177
Eisenegger, Christoph, 10
Enlightened self-interest, 5, 31, 38, 61, 81, 86, 91, 116, 130, 133, 158, 167, 175
Esping-Andersen, Gøsta, 108, 113, 125
Eusocial insects, 22, 23
Evolution, 22, 23
Exotic preferences, 58
External validity, 66
Externalities, 85, 90, 92, 93, 97, 104, 109, 124, 147, 149, 160, 162, 163, 165, 166, 170, 173, 177

Falk, Armin, 60
Fascism, 108
Fasolo, Barbara, 139, 142
Fehr, Ernst, 10, 70, 72, 130
Ferguson, Alex, 20
Fig wasps, 25
Fishing, 117
Flourishing, 152, 155, 156, 157, 158, 159, 165, 167, 173
Fulfilment, 156, 157, 165

Galizzi, Matteo, 72
Gambling, 164
Generalised reciprocity, 5, 12
Genovesi, Antonio, 79
Gestalt characteristics, 152, 153, 155
Gintis, Herbert, 44
Gneezy, Uri, 129
Golden rule, 1, 169
Gossip, 35, 108
Gouldner, Alvin, 4, 104
Greatest happiness principle, 151
Grooming, 26
Group selection, 24, 25, 41, 54, 60, 95, 119, 142, 173

Haidt, Jonathan, 14, 44
Haig, David, 6
Haldane, J. B. S., 40

Hallsworth, Michael, 144
Hamilton, Alexander, 88
Happiness, 147, 151, 157, 173
Harbaugh, William, 98
Hardin, Garrett, 116
Harm principle, 150, 160, 166
Hausman, Daniel, 154, 155, 156
Heath, Anthony, 47, 76
Henrich, Joseph, 13, 34, 35, 41, 42, 50
Herrman, Benedikt, 70
Hibbard, Judith, 140
Hierarchical punishment, 101, 104
Hierarchy, 28
Hillel the Elder, 1
Hobbes, Thomas, 38, 39, 176
Homo reciprocus, 166
Hospital star rating system, 139
Hume, David, 5, 39, 81, 88, 155
Hunter-gatherers, 33, 41, 45, 49, 50

Identity, 105, 110, 136, 160
Income/wealth concentration, 124, 126, 130, 172
Incomplete contracts, 129, 131
Indirect reciprocity, 5, 6, 12, 34, 35, 108, 120, 143, 167
Individual selection, 24, 29
Inequality, 125
Infants, 33, 95, 168
Information asymmetry, 81, 82, 85, 89, 90, 131, 133, 139, 161
Intentions, 59, 60
Inter-group learning, 120
Internalities, 147, 149, 165, 166
Intrinsic motivation, 136

Jacobsen, Patricia, 131
Japanese macaques, 29
John, Peter, 158

Kahan, Dan, 135
Kahneman, Daniel, 147, 152
Killer whales, 25
Kin selection, 23, 28, 40, 53
Kirchsteiger, Georg, 59
Knaves, 88, 90
Knights, 88, 90
Kollock, Peter, 131
Kolm, Serge-Christophe, 3, 77, 175

INDEX 193

Kropotkin, Peter, 20, 24, 25, 45, 99, 113, 122, 135, 175

Layard, Richard, 154
Le Grand, Julian, 87, 88, 89, 91
League table competition, 119
Liberal economic tradition, 84, 86, 148, 160, 161, 165, 166
Libertarian paternalism, 147, 148, 151, 157
Liberty, 147, 149
Liking reciprocity, 4, 10, 113
Loneliness, 125
Loss aversion, 149, 166
Lowndes, Vivien, 138

Machiavelli, Niccolò, 89
Madison, James, 88
Malinowski, Bronislaw, 52
Market for lemons, 131
Matching pennies, 30
Matching reciprocity, 4
Mauss, Marcel, 1, 46, 47, 76
McKelvey, Richard, 67
Meerkats, 43
Messaging, 144
Mill, John Stuart, 82, 85, 86, 92, 148, 150, 160, 166, 176
Missed hospital appointments, 144
Moralistic aggression. *See* Negative reciprocity
Morton, A. L., 137
Mutual aid, 21, 24, 38
Mutualistic symbiosis, 25

Nagel, Thomas, 83
Nash equilibrium, 31, 63
Nash, John, 31
National Health Service, 121, 122, 139
Nationalism, 107
Navarro-Martinez, Daniel, 72
Negative reciprocity, 1, 12, 22, 27, 33, 36, 50, 64, 71, 80, 99, 101, 104, 109, 116, 118, 122, 129, 136, 143, 164, 167, 168, 171, 177
Neoclassical economics, 84, 86, 92, 151, 154, 170
New Testament, 1
Nowak, Martin, 2, 4, 6, 22, 25, 35, 60, 71, 101, 108, 118, 177
Nudge, 147, 148, 149
Nuti, Sabina, 140

Obfuscation, 161
Old Testament, 1
Olson, Mancur, 115, 118
Opportunity, 160
Organ donation, 144, 162, 173
Ostriches, 25
Ostrom, Elinor, 34, 49, 99, 105, 114, 116, 117, 121, 130, 136, 172, 174
Outgroups, 95, 105, 107, 109, 119
Owen, Robert, 137
Oxytocin, 10, 11, 63

Palfrey, Thomas, 67
Parsons, Talcott, 2, 80
Paternalism, 148, 150, 161, 166
Pay-for-performance, 134, 135, 145, 172
Peace, 86
Peak-end evaluation, 152
Peer punishment, 101
Phishing, 89, 94, 98, 161, 165, 167
Pinker, Robert, 91
Pinker, Steven, 43, 100, 105, 124
Pipesuckers, 93
Pollyanna Fallacy, 112
Power asymmetry, 81, 85, 98, 109, 171
Present bias, 84, 149, 150, 160, 166
Prestige-cue, 34
Priming, 15, 137
Principal-agent problem, 131
Prisoner's dilemma, 62, 63, 101, 103
Public goods game, 68, 69, 70
Public reporting, 140
Pure altruism, xiv, 3, 14, 17, 87, 91, 112, 114, 125, 170, 171, 174, 175

Rabin, Matthew, 59
Rationality, xiv, 30, 88, 118, 129, 131, 149, 151
Reciprocal altruism, 1, 4, 12, 17, 26, 64, 68, 71, 78, 79, 80, 97, 115, 168, 170, 171
Reciprocity anxiety, 96
Redelmeier, Donald, 152
Reef cleaner fish, 25
Regulation, 117, 147, 148, 149, 161, 162
Relative income, 124
Relative price mechanism, 129
Repeated games, 69, 101
Reputation, 6, 12, 33, 35, 38, 50, 119, 132, 133, 138, 139, 140, 142, 145, 160, 162, 164, 168, 172, 177

Reputational competition, 142
Resentment, 96, 98
Retaliation, 99, 100, 101, 102, 104, 110, 171
Retribution, 99
Reverse reciprocity, 6, 12
Rhinoceros, 93
Rousseau, Jean-Jacques, 39
Rustagi, Devesh, 73
Rustichini, Aldo, 129
Ryan, Richard, 49, 117

Sandel, Michael, 78, 82, 129
Sapolsky, Robert, 4, 10, 11, 24, 33, 40, 49, 50, 107, 114, 125
Self-determination theory, 49
Sen, Amartya, 155, 159
Sethi, Rajiv, 120, 146
Shiller, Robert, 32, 85, 94, 137, 161, 166
Shirking, 130
Shrimp fishermen, 73
Silk, Joan, 44
Skelcher, Chris, 138
Smith, Adam, 63, 76, 79, 81, 86, 89, 92, 132, 176
Smith, Eric, 17
Social media, 109
Social norms, 13, 14, 34, 50, 58, 115, 116, 117, 120, 124, 125, 126, 168, 169
Somanathan, Eswaran, 120, 146
Spillover effects, 11
Strong reciprocity, 15
Sugden, Robert, 34, 39, 68, 71, 79, 81, 82, 83, 85, 124, 148, 160, 161
Sunstein, Cass, 88, 149
Superorganisms, 23

Tabellini, Guido, 85
Taylor, Michael, 172
Temporal monotonicity, 153
Testosterone, 10, 11

Thaler, Richard, 88, 147, 149
The gift exchange, 47, 76
The Qur'an, 1
The Torah, 1
The view from nowhere, 58, 83, 157
Thurnwald, Richard, 49
Tit for tat, 2, 63, 69
Titmuss, Richard, 77, 87
Tomasello, Michael, 29, 33
Total prestation, 46
Tragedy of the commons, 116
Treib, Oliver, 138
Trivers, Robert, 1, 25
Trust, 10, 17, 32, 34, 38, 67, 78, 85, 124, 125, 126, 131, 133, 135, 138, 139, 142
Trust game, 67
Tuscan performance mechanism, 142
Tuscany, 140

Ultimatum game, 7, 47, 64
Utilitarianism, 151
Utility, 57, 83, 87, 147, 151, 153, 155, 156, 157, 165, 173

Vampire bats, 26
Veterans Health Administration, 119

Wages, 129, 136
Welfare, 147, 151, 157
Whistle blowing, 102, 109
Wilkinson, Gerald, 26
Wilson, David Sloan, 44, 111, 118
Wilson, Edward O., 22
Wynne-Edwards, V. C., 24

Xiong, Xiling, 96

Yamagishi, Toshio, 17

Zak, Paul, 10
Zero contribution thesis, 115